WEIRD

WEIRD

Lynette Eklund

WEIRD

A Monster Maker's Journey From Small Town to Hollywood with OCD

HISTRIA
A&E

Histria A&E
Las Vegas ◊ London ◊ Palm Beach

Published in the United States of America by
Histria Books
7181 N. Hualapai Way, Ste. 130-86
Las Vegas, NV 89166 USA
HistriaBooks.com

Histria A&E is an imprint of Histria Books dedicated to outstanding books that focus on arts and entertainment. Titles published under the imprints of Histria Books are distributed worldwide. We appreciate your support of copyright by purchasing an authorized edition of this book and for respecting intellectual property laws by not reproducing, scanning, or otherwise distributing any part of it by any means without permission. You are supporting authors and enabling Histria Books to continue publishing books for everyone.

All rights reserved. No part of this book may be reprinted or reproduced or utilized in any form or by any electronic, mechanical or other means, now known or hereafter invented, including photocopying and recording, or in any information storage or retrieval system, without the permission in writing from the Publisher. No part of this book may be used or reproduced in any manner for the purpose of training artificial intelligence technologies or systems.

Library of Congress Control Number: 2024953111

ISBN 978-1-59211-594-5 (softbound)
ISBN 978-1-59211-663-8 (eBook)

Copyright © 2025 by Lynette Eklund

1. Van Nuys, California — Stan Winston Studio

FADE IN.

Ever so slowly, Alpha Raptor turns in my direction, with her green-veined gold eyes looking just over my head toward Chris. She's a beauty. She'll be even more beautiful once her skin colors are as intense as her eyes.

I stroke the folds of her throat. "That's good. Hold her there."

Stabbing a curved needle into her skin as Chris pushes a brush deep under her upper lip, she shudders.

We both pull back and wait to see if she will keep moving.

She doesn't.

Chris pops his headphones back over his ears, leaving me listening to just the ch-ch-ch of whatever song he's listening to.

I pierce Alpha's throat a second time.

She throws back her head and tries to kick me.

"Get back!" Chris pulls back his hand just in time to keep Alpha's jaws from snapping shut on his hand.

Alpha whips her head toward me.

I dive off the wood crate I've been sitting on and jump to my feet just in time to see David, who's been working on her other side, dodge her tail as it swings in his direction.

Thrashing and snapping, she bucks and dives, ducking her head only to throw it back, her teeth gnashing, daring anyone to come near her.

I don't know what's wrong with her, but with her body bucking — and that mouth chomping at fourteen-hundred psi — I'm not about to try to find out. With that much strength, one bite with those teeth would crush a man's hand.

I'm sure this isn't how most people spend their days at the office, but being threatened by Raptors is pretty typical for me. I'm a female Hollywood monster-maker. The funny thing is that's not the weirdest thing about me.

I am — simply put — weird. This is not an opinion or a self-deprecating comment. I'm not asking anyone to say something to make me feel better about myself. I am simply weird.

I have Obsessive Compulsive Disorder, OCD. I'm not "a little bit OCD," — as you hear so many people too casually claim these days. I'm riding an OCD freight train at full speed, making pursuing my dreams even harder.

When I was eight, I told my parents, "When I'm nineteen or twenty, I'm going to move to Hollywood to work for the movies." Not proper wording, but those words became my mantra. I didn't know exactly what I would do in Hollywood; I just knew I wanted to be a part of movie-making. I was accountable once I said it out loud, and those words became law. That's the way the OCD I have works. It's about rules, and almost all of it is mental obsessions — not physical.

Obsessive compulsions are not amusing. They are real obsessions that take a great deal of energy to handle. By the time I was fifteen, I was backtracking in stores to keep from tangling the invisible string trailing my path, noting which limbs I put in my clothes first each morning so I could do the opposite the next morning, rotating which stuffed animal I covered with a blanket first each night so they all got equal attention, concerning myself with what impression I'll leave if I suddenly die and someone else sorts my belongings, replaying words or scenes in loops in my head for hours on end, holding my breath when I stood too close to another person, and washing my hands to the point of making them so chapped they bled. When I wasn't avoiding sugar to keep from becoming diabetic and having my toes fall off, I was shoveling three-thousand calories a day into my five-foot-five, one-hundred-and-two-pound frame — mainly in the form of pre-packaged food that I was sure wasn't poisoned.

My Rule #1 of many Rules was: *Failure is not allowed — ever. Period.* I couldn't fail — not my parents, my siblings, my teachers, my instructors or directors, not my stuffed animals or my latest in-progress craft project. I had to always be accountable, wanted — needed. Followed closely by Rule #2: *I keep my weirdness a secret* because weird is different, and different is not perfect.

Now, as an adult, I no longer consider myself disordered — if that's even a word. So, I have OC, but not D. It's a matter of who's in control. Yes, a couple of mornings ago, after adjusting the bathroom scale to align with the floor pattern where it must sit at all times, I put my hair in a ponytail and reached in the drawer for a set of always pre-coupled bobby pins. Just as I started to separate the pair, I spotted a different pair of bobby pins sitting on the counter — and bing! I was in a quandary. If I put the pins in my hand back without using them, I could hurt their feelings. But the other two pins have been lying there all night, assuming they would be used in the morning. After pondering for a couple of minutes — these are not fast decisions with everything that needs to be considered — I verbally apologized to the two pins on the counter and assured them that I would use them again. They seemed satisfied, so I used the two new pins for two days, at which point they seemed okay with returning to the drawer and returning hair duties to the two pins patiently on the counter.

I know my obsessions make me sound disordered, but they are simply a part of me, just as my Masks have become a part of my daily living. People call me hyper. They call me stubborn or driven. If they knew my actions were actually because of Rule #1, they'd probably pity me instead. But my Masks, combined with my OCD, have given me the drive to follow my dreams and succeed. So, at this point, I just say I am weird.

As per my eight-year-old vow, three months after my twentieth birthday, I packed my meager wardrobe, a three-foot-tall stuffed white rabbit named Cecil I rescued from an abandoned car in the middle of a field, and Tracy — an armless mannequin torso I saved from Lord and Taylor's dumpster behind the Galleria in Houston — into a 1978 Cordoba and moved to where many weird people flock. The Island of Misfit Toys. Hollywood — where getting attacked by a Raptor is just another day at work.

I'm now working for Stan Winston, one of the biggest names in the creature effects industry, the guy responsible for the creatures in the *Alien* movies, *Terminator* and *Predator* films, *Edward Scissorhands*, and yes, all the life-sized dinosaurs for *Jurassic Park*. He's assigned me to fabricate the Raptor puppets for *Jurassic Park: The Lost World*.

Puppets. There's a term that used to bring up an entirely different image in my mind. I used to think *puppets* were hand puppets and marionettes, but that word encompasses so much more in Hollywood. *Puppets* means any creature manipulated by a puppeteer, whether by hand, rod, string, cable, radio control, programming, or a combination of methods. Many times, even suit performers are also puppeteering while inside a creature's body. These life-size dinosaurs are some of the most elaborate puppets I've ever worked on, but they are still *puppets* nonetheless — and I'm redesigning the way their anatomies function.

After the robotics are built and the wiring is complete, I attach shells for bones, then musculature and skins to turn those robots into creatures.

Before I was finally hired, I'd submitted my resume many times over the years. I still feel like an outsider in a class full of cool kids, but I'm used to it. I've spent every day of my life feeling this way. It doesn't help that Kathy, the head of Stan's fabrication department, only tolerates me because her attempt to get me fired failed.

The Raptors are over half-done now. Chris, David, and I have the mechanics under well-moving carbon fiber skeletal shells and carved foam musculature that moves like a real animal. With the foam latex skins over the one we're calling the Alpha, all we have to do is attach the skin and finish installing the mouth, and she's off to the painters — but she's still throwing a violent fit.

She rears up again, and we all wince in unison as we hear a loud crack just as David — the only one able to get to her control box safely — pulls the plug.

Suddenly, as abruptly as it began, Alpha stops, her body tightened into a bizarre pose, with her head cocked uncomfortably to one side.

From hip to neck, her skin has several new open wounds where she hyperextended and tore or hyper-compressed ground it between her shells, and much of the stitching David and I just did is ripped loose from the inside.

"Her skull is broken." Chris continues to massage the back of her head. "And at least two of her neck rings."

We all know what this means.

Alpha isn't almost done. She's going to have to undergo major surgery.

By now, Alpha has drawn the attention of a dozen other people in the shop. "What caused that?" one voice asks the question we're all wondering.

"A rogue signal from the airport, most likely."

Until the dinosaurs are fully programmed, they don't have set stopping points and can move until something — like their skulls — stops them. That little Van Nuys airport just one block away… the one that hosts the cool air show… the one that entertained us the Monday after the show as we all spent the morning running outside whenever the roar of some big military plane fired its engines up high to show off during its departure… yeah… that little airport of vintage aircraft… it just killed our Alpha Raptor.

The next few days will be long, but I don't care. The road to Stan's shop hasn't been easy, so at this point, I'm ready to accept almost anything this profession can throw at me. The good parts are a blast and the bad parts… well… with how my head works, I've been making things hard on myself since I was just a kid, so I'm used to that.

FLASHBACK:

2. Illinois — Home
(When I Was Seven)

Sitting on the floor with the threadbare spot in front of the flowered-print sofa, holding the right-handed scissors too big for my hands that always leave a dent on the back of my left thumb over the paper egg carton, I stop. My alligator has to wait until Fred Astaire and Ginger Rogers stop dancing.

I stand up and strike a pose that matches Ginger's so I can dance with Fred. Wearing my imaginary evening gown with feathers on the hem and rhinestones on the bodice, just like Ginger's, I twirl around the room. I could just as well be Cid Charisse in *Silk Stockings* or Vera-Ellen in *White Christmas*, but today Ginger is dancing on our old black and white TV, so I'm Ginger.

I'm skinny and long-legged, so there's hope that I'll grow up to be pretty. If not, surely I'll be good enough to be a Busby Berkley background dancer. I don't have to be the star. I just have to work for the movies somehow.

The back door off the kitchen slams shut. Daddy is coming back in from mowing the yard. Within seconds, I hear Mommy's feet on the stairs as she comes up from doing laundry in the basement. Before either pair of footsteps near the living room, I'm settled back on the floor, dividing the carton flap into four pieces for legs, with my Normal Girl Mask on again.

"Whatcha watching?" Daddy asks as he drops into his fancy green recliner with the heated, vibrating back — although it's too hot for him to want either today.

"Fred Astaire and Ginger Rogers" — the movie title doesn't matter. *Fred and Ginger* is enough. I staple the two lid halves together to make my gator head. "When I'm nineteen or twenty, I'm going to Hollywood to work for the movies."

"Oh, yeah?" I don't have to look to know he's smiling. I can hear it in his voice. Daddy always smiles. "What are you going to do for the movies?"

"I don't know yet, but I'm going to work in Hollywood somehow."

He doesn't say anything more.

I've told Mommy and him this hundreds of times, and they never say anything. They always just smile.

He holds out his Pepsi bottle. "Want a swig?"

If I drink it, I'll become diabetic. My sister said there was a lady who was a diabetic. She ate too much sugar, and they had to cut off all her toes. I want to keep my toes. But if I don't take a sip, I'll hurt Daddy's feelings.

I look at him.

He's admiring my alligator.

Maybe I'll find some blue buttons, so it can have blue eyes, just like his — uh-oh, I forgot. It's Saturday. A baseball game is starting on channel thirteen soon.

My head flies into hyper-drive, assessing and calculating information in seconds, as it does to keep normal people accepting me.

Daddy loves watching baseball — I didn't take the Pepsi he offered me — he can't watch his baseball game because of me — I'm already disappointing him — I can't disappoint him, or he won't want me anymore — the Pepsi — my toes...

My heart sinks. "I'm not really watching the movie very much." I shrug as if Fred and Ginger don't matter. "You can watch baseball if you want."

"Sugar, it's not going to hurt for me to miss a couple of innings. You can finish your movie first."

"I've seen this one before" — four times, actually.

I get up, go to the television, and change the channel to the baseball game before going over to Daddy. I take the bottle and turn it up just far enough for my lips to come in contact with the sweet, cold, fizzy goodness.

I love him so much. I can never disappoint him — even if it means having my toes fall off.

RETURN TO:

3. Van Nuys, California — Stan Winston Studio

Our poor Alpha. My heart hurts for her. With her skin peeled off, her neck, shoulder, and back muscles detached, and her carbon fiber shell parts removed from her head and neck all the way down to her waist, she looks more like a giant Terminator lizard than a Raptor. Her ribs, which I meticulously designed not to collide with each other and to float over her mechanics no matter which way she moves, lay loose over her robotic parts, waiting for a new upper torso shell she also broke during her tantrum. She'll be beautiful again, but not today and not tomorrow. We have several days of work ahead of us to get her back to where she was.

Meanwhile, there are plenty of other Raptor body parts to work on — two insert tails, a pair of digging arms, two mechanical insert waist-up Raptors, two insert mechanical heads with necks, a couple of dummy puppet heads, and a pair of insert legs — but this Alpha is one of our only two full head-to toe-to tail mechanical babies. She needs to be perfect when Spielberg first lays eyes on her.

Not that I enjoy rebuilding a Raptor that has seized itself to pieces, but I love building these things way more than I thought I would.

When the shop was gearing up for the sequel to *Jurassic Park*, waiting to discover which dinosaur I'd be assigned, I remember feeling like a little kid on Christmas eve. All I knew was that not even being able to get an interview to work on *Jurassic Park* was heartbreaking, so whatever Stan assigned to me was going to make me happy.

Then, Chris popped through the door right behind my workbench. "Hey, Netty, I need you to look at something." He led me out to the mold-making area, where the mold for the original Raptors lay in the middle of the floor.

I was going to be working on the Raptors. That big Christmas present was a dud. I didn't want to work on the Raptors. They'd already been done. There was nothing left to figure out — and I told Chris so.

"No. You don't understand. Steven loves the Raptors as the main villains, but he hates the way our puppets worked in the first film. We're going to redesign them from scratch."

We started the Raptors for *The Lost World* with nothing but the mold of the exterior sculpture. Chris asked for my thoughts on everything from the foam latex skin thickness and then had the mold department adjust the core accordingly. We discussed the joint placement, the core design, and places I wanted them to remove so I could replace the hard shell with musculature. Chris coordinated my first job here when I was brought in to engineer the fabrication of Kathoga, the creature for *The Relic* and he'd managed to keep the same crew together for the Raptors. I'd gained his trust, so he readily gave me free rein to experiment and engineer the same way on the Raptors.

He trusted me — trusts me. Stan Winston trusts me …even if Kathy still doesn't.

I still feel so much less than the people I work beside, but at least I'm contributing enough for them to like me today. That's all I can ask. One day at a time. That's how my sanity survives. Yesterday's successes don't count. Neither do tomorrow's promises. I have to justify myself every single day.

Every day, I have to strive for perfection, or I could lose all I've worked so hard to obtain. The pressure I felt as a kid has not lessened one bit, because so much of this job involves me flying by the seat of my pants. At least surviving unpredictability is something I've been doing since my first job, which I landed by attending a party one week after I arrived in Hollywood.

DISSOLVE TO:

4. North Hollywood, California — A Simple Little Apartment

I park two blocks away and walk back — alone — to a little twelve-unit, two-story apartment building that looks like something Fred and Ethel Mertz might have owned in *I Love Lucy*. People spill out into the alley on the south side of the building, with the back and front security gates propped open. It doesn't take a genius to know which apartment is Tim's. It's downstairs with the door standing wide open.

I certainly hope the person who told me to come is here.

There's no music other than the steady hum of conversation that grows louder as I slide behind my Friendly-Casual Mask and take the two steps up into the well-lit living room.

The place is elbow-to-elbow people. Bodies step away from one conversation only to join a different one. There's a lot of big hair, heavy eyeliner on girls and guys alike, and enough black clothing to make goths, punks, and witches feel right at home. I'm not dressed in black, but I am wearing a rust-colored layered outfit of my own design with just enough Japanese flair to keep me from looking too out of place — though I wish I'd gone heavier on my eye makeup. Since I'm one of the few not holding a plastic cup, I cram my hands in my pockets. At five-seven, this gives my skinny body the illusion of having hips, especially with my twenty-two-inch waist cinched by my wide olive-green sash belt. I think very hard about leaving, but if I go, I'll fail my new friend — my only friend.

As eyes glance my way, nobody stops talking to find out who I am or why I'm here. Not one soul seems to care.

Desperate not to look like more of an idiot than I already feel, I weave through the mass of strangers in search of the one familiar face that promised to be there.

It's a two-bedroom apartment, sparsely furnished by Garage Sales Unlimited, with no bed anywhere. The only interesting things are the turtle in a gold rubber washtub on the kitchen counter, and a Burmese python in a large aquarium in what should be a bedroom but is set up as an office. The other bedroom is for storage and the only room not lit.

Besides never finding a bed, I still haven't seen my friend. Not willing to give up quite yet and having him thinking I'd chickened out, I backtrack through the bodies, and toward the rear door leading onto the back patio.

The L-shaped building with a detached garage should've accommodated the residents quite nicely, but someone in the building is getting ripped off because the landlord has given the entire first double-car garage with the door that conveniently opens into the courtyard to this Tim guy, and Tim has turned the space into an art studio of some kind. But tonight, there's a keg on the edge of the worktable, along with a few bags of chips. Other than that, the room is white dust that has become one with the surfaces and is so packed with people leaning against the counters along the walls that I don't stay. It's not like I'll eat the food anyway. It might be poisoned.

The fear I have of being poisoned started when I was seven. By the time I was eight, the obsession owned me.

FLASHBACK:

5. Illinois — Home
(One Night When I Was Eight)

Tonight is card club night for Mommy and Daddy. They'll only be across the street, but they won't get home until late, so they won't have to watch me die. I sit at the dinner table alone, everybody else finished, as I cram in another bite of mashed potatoes.

My head whips into Hyper-drive again. I'm not sure how many bites of potatoes everybody else ate, so I don't know if I've eaten enough to get the antidote for the poison — If I get it wrong, I'll die — The perfect family is four people — They already had a girl and a boy — Pictures in magazines only ever show four people in a family — They don't need me — They never treat me like they love me less, but they're nice to everybody — They could afford so much more if they didn't had to split everything three ways. Even worse, I started as not just an unplanned pregnancy, but as unplanned twins. Around the four-month mark, my twin sister bailed out and I went to full term alone. Maybe I was supposed to bail, too, but I didn't. Now, Mommy and Daddy are stuck with me — unless they poison me.

I stare desperately at my plate.

"Lynette. Hurry up and finish." Mommy dashes past with her lipstick on her way to the bathroom.

She wants me to eat more. Maybe I got the antidote balance right. I replay her words, precisely listening for a hint of frustration in her tone.

A knock at the back door instantly pulls me back to the kitchen. Cindy is early.

All three of us kids rush her at once. My sister, Julianne, wants her to color with her. Greg wants her to play Chinese Checkers. I try to drag her into the dining room to show her the puppet I'm making named Salty.

I don't know the exact minute Mommy and Daddy leave — but I know I swallowed my final bite at six-fifty. The minute they leave, Cindy lets me drag her into the dining room to show her Salty. Mommy found the instructions in one of her magazines and helped me collect the pieces to make him. The lady next door let me go through her box of leftover fabric scraps from her sewing projects, where I found pieces for his shirt and pants.

Salty has a Styrofoam ball head and cardboard tubes from pant hangers strung together with kite string for his body. I don't know how to sew, but I've followed the patterns in the magazine well enough to keep him from looking too silly — although my stitches are way too far apart, so pants only look good when he's upright.

Cindy is always impressed with the things I make, but then she has to be. She's the babysitter.

We're all in our pajamas, watching *Alias Smith and Jones* by eight-thirty, when I start feeling queasy — it's happening. Tonight is the night I'm going to die.

Eight-forty. If I move from my spot on the sofa, I'm going to throw up. Sweat sends a chill through me. A little whimper escapes my lips.

"What's the matter, Lynette?" Cindy kneels down in front of me.

"I'm going to be sick." Just saying the words makes my dam of tears burst.

I'm shaking and weak as Cindy leads me to the bathroom.

"Just sit in here. I'll call you parents."

I can hear her on the phone, but I can't make out the conversation.

Five more minutes go by — five minutes closer to being dead. Cindy returns with a cold cloth to cool down the back of my neck. She offers me a juice glass of 7-Up.

Diabetes doesn't matter. I'll be dead before my toes fall off — but 7-Up in the refrigerator is suspicious. We rarely have 7-Up in the house — and I didn't see her pour it.

I get sick almost every time she babysits. Cindy can't want to babysit me anymore — She's in on it — She poisoned the 7-Up to help.

I accept the glass and humor her by taking a sip small enough to maybe make me sicker, but probably not enough to kill me.

Five more minutes pass. I don't feel better, but I don't feel any worse either — and I'm not dead yet. We stay in the bathroom. Waiting. Cindy is waiting for me to puke. I'm waiting to die.

Ten more minutes. It's now nine o'clock — two hours and ten minutes since I finished my supper. Ten minutes passed when the boy on the news died after his dad poisoned one of the pixie sticks in the Halloween candy they were handing out last year, and his own son ate it. He got sick after two hours. They took him to the hospital, and he died.

Five more minutes tick by. It's now two hours and fifteen minutes since I last ate. I guess my supper wasn't poisoned after all. Mommy and Daddy didn't leave to keep from watching me die. I get to live one more day.

I calm down. Cindy takes me into the living room and lets me nestle beside her on the sofa to watch a little more TV before sending me off to bed.

I missed the end of Alias Smith and Jones — I always miss the ends of shows when there's a babysitter, but that doesn't matter tonight. I survived one more meal.

Knowing Mommy and Daddy still love me enough to keep me, I renew my vow to never tell them — or anybody — that I constantly worry that someone is going to poison me because while I can't stop it, I know it's not normal.

I tuck my secret back into my growing list of personal secrets and drift off to sleep in Cindy's arms.

DISSOLVE BACK TO:

6. North Hollywood, California — Back to Tim's Little Apartment

With so little food at the party, not eating isn't going to draw attention this evening. Stranger than the lack of snacks is a party with no music. These people can only be here for one reason — to talk. About what? I don't know, but hopefully — eventually — I'll find out.

After a half an hour of wandering aimlessly, I have yet to have a conversation with one single soul. My nerves aren't going to hold out much longer. Grabbing a Sprite can from the galvanized wash tub of ice sitting near the garage door as I pass — at least I now know it takes more than a can of soda to become diabetic — I make my way back inside and, to my relief, at last, I see my friend.

"You made it," he says. He introduces me to his girlfriend — having a girlfriend was something he neglected to mention about the *someone* he had to pick up.

The conversation quickly becomes awkward when I realize he didn't pick up anyone. They live together — so he's a weasel and not a very good one. I didn't need him to lie. I never thought we were going on a date.

Quickly, he leads me to the nearest group of people. "This is Lynette. She just moved here from Texas."

"Oh yeah?" One of them says. "What part?"

"Houston."

"Get a Thomas Guide. You're going to need it."

I'd already heard all about the phone book-sized maps of the Los Angeles area from my weasel friend and two store clerks since my arrival — and bought one earlier this morning. "That's what I hear."

"So, what do you do?"

I don't know how to answer that. I don't *do* anything yet. I look to my friend for help, but he and his girlfriend have already escaped toward the garage.

Somehow, I manage not to annoy Fred and Ken — as I find their names to be. Fred is a low-budget director, and Ken works for a creature effects shop called MMI. I don't know what MMI stands for, but I gather it's a fairly low-budget shop of some kind — but even at its budget level, it's too expensive for Fred's films. As we talk, others join us. I'm introduced again, and the conversation continues. Through the ever-morphing discussion, with people joining and stepping away only to have new faces join us — telling me I need to get a Thomas Guide — I cross paths with nearly everyone in the place.

My feet grow tired, but there's no place to sit down, but my feet can fall off before I let them force me out the door. I don't know where my friend is most of the time, but I no longer care. The Sprite can I'm still holding has been empty for over an hour, but I'll faint before I step away and miss something because I now know I'm mingling with the who's-who of the Hollywood creature effect industry.

The air is full of behind-the-scenes talk about working on *Thriller, Dune, Greystoke: The Legend of Tarzan, Starman, Ghostbusters, Terminator, Gremlins,* and *Nightmare on Elm Street.* A low-budget movie called *Toxic Avenger* is also half-talked about and half-eye-rolled over, but I quickly realize that laughing at a film is not the same as laughing at their peers who worked on it because nobody in the effects industry has a career record that doesn't contain at least one good eye-roller — and generally several.

I never hear apologies for the work they did on their schlock jobs. I hear about their challenges in meeting tight deadlines with budget restraints, bizarre requirements to fit storylines, producers with no imagination tying their hands by controlling the design process, and stories about dealing with big talkers with no skills to back up the talk.

Their names don't impress me — because honestly, I don't know who Rick Baker or Steve Johnson or Camilla Henneman are — until I start attaching the stories to the faces. These stories are what dreams are made of, and it's all I can do to keep my mouth from hanging open in awe as I hear how the silicone mold never cured on the newborn Rick Baker sculpted for *Starman,* and how Rick sat in a chair laughing at Tim and the others as they cleaned off the silicone with Q-tips; and design concerns about a movie called *The Fly* that wouldn't be out until next year; and how Fred planned to make his new script, *The Tomb,* his biggest film yet.

As Fred talks on, I'm no longer able to hear him.

It never dawned on me before that monster-making was a career option. I mean, I'd seen *Jaws*. I knew the shark wasn't real. But the idea of people making a career building monsters… The enthusiasm these people have for their work pours out of them, like little kids telling me about their first roller coaster ride. Their eyes, their body language, their voices expressing passion I never imagined could happen over a job for a paycheck.

I scan the people around me. Tall and short, muscular and chubby, fashionable and funky, gorgeous, odd-looking, confident and dorky, they all have one thing in common: They spend almost every waking hour striving for perfection — no matter the schedule or budget.

I have found my people.

I've only been standing among them for two hours, but I've already decided — I'm changing my career path. I'm not going to use my craft background to do beadwork and armor for period films. I'm going to be a monster-maker.

As the night winds down, I still haven't met this Tim guy, but I'm not about to leave this life-changing party without meeting him and thanking him for a spectacular time.

Swimming through the crowd, I finally find him coming up the hallway toward the living room.

After the introduction of myself that I now have down to a few good sentences, he says, "I don't know many shops that will give you a chance with so little experience, but here," he pulls out a scrap of paper and a pen from his pocket and writes two phone numbers on it. "The first one, John, is a friend of mine. Tell him I told you to call. He and another friend are starting a business doing toy prototypes. Being new, they may give you a shot. The second one, Jody, drinks her lunch and can't keep help, so she usually has openings. Tell her I told you to contact her."

Everyone else at the party has been friendly, but he's the only one giving me potential work contacts.

My entire Hollywood dream hangs on connecting more links to a tiny chain. I can only hope I'll gain another link that will pull me closer to my goal.

Monday, I call both phone numbers, hoping to get my first job — and it works.

My first boss is a drunk.

FADE TO:

7. North Hollywood, California — Little Shop of Chaos

I'm working for Jody for two weeks' pay that, after taxes, my new Thomas Guide equated five hours of my salary.

Jody is a short, round lady with boy-cut hair and a big smile. She welcomes me and another girl, Caroline, into the shop at the same time. I don't know who Caroline knows or how she got the job, but at least I have the advantage of having been referred by Tim — who Jody clearly likes — and I get the distinct impression she doesn't like many people.

She sets us up with her assistant at a round table like I just entered an elementary school art class and announces she has a meeting that won't allow her to return until after lunch.

She assigns us to putting the padded helmets and vision scrims in fifteen Big Boys heads. Apparently, Big Boys Restaurant Corporation initiated a promotional campaign to let the public decide whether to keep Big Boy or retire him and replace him with something more modern. So, while the public thinks they're making the decision, we're already building the new Big Boys for his *Thanks for Saving Me* tour.

I quickly catch my stride, thoroughly enjoying the calming order of doing the same steps in the same order. Fifteen Big Boy heads aren't enough repetition to get boring, but they are enough duplication for me to hone the steps toward that perfection I must have.

The three of us chat, always keeping our hands moving. And while Jody's assistant doesn't state anything directly, with Tim's tip, I know from her tone that statements like *Jody is very picky about the edges*, or, *Be sure you get that Velcro perfectly straight or Jody will have you do it over* have warnings in them.

After a brown bag lunch in my car of chips, Coke, a bologna and ketchup sandwich, and a Ding Dong, I go back inside and get back to work on my Big Boy heads.

Jody returns shortly after lunch and saunters over to check our work. Pleased with what she sees, she wanders back to one of the cutting tables and starts working on a pattern.

The shop is quiet now. The only noise is the sound of the air blowing from the vents overhead, the hiss of scissors cutting paper, and the soft tap of our glue brushes on the inside of the giant plastic Vacuform heads. I gather up an armload of foam scraps to throw away. Every step I take feels like I'm in a spotlight that is directing me in front of a target, with Jody at the other end of the room, her arrow already nocked, and bow drawn.

As I drop my load in the trash can, Jody screeches, "Get out!"

I whip around to see Jody nose to nose with Caroline — thank goodness — who stands frozen, pink-cheeked, and mouth opened, afraid to move.

Jody throws her arm sideways, pointing to the door. "Get out!" She keeps screaming and ranting on about God-only-knows-what as she stays on Caroline's heels, all the way to the worktable for the girl to collect her things, and then all the way to the door, where she anchors herself in the doorway, screaming at poor Caroline, even while she starts her car and drives away.

I have no idea what Jody is saying — nor do I want to get caught trying to figure it out. Instead, I take the gorilla approach. I stay perfectly still and avoid eye contact until Jody storms into the back room and slams the door.

Twenty minutes after lunch, on my first day at my first job, and already I've learned that Tim was in no way exaggerating. Mornings are going to be relatively sane, but the afternoons… Oh, boy.

The poor girl was apparently screamed out the door for using scissors designated for fabric to cut paper.

Until I'm in my grave, Jody will join the team in my head that threatens me if I ever break one of my Rules — the newest Rule being: Never use fabric scissors to cut paper.

(DAYS LATER)

I survive the next few days by being quick and responsive in the morning and wearing my Cloak of Invisibility in the afternoon. This is one time my Cloak of Invisibility is my friend. Back in high school, it was so powerful that the yearbook photographer never snapped any shots of me, and when the cast went out for pizza, they'd forget to invite me — and then apologize on Monday, saying they wish they'd thought of me; and when my dance partner got thrown out of the show for sneaking onto the school roof, I was cut from the dance number *I* choreographed; but now, being invisible in the afternoons is the best thing in the world.

With the Big Boy heads complete, Jody has shifted me over to making rhinestone buckles and appliqués for twelve white Elvis Presley jumpsuits for what she says is a TV pilot. I can't think of a worse position to be in — other than unemployed — than working directly with Jody, but here I am.

I've never used Stitch-witchery before, but I'm confident enough in my learning abilities that I'm certainly not admitting that to Jody. I watch closely, listen hard and absorb every bit of information I can on the first pass — because I doubt very much there can be a second.

Surprisingly, she seems to like me. Whatever she thinks is fine with me, as long as the thought is friendly and not accompanied by a drunken rage.

I steam and cut, iron and trim, rolling along quickly and efficiently.

Grateful she has an industrial sewing machine slow enough for me not to sew through my fingers, I switch its spool of white thread to metallic red thread to match the red lame' and settle in for a safe afternoon. But no matter how many tests I sew, the thread keeps breaking.

I check the machine threading and adjust the tension. I change the needle and sew more tests. I try anything I can think of to keep from asking Jody for help, but I'm getting nowhere, and eventually she's going to catch on. Knowing if I don't get these appliqués done soon, she'll scream me out the door for incompetence, I present myself to the firing squad.

"I've tried everything," I tell her.

Without a word — thank goodness — she stomps over to the machine, but then she doesn't even sit down and look at it. She yanks the spool off the top, holds it up to me and says, "You can't use this thread. It'll never work. Who told you to use this thread?" Every sentence growing louder than the one before.

Since I'm clearly going to be driven out the door in the next few seconds anyway, I might as well go down in flames. I match her tone, "It was on the rack. And nobody told me *not* to use it!"

We both freeze.

I don't know what she's thinking — but I'm thinking I need to get my feet moving before she swings that arm of hers around, because I'm standing close enough for her to knock me cold.

After five of the most uncomfortable seconds of my life, she comes back to life. "Well, it's only good for hand work. It's too fine for the machines. Here, use this one." She hands me a different spool of red thread and walks away.

I return to my work completely intact, my head looping the word *convoluted* over and over — because her assistant used the work in a sentence, and now I'm stuck. *Convoluted*.... I wind a new bobbin ...*convoluted,* thread the machine ...*convoluted,* and start sewing on appliqués ...*convoluted*...

I hope Tim won't regret referring me to her ...*convoluted*...

FADE TO:

8. Reseda, California — Teddy Ruxpin's World — Alchemy Ii

After two weeks of working for a drunk, I don't want to ever have work in that kind of tension again. But to keep from going back, I need to snag a job from the only other phone number I have. I call Alchemy II again and talk to John — again — who refers me to Linda — again. I tell her I'm available — again — and she says they won't have any decision for about another week — again.

A week is seven days, so the following Monday, I call her again. This time, she says it'll be a few more days.

A few means three, so three days later, I call again.

This time, she offers me two weeks of work. I don't ask what I'll be doing — I don't care. It's a place willing to give me a chance. Two jobs in the first six weeks I'm in Hollywood. I'm on my way.

Jody calls me later that week to hire me back for a new project. I don't ask what that job is, either. It doesn't matter. Linda has saved me — at least temporarily.

While it's a relief not to have to return for another round of Russian Roulette so soon, it's nice to hear I did well enough for her to want me back. If I can say nothing else about Jody, the quality of her product is close to perfect. With her wild temper, to do anything less would be utter failure — and failure isn't something that can simply happen to me before I try again; it's a lifelong threat in a head game I cannot bear. The battle between staying committed to my dreams and staying braced for ultimate rejection eternally whispers to me in my head, and Jody's call validates my work in a way that supports both of these obsessions. It's that validation I've striven for, but one I've never trusted when it comes.

FLASHBACK:

9. Illinois — Highland Community College

At fourteen, besides repeating words in my head for hours, counting stairs — even though I don't bother remembering the number, and so many other obsessive habits that I keep hidden from the world, so they'll never know I'm weird, I've tipped enough Pepsi in the grass at picnics by now to grow an oak tree. I won't even get into my long list of bathroom and tight space Rules. I've avoided eating enough meals at friends' houses to feed a small country. I haven't had a piece of Halloween candy in years, and I'm so skinny most boys aren't interested in me — unless they need another fast runner for backyard football.

Mom even took me to the doctor to see if I had an eating disorder. Since he couldn't diagnose me as anorexic or bulimic, he told her that I'll eat when I'm hungry. That statement is only half-true. I eat, but a bite to avoid being poisoned when I'm able to match others bite for bite to avoid being poisoned, or when I'm so hungry I'm willing to gamble on dying — but I don't intentionally starve myself.

I could be this skinny simply because I'm on the move from the second I wake up to the second I go to sleep, out of fear of disappointing somebody. I practically jump out of bed when the alarm goes off so I can be sure to see what the others are having for breakfast and identify the safe food. I push hard to keep my grades up to keep my parents wanting me; I play the flute in band; I work at the family ice cream parlor; I help keep score and calculate the stats for the baseball team my brother plays for and my dad coaches; I go to the roller rink on Sunday nights; and when it's not snowing — since I'm still not old enough to drive — I bicycle our hilly town miles every day. I do it all because I can't *not* do it. I cannot fail anyone or anything — and certainly not my dancing.

I have to dance.

I know now that Fred Astaire and Ginger Rogers have long since retired, and those musicals aren't being produced anymore, but John Travolta is bringing in a new kind of musical. Since I still have no other plan for Hollywood, and I've already proclaimed my dream aloud — even if it is just to my immediate family — I cannot fail.

A statement by me about myself immediately becomes an unbreakable Rule. Breaking any Rule is failure. My head repeats this to me all day, every day. Failing people is not perfect. If I'm not perfect, I'm dead weight. Extra. Unwanted.

This summer, five days a week, besides bicycling to rehearsal with the children's theater at the park mid-afternoon, I'm studying ballet for two hours under the instruction of Ed Parish, a retired dancer from the New York Ballet Company. Two of my girlfriends signed up, too. Everything about Ed terrifies me. His posture, his tone, his expectations. And he picks on me constantly.

"Pull up more. Don't let your leg drop."

How can I not let my leg drop after he's had me hold it up there so long, I'm getting a Charlie horse in my thigh?

Two of the eight girls in the class already have their pointe shoes. I won't get mine until after this class. Of the two, Maria is clearly destined to be a ballerina. She's my mark to follow, those it's idiotic to think I can keep up with her.

Of the two guys in the class, one, Dagoberto Nieves, is Ed's foster son, and the youngest dancer in the American Ballet Company. He's just using the class to keep in shape while the company is on hiatus and makes the rest of us — except the one — look like a bunch of clunks.

After only one week, one of my girlfriends and another girl drop out. The next week, my other friend quits, too. But I can't fail. I'm sticking this out.

With my friends gone, I have to bicycle the three miles to class every morning. And every day, Ed targets me, while he lets the other girls get away with doing so much less.

Ed pushes on my stomach. "Pull up, or your pirouette will always fall off. Watch Dago." He gestures to Dago, who comes to the center of the room and does a plies-turn, and then another, and another, until he finishes with five consecutive perfect turns, his head snapping around so he never loses sight of himself in the mirror.

By the end of the two hours, I'm fighting back my tears. I'm never going to be a Dago. He's shown me that. My thighs burn and my heart dies as I pedal the three miles back home.

My parents paid for me to take these lessons because I practically begged to go. I can't quit — that would be *failure* — but there's no way I'm going to sign up for any more of Ed's abuse. If he doesn't want me around, I'll do my best until the class ends, and then he won't have me to endure my mediocrity anymore. After all, my plan isn't to become a ballerina. Ballerinas go to New York, and my success is in Hollywood.

(Years later, I learned that Ed told my mom that he was tougher on me than the others, because he saw potential in me. But with my internal mantra of failure and rejection, it never occurred to me that anyone of his caliber might appreciate me. Had I known, I would've let him drill my pirouettes into the floor and reveled in his attention, and my life might have been very different.)

DISSOLVE BACK TO:

10. Reseda, California — Back To — Alchemy II

Jody gave me a chance. She allowed me to feel the beginning of what my dream could be — like Ed had with his intense ballet training — and she believed I could meet her standards, just like Ed had.

I blew it with Ed. I won't allow fear to kill an opportunity for me again.

Jody asks me to let her know when I'll be available again, and I assure her I will — because work is work, and with her shop being my only other connection, what choice do I have — but if I have anything to do with it, I'll make sure this two-week job at Alchemy II goes longer than just two weeks. Watching her outwardly scream Caroline out the door within four hours of starting also showed me just how literal my rejections might be, and while I won't let that stop me from working for her, I won't default to that kind of emotional torture just because the job is easy to get.

When I walk into Alchemy II and meet Linda in person, I realize I'll be making toys for a very tall elf. Linda is taller than me, and I'm five-seven. She's also an extremely thin woman in her upper twenties, with brown curly hair, a nose that turns up on the end, and enormous eyes. She's friendly and calm — a relief to see after working for Jody — and after the standard paperwork forms, she whisks me through a quick tour of the facility. Fast because the entire place is nothing but a small building with a few offices and three work rooms.

The high-ceiling warehouse work area — which still isn't very big as warehouse space goes — is where the half a dozen mechanics work, along with one lone sculptor sitting at a table facing the wall. At one end of the room is a set of double doors leading into the mold-making area run by a father and his two sons.

Between the offices and shop floor is a modest-sized sewing room. The place is bustling with people, everyone working to complete a dream born in the mind of a man named Ken Forsse.

"His idea is to create a toy bear that can be a friend to every child," Linda explains. "Teddy Ruxpin will be able to read stories to kids, so they won't have to wait for someone to read to them. He'll have a buddy named Grubby, who can plug into a jack in Teddy's back so they can tell stories together.

"Instead of kids playing records or cassettes that recite stories to them as they follow along in the book, Teddy will be different. He'll be the first animatronic toy. He'll blink and move his mouth, so kids will have a moving, talking friend reading to them. And each story will come with a whole outfit for Teddy to wear, so he can dress to match the stories he tells."

I will be a part of a historic breakthrough in the world of toys — we all will. The excitement among the workers is contagious, and I'm ready to jump aboard.

Teddy's body is well underway, but while his mechanics and programming are being perfected, he's still headless.

The fabrication room is small, but it's certainly busy. There are piles of clothing pieces for Teddy and Grubby everywhere. Six creepy, faceless bears made in cheap white fur hang on the wall, wearing copies of the completed outfits — a winter coat, pants, and boots; pajamas with slippers; hiking overalls with a jacket, hat, and boots; a raincoat with a hat and boots; a flight suit with a jacket and scarf; and a sweat suit with tennis shoes.

I'll be joining the crew in making the salesman sample copies — thirty-six copies of each, to be exact.

Sue, a confident blond girl only a few years older than me, takes me to a strange-looking machine called an overlock and sets me up with a stack of rain cap pieces. Not wanting to admit I've never used an overlock before — let alone an industrial one — which means it's a machine capable of moving fast enough to sew over your fingers before you can get it stopped — I stand casually and uh-huh at the correct times, to give Sue the impression I know what I'm doing, so Linda doesn't have a *Jody Attack* and scream me out the door before I even start — and thank God the machine running four giant cones of thread simultaneously is already threaded so I don't have to blow my cover right off the bat, the same way I did when I started college and claimed I already knew how to sew when I didn't even know how to thread the machine.

As Sue demonstrates the machine's features, my blood slams into my toes as I realize the slivers of fabric on the floor under the machine are strips the overlock chops off as it sews — meaning there are no second chances on anything. My failure will be instantaneous, unrecoverable, and potentially very bloody.

I sit down with my pile of parts to face the piece-munching, finger-chopping, job-swallowing machine, with a smile glued on my face, so Sue can't tell that even my bones are sweating.

Braced for a *Jody Attack*, I put the first pieces through the machine. It works! I do it right! Every piece I sew I do under the shadow of Jody hovering over my work in my mind. I'm obsessed with Jody. She's become the reigning ruler of the Fear Room in my head.

I must be perfect. Every time. Perfect.

Soon the excitement of discovering a new skill that is coming surprisingly easily and the rewarding purr of the overlock, as turning out piece after piece of absolute perfection lets me slam that Fear Room door closed, even if only for a few moments. I love this machine.

The way it trims off the excess makes everything so neat and cleanly finished. In no time at all, the overlock and the industrial sewing machine I used for the top stitching and I become fast friends, and I find myself volunteering to sew tiny rain boots over raincoats and hats. This wins great brownie points with the others in the shop. They comment repeatedly on how grateful they are that I'm willing to do the boots and shoes and have no idea how I can do them so quickly.

My secret to success is in the math. Just as with Elvis and the Big Boy heads, repetition begets perfection.

I made almost three-hundred tiny, multi-pieced boots for Teddy on an industrial overlock. Then, Grubby gained a hiking outfit and raincoat set. (Grubby's rain set ever went into production. I think after they mass-produced his hiking boots, the factory probably cried, uncle!) The difference between Teddy and Grubby is that Grubby has six feet instead of two. Multiply that by the thirty-six salesman samples, and you have well over two-hundred more tiny boots. Over five hundred teeny-weeny boots out of such merciless materials trained me on industrial equipment better than wax-on-wax-off taught martial arts to Daniel in that Karate Kid movie that just came out last year.

Two months later, I'm a fearless sewing professional on any industrial machines I sit behind. That's two months — not two weeks — and then two months turn into eight.

(EIGHT MONTHS LATER)

Ken Forsse strolls into the workroom, followed by the other office heads carrying giant boxes. This large, slightly portly smiling man with wavy white hair resting on his shirt collar and a thick, white beard is devoting his life to making toys designed to keep children from ever feeling friendless ever again. He truly is Santa Claus, and we are his toymakers.

The giant boxes he's brought in are the very first cases of Teddy Ruxpins, straight from the manufacturer.

Ken hands me a Teddy. "Thank you."

I'm hesitant to even take it from him. *He's* thanking *me*. I doubt he even knows who I am. I'm just one of a couple of dozen people making his prototypes. I'm not one of his main people. I'm invisible.

Still, at least for that moment, I can pretend to be somebody who matters. I thank him back — for the Teddy Ruxpin toy that is already becoming the chatter of the world, even though it's just getting ready to hit the shelves because I know the odds of me being able to buy one of these expensive toys will be nearly impossible; for taking a chance on me when I had so little experience to offer; and for not forgetting to include my name on the list of people to get one of these cherished first Teddys.

It would be so cool to have his name — Teddy Ruxpin's creator — and the date on the corner of my box.

I scan the room. Nobody else is asking.

I've been working for this man for months and will still work for him tomorrow and the next day. He's either going to think it's weird that I'm asking for the autograph of someone who signs my paychecks every week anyway, or he's going to think I'm a money-monger getting ready to sell my Teddy for big bucks and ditch my job. He'll hate me.

He passes by on his way to the mechanic's area.

I grab a pen off my workbench. Still, nobody else moves to get Ken to sign their boxes. I'll be the only one with a signed box. I'll be the only one looking greedy.

I can't have him hate me.

I turn away and place my Teddy, along with the pen, next to me on the table. Teddy smiles at me through the plastic window of his box. I know he's a first bear. I know he's special. That will have to be enough — and it is to me because this friendly little Teddy bear is not for sale.

(JANUARY)

I have friends. Mostly monster-makers — mostly guys. We go out for dinner, go to movies, go to The Comedy Club and The Improv. We fire up a grill for group potluck dinners and have get-togethers for Thanksgiving since our families all live in other states and go to Bronson Caves for Easter picnics. We stay up half the night eating pizza and watching monster movies we've rented from The Odyssey — which is right across the street from Blockbuster but has a way better classic movie collection.

I date Tim some and act as mock dates for Ken Hall and his brother Cleve — meaning they want to go someplace with a date, so I dress the part and go with them platonically.

Every couple of months, one person or another throws a giant creature effects industry party at their house or apartment, where the same fifty or sixty effects artists get together to keep up with the news about upcoming projects and behind-the-scenes stories. Very few people have real dates with them. I don't know why, other than the fact that there simply aren't that many females in the effects industry, and we rarely have time to mingle with anybody else. So, we just go to parties and talk to the people we work with.

By far, the best attended party is Ve Neil's Halloween party (Nowadays, most people know Ve for being a judge on *Face Off* or her work designing Beetlejuice's makeup, but back then, she was just another one of us.) Every creature artist spends weeks — months — challenging themselves to create elaborate and outlandish Halloween costumes for just that one night. It's one of the few times they're free to do what they want to make instead of what the producer and the script demand.

I can't make anything as elaborate as theirs, but I hold my own well enough after being inspired by some black and gold geometric patterned trim I found at the fabric store. I make a cape of orange, yellow and red Plexiglas diamonds, stiffen a wig, and use latigo to lace together a geometric-trimmed top and long loin cloth, creating my own Aztec Fire Goddess. Mine may not have been the wildest, the coolest, or the most elaborate costume parading around Ve's pool — that nobody abandoned their costumes to swim in — but my design kept me from being invisible, at least for that one night in October.

But today is just an ordinary Tuesday, and I'm invisible. This past weekend, even though the desert air gets pretty cold in January, Carl Surges had a pool party. He heated his pool to ninety-seven degrees and his hot tub to a hundred-and-two, so unlike at Ve's party, most people spent most of their time indoors, or in the pool.

I talked to a lot of people there and had a terrific time, but those people won't remember me. I was dressed as myself. I'm still just a young, generic brown-haired skinny girl, who looks like so many other brown-haired skinny girls that there's nothing to remember. About the only thing that makes me different is that I'm the one looking normal. I don't have cool heavily gelled hair, or spikes on my clothes, or heavy black eyeliner. My ears are only pierced once — another of my Rules.

So, here I sit on the tenth month of my two-week job, stuffing Teddy's hand-puppet friends called Fobs, reminiscing like Cinderella after the ball. Invisible.

Linda pops out of her office, carrying a portable television and plunks it on one of the tables. "The Space Shuttle Challenger is launching in one hour. This is history in the making, and I'm not going to miss it."

I'm excited. I thought I was going to have to miss it. The Challenger will have the first average person aboard — a high school teacher, named Christa McAuliffe. This is so cool. A normal person. Not a scientific genius or an engineer. Just a normal person like…

…like I pretend to be.

We're like a bunch of kids on the last day of school before Christmas break, watching the clock, trying to do our work just well enough to keep from getting in trouble.

"It's time!" Linda calls from the other room.

We shuffle our shoulders so everyone has a clear view of the screen, and we wait.

The countdown begins. "T-minus ten… nine…eight…" Hugh Harris keeps the countdown going. At "Liftoff" the Challenger pushes itself off the platform, climbing so slow that it looks like it's going to lose its fight against gravity.

Imagining what the astronauts must be feeling at that very moment, I'm overwhelmed by the adrenaline inside my own body. Laughter escapes my lips and soon the entire group, with our eyes locked on the screen and my mind riding the rocket, celebrate as if we have contributed to the mission.

The Challenger explodes.

A shuttle, carrying astronauts and a schoolteacher, disintegrate right there on national television.

I'm mute. I can hardly fathom what I just saw. This isn't just a story of something that *had* happened, something that we would later hear about, like the moldmaker I knew who died in a shootout with the police last fall. I just saw real people — in real time — get blown out of existence.

The news plays the scene in a virtual loop, while they talk about how horrible it is, and I watch those people in that rocket die over and over again. My head races to thoughts of Christa's family, her students, and the other astronauts who probably dreamed of riding off into space since they were little kids. I feel as if I'm with them, still alive but looking at their trip through a window, their disappointment for their dream that will never come true and of their chance to say goodbye ripped away from them with just enough time for them to have these thoughts themselves before they were vaporized.

Thirty minutes later, with my mind still clawing to accept what I just witnessed, my hands are threading a needle to sew together the parts of the next new toy.

Life goes on — especially in the entertainment industry.

People have bad days — *I* will have bad days. People die — *I* will know people who die. I must remember that there will always be people out there who don't know me, and whose lives are not a part of my personal issues. Maybe they'll even have contractual obligations like Ken and Alchemy II has to Worlds of Wonder. We're all part of one big chain with our lives linked end to end. Those people who don't know me won't allow — or just like Ken and Alchemy II — *can't* allow my issues to become their burden. Those people still need their jobs. My deadline is their deadline too.

Not for one second do I believe Ken doesn't care about the impact the Challenger's explosion might have on Ms. McAuliffe's family, her friends, her students, and so many others terrorized by what we witnessed. But stopping my life from moving forward because of something I cannot change, when hundreds — if not thousands — of people are relying on my seemingly irrelevant contribution to any one particular day of hand-sewing seams shut on Fobs to keep that chain connected.

I have to meet my deadline so they can have work to keep their jobs secure. I am a link in a much bigger chain. To not fail, I must always honor *The Chain*. It is my responsibility. It is my new Rule.

(ONE MONTH LATER)

With my friends talking about working on *Captain EO*, *The Fly*, *Big Trouble in Little China* and *Aliens*, I'm dying to try my hand in the creature effects industry, but I can't figure out how to tell Ken Forsee, who has given me so much, that I want to quit. Quitting is so permanent — and when it isn't, it's so hard to come back from.

FLASHBACK:

11. Illinois — Sophomore Year of High School

Knowing the band leader forces the football players to march in the halftime show or flunk band, joining theater means the conflicting performance schedule will cause me to flunk band, so I am going to have to give up the flute I've played since fifth grade. I justify it as: This isn't *failing*; this is a responsible choice.

The posters go up announcing the audition dates for *The Prime of Miss Jean Brody*. My stomach back-flips.

I've been in several plays at the community college, but they were musicals. This is a straight drama. The only acting I've done is with the summer children's theater in the park. I had a lot of fun being the lead villain, but I doubt if it's enough experience for this well-reputed school theater program.

Theater in Freeport is huge. The town population is just over thirteen thousand, but it boasts three live stages, a band shell in the park, and a concert hall. People drive from Chicago — two-and-a-half hours away — to sit in the high school's eight-hundred-seat theater in this dinky little farm town.

If I land a part, I'll be into the big league in this little town.

On my way to class, I walk past a poster, certain I'll miss the date, I reread it. *September twelfth and thirteenth, with call backs on the fourteenth* — two days away.

After English class, I pass another poster. *September twelfth and thirteenth...*

The next day, I pass the same poster by the Mass Media room. *September twelfth and thirteenth, with call backs on the fourteenth* — one more day.

I reread everything. If I see a poster, a billboard, or even a *Home Sweet Home* sign, I have to read it and reread it, as long as it's in view, just in case I missed something. I'll read the same graffiti in the same bathroom stall every single day. I know what each stall wall says before I even enter, but I still read the stupid walls every time anyway. I can't *not* read it. My friend's house has a mirror with a poem on it. I read it every single time I see it. I still can't recite the poem — because I don't really care what it says — but still, I have to read it anyway.

It's the big day. After Mass Media, I read the poster again. *September twelfth and thirteenth, at three-o'clock.* Three o'clock. All day long I reread the posters and recalculate how much time I have.

Entering the choir room after school, I do a quick head count — something else I always have to do. I recount each time more enter, updating my tally like a dog shepherding its herd. So far, there are twenty of us for sixteen parts. I can't be cut.

I check the clock. Two-fifty. I still have ten minutes.

More girls enter. Now there's room for the director to cut some of us.

By the time Mr. Estrem, the director, closes the door, I know he's going to cut at least three boys and eight girls, and my confidence dies right there in the second chair from the left side of the room.

My line reading is okay, but not leading lady material. That's not a *failure* though because I'm just here just to get warmed up for the musical.

When I arrive the next morning, there's already a swarm around the cast list posted outside the drama classroom door. I wedge my skinny frame between a pair of shoulders and squeeze my way through until I can see the list. As I read down, I notice a few missing names, and in my head, the count I tallied three days ago starts erasing the extra faces until I can see the kids left who make up the cast — I am one of them.

Six other girls and I have landed the part of *Student*. Still, I'm in and many others aren't — so I didn't fail.

At the read-thru, whenever we come to a place where the line is for *Student*, I lift my hand, but Mr. Estrem passes me by and gives the line to someone else. Another line. I lift my hand. Again, he passes over me. Line after line, he looks around, as if I'm invisible.

He isn't going to give me one single line.

We hit another batch of lines, and I don't even bother to wiggle a finger. It doesn't matter. I'm invisible.

Ellen whispers to me, "Do you have any lines yet?"

My head moves side to side so slightly, that I'm not even sure she can tell.

"Lynette doesn't have any lines yet." She says big and bright.

Mr. Estrem looks at me and pauses, before turning to Beth, who already has five lines — I'm counting. "Beth, why don't you take this one."

We haven't even started rehearsing and already the director hates me. But unlike with Ed Parish, this time, the entire cast can see I'm not wanted.

The next Monday, when I show up for the first rehearsal, my whole body is vibrating. *Don't back down*, I tell myself.

After I told my parents what happened at the read-thru, I told them what I wanted to do. I've since told Ellen and several others in the cast, too. I've stated it aloud, so now I have to follow through.

Now, I wait.

Mr. Estrem enters the back of the enormous theater, and I march straight toward him.

The walk is long. The entire way, I remind myself that I have to follow through with my witnessed decree or I'm a failure.

I hold out my script to him. *To stay is to fail.*

"What's this?"

"It's my script. If you don't want me to be in your play, you can find someone you do want."

The walk to approach him was slow. My exit is much faster — but I don't run. I walk out the door, never looking back to see if that dumbfounded look on his face has left, feeling the power of finishing *The Prime of Miss Jean Brody* on my terms — not his. I didn't allow him to make a failure of me by ignoring and humiliating me in front of everyone, and it felt good.

What a stupid thing to do.

Mr. Estrem also directors the musicals.

I had to quit. I said I would. If I stayed, I would've failed everyone I told. But now that I've quit; I've failed me.

DISSOLVE BACK TO:

12. Reseda, California — Back to Alchemy II

Before I can find a way to leave, my Chain grows a new link. Teddy Ruxpin becomes the number one selling toy in the nation in December, so Ken Forsse writes a live action children's show based on Teddy and the other characters from his world. Film work is coming to me.

Of all the characters, Linda assigns me to construct the six Bounders. She hands me a drawing of something that looks like a fanged unicorn tadpole. No arms. No identifiable body. Just legs attached to a wacky muzzled head.

She gestures toward the sewing room. "The actors are waiting for you to take their measurements."

The place is empty. I turn to leave, but then I hear a voice.

There are five men and one woman standing at the other end, their heads hidden behind projects on the worktables. They all act as if there's nothing unusual going on, but then why shouldn't they? I'm the weird one. I'm five feet seven inches tall, and they range between three-six and four-foot-four.

In no time at all, they use the term *dwarf* and point to the short upper bones on Art that show he has a different form of dwarfism than Cindy who has the prominent forehead. While I'm not sure calling them dwarfs is proper to the rest of the world, among the Little People of America, they strut their irreplaceable advantage with pride.

I'm going to have the pleasure of working with this group of little people for the next three months. I can only hope they can teach me how to be as comfortable in my skin as they are in theirs.

Linda explains to me how character suits are built by Alchemy II, laminating three layers of quarter-inch foam sandwiching cheese cloth between then by a lot — and I do mean a lot — of Barge rubber cement. The build-up is done over a Styrofoam form of the character covered in aluminum foil. When the layers of lamination are complete, the piece is slit and slipped off. Wha-la, a foam body with no major fabrication skills needed.

I don't know how to foam sculpt, but I'm sure this can't be the standard process because all the Barge fumes make it toxic as hell. Still, she's the boss, so she gets to make the rules.

While laminating three patterned layers of foam with staggered seams from one layer to the next, I learn a lot about patterning sheet foam. I also realize there are lots of similarities between cutting and sewing fabric into shirts or pants and cutting and gluing foam into a torso or a leg — or even a giant bouncing mouth.

My math brain runs the numbers, as it always does. Three layers on six characters means eighteen foam pattern sets. A *Karate Kid* wax-on-wax-off job to hone my skills.

With so many characters to build for this pilot episode, Linda hires some of the top suit-building freelancers in the film industry to oversee their construction. The first is Arden Ashley, known by many as the queen of walkaround suits. Her reputation is so big that more than one person tells me that she can make or break people. If she works with me and decides I'm worthless, my career in the effects industry will be over before it starts. Next Bill Bryan, whose claim to fame is building and wearing the Marshmallow Man in *Ghostbusters*, joins the team. With Arden taking charge of the lead characters' bodies and Bill foam fabricating many of the heads, I'm poised to sponge up as much knowledge as I can.

When Arden overhears me expressing my doubts about this bizarre lamination method for the body pods and the simpler heads that don't need Bill's special touch, Arden concludes I'm worth teaching. On the sly, she teaches me the basics of real foam suit construction, from body pods theory, to joints, to basic figure finishing while I build the body for Louie — a one-off character who only appears briefly, so the carving team didn't want to carve more than just the head for him — and in the process, I learn just how unusual this lamination technique is — and why.

Learning from Bill is tougher. Because we're so crowded, Linda has moved me and my Bounders to the main warehouse space and has Bill at a bench she added to the room with the overlocks. I can go all day without ever seeing him at all.

I desperately want to see how a real foam fabricator creates something as elaborate as a head. A body is one thing. It has arms and legs, just like clothing has sleeves and pants. It makes sense. But a head... Where do you even start? I can't let this chance go to waste. But he's the Marshmallow Man and I'm nobody. He's not going to want me taking up his time.

The bathrooms are at the other end of the building. Rather than going down the hall, if I pass through the sewing room, I can go right by his workspace. If I'm quiet, maybe he won't even notice me — after all, nobody else does.

So, I set my little brain secretary to strategically track my bathroom trip count and the time between trips, to assure I don't appear to have health problems. During my tour, I notice he's seaming and gluing the foam similarly to the way I'm doing for the lamination method, but he's using a foam I've never seen before. I'm dying to know more, and so is Sue.

"Let's just go ask him," she says. She's my superior — he'll talk to her.

Shadowing her, so if he doesn't want us bothering him, I look like I only paused because she did, we both "head to the bathroom" through his work area.

She pauses. "What kind of foam is that?"

He picks up a head, flipping it around so she can see the inside as well as the outside, while I stay hands off and two steps back to be sure he's not offended by an eavesdropping underling. But not only is Bill not offended by Sue's questions; he seems enthusiastic about giving answers.

The foam, called L200, is relatively new to the film industry. It allows him the same firm structure the lamination gives the Scott foam, but he can do it in one three-quarter-inch sheet, so it's faster and uses only a fraction of the glue. I've heard of the foam before — enough to know there are very few people in the industry who've mastered it. Now, feeling a flat sheet of it, I have no idea how he's getting that stiff foam to take on such organic shapes, but I can see that it takes good patterning skills to handle it — and I know how to pattern better than most. So, I create my next Rule: *I'm going to master L200.*

There. I've said it. It must happen.

After Bill finishes the heads, Linda moves Bill to the main warehouse, near me. "If he needs help with anything on the Wooly Whats-it, you're his assistant."

I can't hide behind Sue this time. I don't know if he'll want my help, but I hope so hard there's probably a hovering neon arrow pointing to the top of my head.

The Wooly Whats-it is a pink, long-furred character, worn by a six-feet, six-inch tall man. Bill constructs the suit like a giant baffled beanbag with arms and short legs coming out of it, while asking about me and chatting along as if I'm a real co-worker, seemingly unaware that my Calm Mask is dangling cock-eyed under my chin.

Days go by, and my neon arrow starts to fade — until I hear, "Can you sew the fur cover while I assemble his head?"

I'm in!

While I drape and sew the pink cover for the body, I have the chance to work directly with a master foam fabricator — and he's as nice as he can be the whole time. He's generous with his knowledge and willing to answer any questions I ask.

Tim told me once that it was better to share information than to hoard it. He said if a person is incapable of learning it, nothing he says will help them anyway, and if they're smart, they'll learn it somehow. So, in an industry this small, you might as well teach them and make another friend.

I don't know if Bill considers me one of the incapable ones or smart ones. I guess I'll find out someday.

Making Wooly under such a tight schedule, Bill has to build his under-body with a lot of hand-sewing and raw seams, so Wooly isn't doing so well by the time he's done on-set. Since I fur-covered Bill's original Wooly Whats-it, when filming is complete, Linda has me rebuild the big guy for pick-up shots and public appearances, giving me a chance to duplicate the extremely complex understructure Bill engineered.

Running Bill's full beanbag process from theory to completion is a training like no other, and I come away from Wooly with knowledge I'm sure I'll use again someday — that is if I can apply what I learned and become one of the *smart ones*.

(MONTHS LATER)

I'm starting to feel the weight of my current Chain, and I'm not sure what to do about it. Even though I hear the inside scoop about movies long before they hit the theaters and I'm dying to join the excitement of the high-pressure fast-paced creature effects world, I stay with Alchemy II beyond Teddy's live action TV pilot and through more toy prototypes because Alchemy II has become such a part of me that I can't figure out how to give myself permission to quit.

FLASHBACK:

13. Illinois — High School

As it nears time for auditions for the musical, Mr. Estrem makes of point of telling me to try out. Disco is big, and I have a reputation as a fairly showy dancer. Any time it's slow at our family's ice cream parlor, we push the tables aside, turn up the music and dance. One of our workers and I rehearse whole routines, so we can go to the dances and clear the floor just like in *Saturday Night Fever* with our acrobatic spins, dips, and lifts. Apparently, Mr. Estrem has gotten the word that if he wants the best dancers in school for *Funny Girl*, he needs me on his roster.

He casts me as a Ziegfeld Follies girl, and I get to dance and strut like I know how to do. I even choreograph one of the dance numbers.

My junior year, the musical is *Anything Goes*. There are a group of backup dancers called Angels. That's the role I want to be, and I know my dancing is worthy of the role, but at auditions, I'll still have to read and sing.

I hate my singing voice. I have to nail this singing to be an Angel. If I don't, I'll wind up being third-girl-on-the-right.

"Lynette." The director calls me up.

I go to the piano and scan the choir room's terraced seating. Every face stares directly at me. The first row is face-level, and the sets of eyes locked on me are the confident ones, who know they'll get lead roles.

From our two song options, I pick *The Heaven Hop,* because it's the easier one.

The piano starts, and I'm suddenly taken back to one of the old black-and-white movies I watched called *Born Yesterday,* a movie about an airhead gangster's girlfriend who gets tutored on how to act more dignified. The character singing *Heaven Hop* is also an airhead gangster's girlfriend. I open my mouth and sing in a deliberately ugly but on-pitch voice that's something between a Bronx bimbo and screeching.

Giggles break out around the room — but they're my instigated giggles, not kids laughing at me behind hidden hands and smirks. I'm so thrilled by their reaction that I blow some of the words, even while I grip the music score so tightly, I'm crimping the pages. But I sing. And when I return to my seat, I hear applause.

The list for call-backs is up the next morning, and my name is on it for consideration for Bonnie — that supporting gangster's girlfriend part. The idea of memorizing all those lines, and maybe forgetting some of them in front of an audience of hundreds… I'll never survive.

Before the school day ends, I run to Mr. Estrem's office. "I don't want to be Bonnie. Please don't make me go to call-backs." I know to him I must sound neurotic. I've already walked out on one of his plays. Now, he's considering me for a major supporting role, and I don't want that either. "I want to dance. Bonnie doesn't dance. I want to be an Angel. Please don't ask me to be Bonnie."

An Angel I become. I'm good at it — and so are the two girls he casts to double as Bonnie.

I know I'm a decent dancer — but I don't have the guts for acting. I'm skinny. I have a pointy chin and crooked teeth. I'm not pretty like Seong. I'm flat-chested, and if my hair is even slightly short, people think I'm a boy. I don't have Bonita's spectacular singing voice. I can do the splits, but I can't do the Chinese splits too, like Donna.

I've vowed to my parents I'm moving to Hollywood, but performing isn't going to get me there.

A dancer who sings like Judy Holiday and is afraid to memorize lines is just a dancer. My days as a performer are numbered, and I know it. I'm going to have to look for a Hollywood job idea behind-the-scenes.

DISSOLVE TO:

14. Reseda, California — Back To Alchemy II

To appease my dream of being a monster-maker, by night, I become Batman. Donning my In-the-Know Mask, my friends ask me to save them from the patterning and sewing they don't know how to do themselves. I moonlight for friends whenever they need help with a deadline. Instead of sleeping, some nights, I find myself microwaving foam latex Pinocchio noses for an optometrist commercial.

Other nights, I sew small spandex core covers Tim needs, to produce foam latex skins for the miniature stop-motion shark he and Ted Rae are making for *Jaws: The Revenge*, along with detailed curtains, a duffel bag, and other tiny pieces Ted needs for the miniature boat their mini shark will attack in the scene he'll be filming.

By day, I put on my Normal Mask and go to work, where I work at the table on the main shop floor, listening to cassettes on my Walkman, virtually unnoticed.

I always have to start with my set listening routine. First is the soundtrack from *Amadeus*, where I use cranked-up Mozart to get my head running full-speed ahead. Second, the soundtrack from a rather tedious to watch art film called *Koyaanisqatsi* to settle into my typical fast but steady rhythm; then I shift to the Art of Noise album *No Sound* to keep from getting too tight. After finishing those three — always in that order — I free myself to listen to whatever I want. My choices swing from Bob Marley, The Nylons, Styx, Vollenweider, Stray Cats, or any number of movie soundtracks, my favorite go-to options being *Out of Africa*, *Bladerunner*, *Footloose*, *The Mission*, *The Cotton Club*, and *Ragtime*.

With Teddy and his friends done, we're creating more animatronic toy prototypes of other characters. After Mother Goose with the Ugly Duckling, I'm now working alone because Linda assigned me to the covering, cosmetic finishing, patterning, and, yes, even the umpteen salesman samples of Charles Schultz's Woodstock. Just as Teddy Ruxpin and Grubby have their hand-puppet friend, the Fobs, Charlie Brown and Snoopy will have Woodstock. Since she couldn't find fur that was the right color and length in the quantity I need, she had to settle for the right color and quantity. This leaves me shaving down yards and yards of bright yellow fur with a dog shaver, and nobody wants my big yellow fluff-mess all over the other projects.

Everybody else is in the fabrication room, working on either Charlie Brown — which is going very badly because that giant round head of his doesn't translate to something that can have an animatronic mouth at all — or Snoopy, who's looking good. My little yellow bird, with its body that, when it's squeezed, causes his head to throw back, so he looks like he's blinking, chirping, and flapping his wings all at the same time, is mine — all mine.

I've finished Woodstock's prototype and am halfway through shaving my third yard of fur when in walks Linda with a girl that can't be ignored. Her golden hair stands straight out, bobbing and weaving with every step she takes or turn of her head, like a dandelion seed ball dancing in a breeze. I run through Tolkien's characters, trying to place her. She doesn't even fit the description of one of his fantasy races of people. With her dark eyes, broad nose, and open smile, she's unique — I envy her already.

"This is Terri Hardin. She's going to be your help on Woodstock." That's all Linda says before she disappears, leaving me with this person I'm supposed to boss around. I've never been in command of anyone other than myself, and from Terri's relaxed confidence, I'm betting she has a lot more experience than I do. She should probably be the boss of me.

While we shave more yellow fur, Terri tells me she just finished work on Michael Jackson's *Captain EO* for Disney, where she worked with Tim. Before that, she worked with quite a few of my other friends on *Ghostbusters* — I was right about her experience level. She apparently knows everybody I know and then some.

I call the effects people I socialize with *friends*, even though I'm not sure we are. I think they tolerate me being around mostly because of my friendship with Tim Lawrence and Ken Hall, and they like them. Even at the parties, I still wear Masks and pretend I belong to keep from sliding into a corner.

Terri tells me she doesn't frequent the regular effects artist parties, with invitations spread only through word-of-mouth, so fans can't find us. She doesn't say why. She just doesn't.

As we trace, cut, sew, and glue, Terri's stories about the jaw-dropping projects she's worked on are inspiring and crushing. I'm going to have to leave Alchemy II to gain stories of my own if I'm going to be completely happy living in Hollywood.

Over the next few weeks, we become more than co-workers; we become friends. I learn that her unusual look comes from having a Black dad and a white mom.

"But my blond hair and light skin come from my dad's side. My mom has dark hair and an olive complexion." She goes on to tell about the challenges she had as an interracial child, not being accepted by whites because she looks strange, nor being accepted by the Black community because she's too white.

I can hide my weirdness, but hers is right out there for everyone to see, draw their own conclusion — no matter how uninformed it may be — and act upon. I admire her and wish I had even half the guts she has. I wonder, though, if her confidence is a mask like mine or whether she's walked the walk long enough to know how to survive in a world that hasn't wanted to accept her from the get-go.

I don't tell her everything about me because I want her to be my friend so very much. I need someone like her in my life. So, I tell her the same things I tell everybody else, the normal stuff — the safe stuff — and continue to keep the weird parts of me my secret.

By the time Terri finishes her time at Alchemy II, which was only long enough to help me with Woodstock and for me to help her with a core cover for her mermaid tail, we're socializing outside of work. With the effects industry being nearly all-male, she's my only close female friend, and I am hers.

I want to be a link in her Chain.

RETURN TO:

15. Van Nuys, California — Stan Winston Studio

It takes a long Chain to reach from one of the newest shops in the industry to one of the biggest, but somehow, I managed to hold on until I got here. I fill another flaw in the set of Raptor hands I'm patching — one of the few jobs I do at my assigned workbench.

With the Raptors being so large, I usually work out on the main floor, leaving my table to get piled with whatever anyone brings in the room and doesn't know where to put it.

I hate that. This is *my* table — that became the Rule the second Kathy assigned it to me — all four by eight feet of it. My tools sit to my left — never the right. My snacks go in the drawer; work-in-progress goes on the right, and my current project sits directly in front of my chair, which is very specifically one-third of the way from the left edge, so people entering through the door come in over my right shoulder where I can see them with a glance. All calculated and reasonable.

No sooner than I fire up the heat gun to spot-bake the foam latex patch when that door over my shoulder opens, and in comes Lindsay McGowan, one of Stan's up-and-coming project coordinators, with one of the guys from the mold department. They dump a complete neck-to-tail fiberglass shell on the floor and a bulky foam latex skin on my table.

I sigh and shut the heat gun back off.

Lindsay smiles with that smile of his that makes him completely unintimidating. "Do you think you can turn this into a suit?"

As far as I can tell, he didn't consult Kathy first and came directly to me — one more reason for her to hate me.

"What is it?"

"A baby Triceratops. It'll be in a cage, crying for its mother in a separate cage. They want to add it to a scene they're filming next week."

Spielberg loves pulling heartstrings. The man is always thinking, and this'll add a nice touch.

Maybe this will be my chance to... "Who's going to wear it?"

"Me," Lindsey says.

Hope dissolving faster than a slug in salt, I straighten my Professional Mask and kick myself into hyper-drive. I calculate how long it will take to cut apart the fiberglass form, joint it, add closures, pad the interior, skin it...

"You'll get the head tomorrow."

I don't have time for mistakes. If I stick to what I know, "I can do it."

The baby will be adorable ...alone — I feel it ...what it wants right there in eyeshot, but still out of reach — I feel that too.

It's not very often that I don't get to improve something during the construction process, something to make a puppet or suit lighter, more comfortable, faster — better than I've made before. Since early in my career, I've been obsessed with making things better than I've made before. Not only do I enjoy creating new ways to use materials, pushing the envelopes when it comes to construction, finding unique processes to make things move more realistically, at this point, my head speed runs every theory it can imagine whether I have time to implement it all or not.

I don't have time to do much for this baby, but I'll do everything possible. I must improve every single time. If I don't, somebody else will do what I do, and nobody will want me anymore.

DISSOLVE TO:

16. Reseda, California — Alchemy II

It's one thing to do midnight sewing jobs, but working with Bill Bryan and Arden Ashley, I learn fast that to play in their world, I'm going to have to improve my skills — a lot.

Teddy promises to hold his position as the number one toy in the world for the second year in a row. With his growing fame, he's invited to be the spokesperson for Missing and Exploited Children. For that, Teddy will go on a national tour, so we need to build walkaround suits of him. This means more Styrofoam-carved forms and toxic laminating.

I can't take it any longer.

After watching Bill sheet foam sculpt L200 heads and seeing photos of things Terri, Arden and Steve Sleap patterned for Shafton Inc. — the company building Smoky the Bear, Woody Woodpecker, among others — I know for a fact that absolutely no professionally built suits are made with cheesecloth and gallons upon gallons of rubber cement.

While I live under the constant mental threat of being hated, my Rule: *You must always be perfect* takes over. But this insane technique is stopping me from doing my best, and I learned years ago that to get what I want, I have to be uncomfortable.

FLASHBACK

17. Illinois — High School (The Last Day of Junior Year)

Most of the kids in the musicals are also in the concert choir. I'm not. To make things worse, my best friend, Todd, is one of the school's biggest triple threats — great actor, great singer, and great dancer — and he keeps asking why I don't try out for choir.

I have a great singing voice — if you like Charlie Brown. Pitch but no style. That's me.

Todd asks me again. "Are you trying out this year?"

The choir director has heard me sing during musical auditions. He isn't going to want me. "I don't have room in my schedule."

"Are you trying out this year?" — "I'm thinking about taking a drawing class."

"Are you trying out this year? — It's too late for me to start now."

"You should at least try." — "I'll think about it."

I'm not auditioning for anything else where singing is concerned. The musicals are terror enough. Luckily, this is the last time I'll have to dodge this bullet. At four o'clock today, choir tryouts for my senior year will end, and I'll be free forever. Besides, Todd and I are meeting by the back door today to walk to Mike's house to play Dungeons and Dragons with the guys in his basement. I can't disappoint them.

Instead of meeting me at the door, Todd catches me at my locker just as I collect the last folder. As we head for the exit, the halls are quiet except for our chatter about how many skeletons Mike will hit us with today — Mike loves his skeleton armies. The lights are already off, but we don't need them. The sun through the glass doors throws a beam that ricochets off the polished granite floor, and enamel-painted lockers, giving us plenty of light.

Todd stops. "Last chance." He points to the choir door."

I look at my watch. Three-fifty. Ten minutes slower, and there wouldn't have been a reason for him to stop.

The pain that hits me every time my friends enter that room and I have to pass it by thumps me again.

"Ah! You want to do it."

Seriously?! I only hesitated for a second.

"Come on." Todd grabs my wrist and drags me through the doors into Mr. Lehman's office. "Hey, J.L., she's here to try out for choir."

J.L. looks from me, to Todd, and back to me. "Are you trying out?"

"Yes, she is," Todd says, drowning out my "I guess so."

I'm so scared I can't remember the words to *My Country 'Tis of Thee* when J.L. asks me to sing it and instead sing the lyrics on a piece of craft paper in our basement.

My turkey 'tis of thee,

So good with cranberry, to thee I sing.

I save your breast and wings.

Your bones are fit for king,

But I can't eat a thing.

I'm di...et...ting.

When my senior year class schedule shows up in the mail, not only do I find myself in concert choir, but in the group of the elitest-of-the-elites — the show choir.

CUT TO:
(SENIOR YEAR)

The show choir is J.L.'s baby. With only eight girls and eight guys, we sing for clubs and events, while working toward the year-end big show — *Showtime!*

This year, J.L. adds a swing-style dance duet to Duke Ellington's swing called *It Don't Mean a Thing*.

This is my chance. While I didn't play Bonnie in *Anything Goes*, I choreographed the swing dance musical interlude for *The Heaven Hop*. I've already proven myself. My stomach flutters as I prepare to do the closest thing to being Ginger Rogers dancing with Fred Astaire.

He asks us who we'd recommend for Todd's dance partner.

Just the idea of the attention has me blushing already. But my Cloak of Invisibility sweeps over me, and all heads turn to Karen.

Forgotten again.

"*I can't...*" Karen's voice fades off, but there's the knowing-look exchange between her and J.L. tells me they've already discussed this in private.

It doesn't matter that they've seen me dance in three musicals and even choreographed a dance I taught several of them to do. I'm unmemorable.

Unwanted.

At last, one lone girl mentions my name, and suddenly, it's like I just stepped into the room. Another seconds the idea, and then the rest offer their unanimous support.

This duet with Todd, full of dips and flips that have the audience's applause drowning out the song several times before it ends, does more than just give me the satisfaction of finally giving me that dance in the spotlight. Todd shows me that his faith in me is stronger than my own, that if I apply myself, sometimes people will appreciate me, and that I'm holding myself back. All of his coercion — and forcing and dragging — shows me that if I truly want to get to Hollywood, I'm going to have to stop hiding from the threat of rejection. I must force myself to do things even when I'm afraid.

I lost the opportunity to improve by hiding from Ed Parish. I missed out on being a lead character in a play by rejecting the offer before the director could reject me. I almost missed out on concert choir and show choir. And by not speaking up, I almost missed out on my dream dance.

I've spent over nine years hiding my obsessive-compulsive habits from my friends and family by forcing myself to do things, not do things, or alter the perception of what I'm doing to appear *normal*. This will be no different.

If I can pretend to be normal, I can pretend I have confidence.

For me to be worth anything, I must abide by Rule #1: Failure is not allowed — ever. Period.

No matter how awkward the process is… I must succeed.

DISSOLVE BACK TO:

18. Reseda, California — Back to Alchemy II

I can never allow being uncomfortable to be the thing that stops me.

I slam on my Confidence Mask and march into Linda's office. "Why do we use this lamination technique?" — if you can call it a technique. Frankly, I think it's simply because the original Alchemy II team members are mainly clay sculptors, not foam patterning fabricators.

I wait for Linda to finish giving me the canned answers I've heard so many times: "Scott foam is an open-cell foam; L200 is a closed-cell foam. So, Scott foam is breathable and keeps the wearer's head cooler.

It's my turn. "I don't believe the foam is still open-celled with two layers of glue-impregnated cheesecloth between the three layers of foam."

"The glue doesn't clog the pores; the cheesecloth is open weave."

The new Teddy head I just laminated is still on my worktable. I take a razor blade and cut off his muzzle, fill it with water, carry it in, and sit it on her desk like a coffee cup. "That's how breathable this foam is now."

That's the end of the conversation, but by the time Ken Forsse has Alchemy II moved into its new, more spacious building, the foam carver is carving a new head for Teddy — but this time, it was out of rigid green foam, so the heads can be Vacuformed. When it comes back, we drill random holes all over the heads, and we have the first breathable, easy-to-maintain walkaround heads Alchemy II has ever made.

I improved their process. I made a difference — and it feels good.

FADE TO:

19. North Hollywood, California — Tim's Apartment

While I am improving, I still don't qualify as one of the big kids yet. So, while Tim and my friends go work for George Lucas at ILM for the next six months on Howard the Duck, I'm left babysitting Tim's turtle — I now know is named Turtle — and Takata, his Burmese python.

A perfect time to save some money for a one-bedroom apartment, I let go of my studio apartment. My studio apartment has served me well, but I can literally throw rocks onto the exit ramp of the Hollywood Freeway from my kitchen door. Besides, it's not the bedroom I want; I need a shop. If I take on freelance jobs to break into the effects industry while keeping my secure job at Alchemy II, I will have to get a place with more space.

Turtle is an easy roommate. He eats fruits and vegetables, and little bits of raw meat. Takata is another story. He eats two live rats every five to six weeks. The snake doesn't scare me, but the feeder rats do. Terri has a pet rat, and he's the sweetest thing ever. Feeder rats are mean.

All I have to do is put him in the bathtub, drop in a rat, and close the shower door. Twenty minutes later, when I come back, the rat is gone. Then, I do the same with the second rat. Once he's finished, he'll push open the shower door and roam the bathroom.

A few hours later, with Takata's aquarium clean and ready for its content resident, I return to the bathroom to find Tim has left out one tiny piece of information — he can turn doorknobs.

A seven-foot animal with no limbs can coil itself into almost any shape and fit almost anywhere, and the game of Hide-and-Seek is on.

It takes me over an hour to find him behind a bookshelf. While this trick is impressive, I don't find it much fun. Still, he doesn't bite or scratch; he doesn't make noise or tear up the furniture or need a litter box; and he doesn't leave fur on my clothes. Still, considering the apartment building has a no-pets rule, Takata makes a pretty good roommate.

CUT TO:
(FIVE MONTHS LATER)

Takata never concerns himself with my comings and goings, so with Tim's time at ILM almost over, he doesn't seem to care that it's time for me to move out.

It's been a good run. Between Alchemy II and hanging out with Ken Hall or his brother Cleve, I've had a pretty good five months. Except… there was that one time…

Cleve Hall (known mostly for his lead in the Syfy series Monster Man) and I watched back-to-back Hammer Mummy movies while dying his hair one Saturday night, and then we decided to go to the Seven Seas, the best-known goth club in Hollywood.

Dressed in seamed stockings, spiked heels, and a leather tuxedo coat and mini skirt, heavy eyeliner, and topped with the biggest hair I could create, I created a goth girl look, and off we went.

I'm not yet twenty-one, but Cleve was the king there, so he got me in with a simple wave to security. Being underage, it's against the rules for me to drink, but ginger ale in a glass looks like any number of drinks. So, I carried my ginger ale while we danced, and I strutted my stuff, trying out my new Cocky Mask. We had a blast.

The following weekend, Ken hosted a party at his apartment, featuring Cleve's famous chili, and Cleve warned me not to mention going to Seven Seas with him. His girlfriend was on the hunt to "kick the ass of the vixen" everyone told her Cleve had been seen with. (Hi, Gabrielle. It was just weird little me.) The party was fun. Being threatened by somebody, I'm certain, could indeed kick my ass… not so much.

But also, during the last five months, I flew up to join the northern California gang for a weekend.

Touring ILM was fun, but by now, I've visited friends in so many effects shops that I've seen enough worktables and mold rooms not to be overwhelmed anymore — inspired to work there, yes, but not overwhelmed. The ILM Christmas party that same weekend was something different, though.

Through the gate onto George Lucas's private estate, up the winding driveway through the woods, the house sits on top of a hill overlooking a massive, perfectly groomed lawn, complete with a baseball field on the right and an atrium/library on the left. (Skywalker Ranch is built up much more now, but at the time, Lucas still lived there on relatively undeveloped land.)

The party was in the most magnificent library I've ever seen, with a stained-glass dome ceiling and a balcony around the perimeter to reach the books in the main two-story room. I was Cinderella entering Prince Charming's castle.

I met *Return of the Jedi*'s Admiral Akbar, Tim Rose; Jeffrey Jones — who I couldn't help still visualizing as Emperor Joseph II in *Amadeus*, even while he was high or drunk — or both — and Tim Robbins, who wasn't known for much, but was known as an up-and-coming. George Lucas made a brief pass through some of the crowd, but he clearly didn't want to be the center of attention — nor the target of the friends and family's fan-attacks — so he slipped out the minute word got too loud that he was there.

Yet, even in this perfect world, as much as I wanted to taste the extravagant hors d'oeuvres spread over two banquet tables, my head continued to tell me the food could be poisoned, and I couldn't override it, so other than a canned cola and couple of chips I gamble on to keep my stomach from growling, I passed up all of it.

As in the fairytale, when the night ends, Cinderella finds herself back in her dull clothes, in her lonely home. But I don't have a home to go to until I find one.

CUT TO:

20. North Hollywood, California — My New... Home?

It doesn't take long to find the cute, older one-story apartment building with a one-bedroom apartment available just three blocks away. My apartment faces onto a quiet little side street, with a magnolia tree just off my stoop shading the afternoon sun from my living room, and the kitchen has a small tile shelf under the corner windows, perfect for vases and plants.

As so many effects artists do, I buy a futon sofa that will double as my bed so I can turn my bedroom into a shop. During the day, I stow away my bedding in an antique window seat I found for a decent price — every day. That's my new Rule. A front room is called the *living room*, not a bedroom. If I die, I can't have anyone finding a bedroom in the living room midday — even if nobody is supposed to be there but me. The only other furniture I buy is a folding card table with chairs for the kitchen.

To make my home complete, it needs a pet. My family always had pets while I was growing up, from the stray German shepherd that delivered nine puppies in the kitchen and the semi-tame stray calico cat we called Funny Company, to the eighteen-pound house cat with the grace of a semi-truck and our epileptic black lab. At one point, we even had a horse tied to a tree in our front yard that Greg won in a dollar-a-ticket raffle at the county fair.

Considering this new apartment is also a no-pets building, dogs and cats — and probably horses — are out of the question. If I put a dry aquarium under the table in my work room, nobody will have to know if I get a snake.

Two weeks is all it takes for me to find Pain — because he could be such a pain sometimes. He's a young Burmese python, barely four and a half feet long. He's much friendlier than Takata — almost sociable. He's beautifully vibrant, and he's all mine.

Two weeks later, Alena, one of the girls in the front office at Alchemy II who wore the Louie suit for the television pilot, stops me in the hall. "I've been asked to perform in a children's video."

"I didn't know you did so much suit performing."

"I'm a gymnast."

That I believe. She's a tiny little thing, but she has some power hips and thighs on her that don't happen without a lot of work of some kind.

"The client doesn't have any particular design, and there's not much money, but if you make the suit for me, you can keep it after the shoot."

My first free-lance job that isn't a part of somebody else's job. All I want to know is where's the design and when do I start.

"There's no design," she says. "The only requirements are that I have to be able to do acrobatics in the suit, and the monster has to be cute, because the point of the video is to show kids that the monster under their bed is more afraid of them than they are of it, and they want it colorful."

Hyper-drive kicks in. Make arms, legs, and hands I learned while working on Teddy's TV pilot. — I've covered heads but never made one — I understand the theory thanks to the repetitive layers on those laminating bodies. I can handle this.

"Oh, and one other thing — they want the mouth to move."

I've always heard the *oh-and* will get you. It's like college all over again.

FLASHBACK:

21. Bauder Fashion College — Arlington, Texas

With my family moving to Houston the summer after I graduated high school, getting an Associate's Degree in Fashion Design Bauder from a college near Dallas, Texas seems logical. I have to get to Hollywood by the time I'm twenty, and I'd grown up liking arts and crafts, so a degree in Fashion Design will qualify me to do costuming — beadwork, armor, fur work… That sort of thing.

There's one catch in my plan. The college expects me to have a basic knowledge of sewing, and I don't — not really.

"I've taken a sewing class," I say during the phone interview. It was only for nine weeks as part of a Home Economics class and I wasn't good at it, but… "Yes, I know how to sew."

Thankfully, they don't ask for a sample garment.

My college instructor, who's also a working designer in Dallas, announces, "In this class, you will make a lined suit. It must have a notched lapel collar, welt pockets with flaps, bound buttonholes, and a kick pleat in the skirt or pleated slacks."

If she didn't see my eyes pop out of my head, I'd be surprised. I don't even know what a welt pocket is — or bound buttonholes, for that matter, let alone how to make them — and I only find out what a notched lapel is because someone else asks.

It's Ed Parish's ballet class all over again. My parents paid more money than they could easily afford for me to attend this college because I insisted on it to the point that I looked at no others. I can't fail them my first week and put them in debt for nothing any more than I could quit Ed's class. But this instructor has the faith in me Ed had. Still, I'm stuck.

After mimicking others in class for the first few days, with lines like "This machine threads differently from the one I'm used to. Can you show me how this one works?" and reading the instruction so intently, I must look like I'm reading *War and Peace*, I meet Sheryl.

I think Sheryl started sewing before she could walk. Compared to the other students, she's still a sewing wizard.

"Sheryl," I start in one evening over our dinner of mediocre Salisbury steak dinner I assume is safe to eat — unless the college wants to genocide the whole dorm. "Can you give me a few tips? I don't know how to sew." Before she can question how or why I'm even here, I push on. "I'm a fast learner, but if Ms. Duran finds out, I'm doomed." I don't elaborate on my definition of *doomed*.

She and I rendezvous in her dorm room several days a week, where she has her personal sewing machine set up on her desk. First, she teaches me how to thread a machine and wind a bobbin. Then, I graduate to straight seams and curves until I'm finally able to make those welt pockets and bound buttonholes.

Meanwhile, in class, I hide behind my Confident Mask and keep busy under the eyes of my hovering instructor by cutting out and marking pieces of my suit and pinning together parts to sew mostly in the evenings in Sheryl's room.

I earn an A on that suit, and to my credit — and Sheryl's — Sheryl never once sews anything on my actual project. That would be cheating, and according to my Rules, cheating is failure, and I cannot — will not allow myself — fail.

DISSOLVE BACK TO:

22. North Hollywood, California — My New… Home?

This time, I'm not faking knowing how to sew a welt pocket. I'll be faking an entire suit …and a head with jaw movement. This project's *oh-and* is a doozy. Even so, I can't stop my head from doing its Hyper-drive calculations.

The body, I can figure out — But I haven't made a head before — I watched Bill make Wooley's head, and it had a mechanical jaw — If I make the jaw separate, make a chin cup for Alena, and add some elastic for a return spring… "I'll do it."

I ask Sue and Jackie from Alchemy II to help me in the evenings, and suddenly, I'm a boss. The word *boss* sounds mean though. I prefer *head of the project*. My crew has more experience than I do, so I can't really boss them around. Besides, by the end of next week, I won't be the *boss* of anything again. We'll be just co-workers again.

I get advice from Arden on how to make a padded torso, and I use my memory to roughly replicate the patterns I used for Louie's limbs and hands, and I make a mediocre-but-sufficient head while Sue and Jackie sew cover the body.

In a week and a half, Alena has a cartwheeling furry rainbow monster suit the client is happy with, and I discover that my perfection Rules and obsessive tracking make me really good at scheduling and delegating — more skills I can add to my toolbox.

Sunday afternoon, while trying to figure out how best to arrange my clothes in the built-in drawers in the hallway, one of the friends from my first apartment building calls. "Wanna shoot some pool this evening?"

I haven't had a chance to show off my new place to many people yet, so of course I tell him to pick me up at my place.

We grab a quick bite to eat at Bob's Big Boy and then hit a billiards hall on Ventura Boulevard. It's nice getting together with him again. We and three others used to bring our dinners and rendezvous at one of the patio tables by the pool every evening just to visit and keep from eating alone. The conversation was so pleasant that I never bothered to buy a television. And after living in Hollywood for well over a year now, I still haven't — though I'll probably pick up one soon.

By the time he drops me off, it's late. On weeknights bedtime is eleven-twenty — that's my Rule. I start getting ready for bed at eleven o'clock — which includes literally *making* a bed to get into. Then I still have a few minutes to read before I turn off the light. Now, it's nearly midnight. My self-assigned seven and a half hours of sleep I'm supposed to get — give or take twenty minutes — is only going to be six-and-a-half.

Calculating... I can gain ten minutes by not reading and another twenty by setting my alarm for seven-twenty instead of seven — That'll only give me twenty minutes in the morning, but I save time by eating Pop-tarts in the car on my way to work. And since falling asleep only takes fifteen to forty-five seconds, if I hurry, I'll only lose thirty minutes.

CUT TO:
(LATER THAT NIGHT)

A hand cupped over my mouth takes me from sweet Dreamland to a thousand-percent adrenaline as fast as I can open my eyes.

"I have a gun. Don't make any noise and I won't hurt you." It's a man's voice. He has me pinned down and he's pressing something hard against the side of my head.

I don't know if it is a gun, but it's blunt and hard, and I'm in no position to doubt him.

He pulls the covers over my head so I can't see him, and he rapes me. My head dashes from one room to another, desperately searching for a Mask to wear, a place to hide. I have nowhere to go. Then it hits me. I'm not allowed to panic. I created that Rule after I wrecked my mom's T-bird, and my dad told me that panicking was dangerous.

Panicking is against the Rules. Like a switch, I shut down my racing thoughts and start thinking as clearly as if I was alone. What am I supposed to do?

A scene from one of my favorite childhood TV shows, *Adam 12*, comes to mind. Every episode, at some point, one of the officers holds a notepad and tiny pencil and asks, "Did you see anything? Can you give us anything that will help us?"

I need to collect information.

My head kicks into hyper-focus. I lift the edge of the blanket to steal a glimpse of anything — a peek, a sound, a smell — anything that might later help the police to catch him. The magnolia tree is shading the streetlight, causing the living room to be engulfed in dark shadows, broken by only a few small stark spots that are almost as bright as if the lights were on.

I lift it a little higher.

He shoves the blanket back down — one of the light pools must be aimed right at me.

I think again about the gun. "I can't breathe." — that's partly true. I'm hyperventilating though, not suffocating.

He holds the edge of the blanket up, so I can catch my breath, and then goes back to his business.

I don't dare try to peek again. I doubt he'll be so patient a second time. Still, I have to collect information for the police. They'll expect me to give them something.

I listen to the rustle of the fabric — jeans, and what sounds and feels like a zip-up canvas windbreaker. The feel of his gloves — cheap cotton garden gloves sold by the half-dozen at hardware stores. His build — lean and relatively fit. Probably not much taller than me. Maybe five-seven to five-nine. His voice — smooth, with a slight clip on some words, as if he's American but lives in a Hispanic community.

It's not much, but it's all I can gather before he says, "Don't move until I'm gone" — and then he is.

Gone.

The second I hear the kitchen door shut I start shaking like I'm naked in the Arctic. I fumble to turn on the lamp sitting on my cardboard box telephone table.

The power is out.

In the dark, I dial 911, my report on the end of my tongue so I can get the words out as soon as I hear a voice.

The call connects. I take a breath to start — and a Spanish recording puts me on hold, telling me *responderemos tu llamada momentaneamente*. I don't speak

Spanish, but I know this means I'm going to have to hope this guy doesn't return even longer, because help is not on the way.

I'm on hold for almost ten minutes with recordings alternating between English and Spanish.

"911. What's your emergency?"

Saying *I've just been raped* into the phone is the hardest thing I've ever had to do in my life.

Dispatch stays on the line with me until the police arrive, find the breaker box, and turn the lights back on.

As one of the two male officers inspects the crime scene — my home — I stand dumbly in the living room with his partner.

After several minutes of silence, broken only by me repeating some of the information I had collected for them — most of which he isn't bothering to write down because he's telling me the zipper was probably his pants and not a jacket — which is both ridiculous and pisses me off. The guy would've to be wearing a pair of unrealistically light-weight jeans with a freakishly long zipper on them. Does he seriously not think I can tell the difference between denim and canvas, or a jacket zipper and a fly? Oh, please!

I point this out and the officer turns his head to me and shrugs. "The chances of us catching this guy are slim. In a city this size, and a place this close to a freeway" — as if you can live much of anywhere in a city that isn't relatively close to a freeway — 'all he had to do was get in a car and disappear to anywhere."

The energy in my head has my brain ready to explode. I am — or he is — saved by his partner's return.

Evidence shows that the guy came in through the back door earlier in the night, by reaching the lock from the nearby window that had a stop on it to keep anyone from fitting through it. Finding me not home, he'd tried to hide in the closet in the kitchen, but the closet was so full of brooms, mops, cleaners, and everything else I hadn't yet found a place for that he didn't fit; he left. The officer's theory is that he'd watched me long enough to know that I was usually in bed by eleven, and my late return threw off his plan.

When I locked up the house tighter before going to bed, I hadn't noticed the missing window screen because the curtain hung over the opening. On his return, throwing that extra deadbolt the landlord had installed so close to the floor that nobody on the outside could reach it through the window, he couldn't reenter the same way. So, he removed the screen over the corner sink, set all the crap I had stacked on the sill on the ground outside, and balanced on that tiny tile triangle to climb over the heap of dirty dishes I had piled in the sink — I hate washing dishes and don't do them until I'm out — to make his way stealthily into the living room.

"It's good you didn't fight him. Another one of his victims tried to resist and he cut her with a knife."

Another one of his victims — "There's more than just me?"

"Yeah. You make four now. With everyone still on edge over the Night Stalker last year, we haven't wanted to go public until we had a good profile on him."

The Night Stalker raped, tortured, and killed thirteen people before he was caught — yet they're not telling anybody this guy even exists?

The first cop wanders off to check my shop — for evidence, or to go to the bathroom. Who knows. I'm still stuck on the fact that I'm victim number *four*, and they have yet to report any of this to the news stations. I guess since he's not been violent by a man's definition of *violent*, he's not enough of a threat yet.

"The gun is new for him. I guess after the altercation, he's decided to upgrade." This asshole is talking like this is one of those old cop shows. At least on those shows, they had the decency not to talk like this in front of the victim.

The other cop reappears, chuckling nervously. "I just got a load of that snake you have back there. Too bad he didn't get loose while that guy was here. That would've put a stop to things, I'll bet."

"Please, don't tell my landlord that I have him. Pets aren't allowed to be here."

He raises a hand. At least I know he can keep a secret — almost too well, if they're not going to alert the public that there's another rapist on the loose.

When I return from the hospital, I change my bed back into a sofa so I sit — alone — with my back to a wall — and wait for the sun to rise. I'm not sure what I'm supposed to do now.

I can't call anybody. Nobody is awake yet. It'd be rude to wake them up for something they can't do anything about. Besides, they won't have time to talk to me. It's Monday. They have to go to work — I'm supposed to be going to work. My co-workers will expect me to be there.

By sunrise, my Rules are leading the charge. I'm supposed to be getting ready for work — so I do. I'm supposed to be going to work right now — so I do. I must honor *The Chain*.

The new building Ken moved Alchemy II into still isn't complete, so the fabrication room is nothing but a framed room with plastic walls, leaving us semi on display. I've spent my whole life pretending to be normal. It's time to pretend harder.

As I cover the head for a David Raccoon a potential for the *Kingdom Chums*, the chit chat in the room sounds the same as any other Monday morning, with Sue, Jackie and Arden talking about their weekend. I even tell them about mine — just stopping short of last night. We laugh and sew, and Arden tells us about the new iris she's added to her insanely huge botanical collection, Mike, who carved David's head form, checks my progress and likes what he sees, and throughout the morning, my pulse settles.

When Sue and Jackie go out for lunch and leave me alone with Arden, I stay in. Arden has a daughter. She's the closest thing to a mother I have nearby. She'll be good practice for talking about my situation.

She's stunned. "Why didn't you say anything before?"

"Because I don't want to be treated differently. I needed to prove to myself nothing else has changed" — and it hasn't.

Nothing about my daily life is different. Last night was horrible, but it was caused by one horrible person — not by Mike or the hard-working Hispanic people working the food truck that sets up in the parking lot at ten-twenty every morning, not by the lean man doing the mechanics on the Teddy's walkaround heads, not even by the guy in his crappy little hatchback who cut me off on the freeway this morning.

Near the end of the day, I tell Sue and Linda but then steer the conversation away from the topic as quickly as possible. There's nothing to tell. Details would be strictly to satisfy morbid curiosity. If I tell them the cops told me odds of them catching the guy are slim, they're going to get indignant on my behalf, or try to play amateur detective and have me telling them details over and over — which is moot because I've forgotten nothing. None of that will let me be normal.

Logic says, nothing I say or do will remove what happened any more than reminiscing over a great day makes that memory go away. It was a bad day.

I'll add a few more Rules to my routine: I'll check the door locks and screens multiple times before (and several times again after) I get in bed. I'll rig the doors and window with noisemakers, so nobody else can sneak in (and adjust this several times to keep a stir from triggering unnecessary fear.) I'll wedge poles in the top half of the window frames so they can't open further than a few inches. Each time I return home, I'll check all the rooms, closets, and cupboards large enough to hold a five-year-old *before* locking myself in — in case I have to make a run for it — by scoping out the rooms as I go deeper into the apartment and again as I backtrack to lock the door. I'll block the closet doors; in case I've missed some cartoon-skinny rapist capable of hiding behind a vacuum cleaner. And I will move on.

Do I want to go back to that apartment? Hell no. But I signed a lease, so I have to live there.

I came to Hollywood to work for the movies. I've only been here a little over a year. Leaving, I'd have to break my lease and give up on my dream, and I won't — can't — do that. Period.

CUT TO:
(THE NEXT WEEK)

After a very long Monday, I stayed the night in Sue's guest room. The next day, I flew to Northern California for a few days to visit the friends who have yet to come home. The day after I return — and spend an hour getting up to check and recheck the doors and windows before falling asleep — my mom arrives. As with the only four other people I've told, I breeze over my retelling and quickly get back to the present.

The police have left my kitchen in shambles. My entire room, from door frames to furniture to floor, is covered in charcoal gray fingerprint dusting powder for me to clean up — movies never show this part. I told the cops the guy was wearing gloves, so after the first few thick fuzzy prints, they could've taken my word for it and not dusted the chairs he never even sat in. At least since I sleep in the living room and have almost no furniture, beyond the door jams — which even *I* don't touch — they didn't dust the entire place.

While my mom and I scrub — and scrub some more — the landlord stops by to tell me he's not going to hold me to the lease, and I can move or stay at will.

There's a second story, one bedroom apartment available in the building where Tim lives, which will also keep me walking distance from Ken and Cleve Hall, who are now a couple of my closest friends.

Shortly after my mom leaves, without even knowing why I'm moving again so soon, Cleve offers to help me carry my few pieces of furniture the three blocks and up the stairs. I'm sure we make quite the sight, a nerdy young girl and a spiked goth guy walking down the middle of the street with a foam block futon sofa over our heads but then, very little about me is normal beyond my outer shell, so away we go.

Furnished, safe, and all moved into my place high above the ground; with pocket doors able to close off the hallway leading to the bathroom and my shop, and another closing off the kitchen, Pain will never live in an aquarium again.

I've already figured out that snakes are much smarter than most people think, but then, if you lived your entire life in a glass box, you'd be stupid, too.

Since snakes don't have eyelids, it's impossible to tell if Pain is simply lying still or asleep — not that they see very well anyway. They see mostly just silhouettes and rely on their tongues, the heat pits below their nostrils, and vibrations for information — he's great at predicting earth tremors as much as a few hours before they happen. After surprising Pain a few times by grabbing him up out of a sound sleep, I started patting out a rhythm on the screen of his aquarium before opening the lid. When he heard the rhythm, he'd lift his head toward the lid, ready to climb onto my arm.

Now that he roams free, I pat out that same rhythm on the floor and call him from behind the sofa, off the curtain rods, or from wherever he's hiding if I don't think to close a pocket door before he wanders into the other room.

I call Terri to tell her I've moved, and she asks the inevitable question. "So soon? I thought you liked it there."

I get as far as *I was raped and didn't want to live in a ground-floor apartment anymore* and she says, "We'll be right over."

We are her and her fiancé, Howard. He goes with her most places as her driver, assistant, and bodyguard. Instantly, he's my bodyguard too.

A couple of hugs and a brief discussion and I'm ready to move the subject to the now — not the then. I don't even invite them to sit down, in case they intend to prolong the topic.

I know I'm supposed to jump when I hear strange noises from the other room or grow tense whenever a man walks near me or I hear an accent similar to my attacker. I'm supposed to keep reliving the moments in my mind, frequently be on the verge of tears, or any number of other trauma responses I've seen in the movies and on the news that rape victims carry with them — but I do none of those things.

I don't want to talk about it because the more I do, the more I confuse people. They'll think I'm faking strength, trying to soldier through alone, suppressing my feelings — but I'm doing none of those things either. I know it's weird, and I can't even have "normal" victim reactions.

Memories don't go away — good day memories or bad. To me, they're all just information I tuck into my highly detailed memory bank where I can recall them very precisely, at any moment. But if there's no need to recall these details for the police, then why should I reenter that room?

I'll never be able to explain this anyone in a way that make sense, but with Terri and Howard I try — and they seem to sort of get that I'm like this simply because this is the way my head is wired.

The only thing I *do* feel is even more different — even less normal — weirder. Because even now, the only thing I'm focused on is the exact same thing I've been locked onto most of my life: continuing to work hard so people will hire me and improving my skills so people will still want me. I know this makes me weird, but it's just …me.

After I assure Terri and Howard that I will absolutely call them if I ever need anything, from then on, whenever we leave my apartment together, on our return, Howard checks the closets for me and then waits until they hear the turn of the deadbolt before they leave me with my legless bodyguard, Pain.

Day or night, at home, Pain is always nearby. He follows me around the apartment, sunbathes in the windowsill when I'm sewing, and rides my waist like a belt when go from room to room — because the poor guy can't crawl fast enough to keep up with me. When I come home, he feels the thump of the front door and comes out to greet me. And at night, he sleeps curled up in the corner of my bed, under the covers.

For anyone breaking into my apartment now, they are going to be in for a rude greeting from a Burmese python.

As for me… after I check the doors — again — I sleep just fine.

(After my attack, the police broke the story to the news stations. Because the guy always cut the power before entering, he became known as the Blackout Rapist.

The Blackout Rapist went on to attack a total of seven women before disappearing.

At one point, the police stopped by to show me a photo and have me listen to a recording of a suspect. The guy's accent was all wrong, and he was way too big to fit through a shoulder-high window and land on that tiny kitchen window without knocking off all kinds of crap — which goes to show how little they regarded my description, because traumatized women aren't supposed to be able to think straight… I guess.

Anyway, later, the police called to inform me there were similar attacks in Northern California and then in Florida. Their consolation to me was saying that while they hadn't caught him, I could rest easy because he had moved out of the area.

Unless he was inadvertently arrested for something else, the Blackout Rapist was never caught.)

FADE TO:

23. North Hollywood, California — My Colfax Apartment

After my confession to Terri and Howard, I put a *do not disturb* sign on that ugly colored room in my head and zero in hard to my goal to become a full-fledged monster-maker.

When the phone rings this time, it's Tim.

"I need some miniature clothes for a stop-motion shot I'm doing for a movie. Are you available?"

"Sure." I'm available for most things as long as I leave seven hours for sleep. "Come on up." Besides, if I say no, he'll hire somebody else, and then the next time he has a job I won't be the name he thinks of first.

A few minutes later, I hear Tim's footsteps on the stairs. I open the door, and he comes in carrying two tiny plaster busts — one of Alec Baldwin and one of Geena Davis. They're only about a foot tall including the base, and they're perfect.

"They're for a movie called *Beetlejuice*. I have forty of each of them. They'll slide in and out of a locked-down torso shell, so I only need one set of clothes. The clothes just have to be the front, with enough side to make them look like full pieces. The backs will stay open, so each frame I can replace pre-painted clay heads and repose their stop-motion arms."

I have no idea what all this clay head stuff means, but what I do understand is that I need to duplicate the actor's wardrobes and that I can do.

He hands me the actual shirts and dresses Michael Keaton, Alec, and Geena wore during filming — all six copies. "They're done with these, so they just handed them all over."

Hyper-drive kicks in. The red T-shirt won't be too difficult, and even the black and white checked flannel shouldn't be bad. I've already learned to do precision to-scale miniatures with the tiny pieces for *Jaw: The Revenge*. Ted got out calipers to verify my top stitching was to scale. Thanks to the vintage Singer Featherweight

I picked up, capable of sewing thirty-five stitches per inch with silk thread, I can do most any miniature with precision. Matching the scale Tim needs will be a piece of cake.

The pattern on Geena's dress is a different story.

The fabric — cotton — is easy enough to replicate to scale. I'll just use rayon so the folds can be more delicate, and it'll easily match. But the print is floral calico — five colors, two different kinds of tiny flowers and leaves, outlining around the flowers, little bitty dots in the flower centers, a repeating pattern of who-only-knows how often…

My head flashes one plan after another, and I have a strategy in seconds. I'll go to the Kinko copy store, scan the dress, reduce it to the correct percentage, and then print a copy of the pattern to scale. Using acetate to make stencils, I can trace each color onto separate sheets, cut them out with an Exacto knife, and airbrush the colors in order onto the fabric, similar to how the fabric is actually done. For the final touches, I can use a fine tip rapidograph pen for the line work. I learned about rapidograph pens in college while doing my fashion illustrations. It'll be nice to put another one of my college skills to use. It'll be tedious work, but the precision, the size, the detail…

I'm excited. "No problem." I can easily do this job in the evenings and over the weekend without it interfering with my day job at Alchemy II.

My first attempt at painting the fabric goes fine until layer four. The airbrush sputters, and suddenly, my flowers have micro polka dots. I hear Ted's voice in the back of my skull as he pulls out his calipers. "Everything you make is going to be blown up onto a huge theater screen; one little mistake is going to be bigger than your head on the screen."

Maybe *easy* wasn't the right word to use for this job. I chuck the piece of fabric and start again.

This time, I don't even get the first layer down, and my stencil comes loose. The paint drifts under the acetate, blurring the flowers.

Trash again.

Piece after piece, I spray and layer and spray some more until, at last, I have enough yardage — or, in this case, *inch*-age — to create the torso of Geena's dress.

I run over to Ted's shop, where Tim has set up his makeshift filming stage.

While I'm checking my muslin prototype of the patterns on Geena and Alec's mini torsos with arms, Ted pops in. "Can you come next door a minute? I need you to take a look at something.

Knowing *something* where Ted is concerned means probable work. I think he may be more obsessive than I am. Or maybe he's just overly picky. It comes across about the same on the outside.

Ted leads me to a miniature set. "This is for a different scene in *Beetlejuice*." — I'd heard *Beetlejuice* is spread all over the industry in individual pieces; apparently, they weren't kidding. "I need some miniature curtains to match these." He shows me a Polaroid.

The little detail I can see in the photo suggests that matching the lace isn't as crucial as matching the off-white and scale of the folds.

"Sure. A trip to the garment district for lace and — No problem."

I finish the clothes for Tim and the curtains for Ted.

When I drop them off, Ted asks, "Can you come in and puppeteer the snake?"

"I'm working at…" My voice trails off, knowing I'm saying *no* to an opportunity to puppeteer without actually saying the word.

"Yeah. There are a lot of the people I want to use who are working during the day, so I'm thinking if we meet at eight o'clock in the evening after we've all had time to eat dinner, we can work until midnight for a few nights and one Saturday. Are you game?"

This job just keeps growing. Trying to keep my Cool Mask from flying off and exposing the spastic nerd I am, I smile casually, "Sure." I can survive a little sleep deprivation for a few days for a puppeteering opportunity.

This movie sounds just about as bizarre as they come, and most people don't think it'll amount to much. None of the actors are all that big. Geena Davis was in *The Fly*, and Michael Keaton has done a couple of okay movies, but that's about it. Still, working with Ted, Tim, Marc Tyler, Steve Sleap, Diana Williams, and whoever else Ted is bringing in on this will make it fun — scary but fun.

I'm fairly certain Steve and Diana don't really like me. They think I'm a dork and only put up with me because we have mutual friends. If I do this, maybe they'll see me as a real person — I doubt it, but it's worth a try.

By the second night, we're showing up in sweatpants and ordering pizza. It's a slumber party without the slumber, and it is fun. I still don't think Diana likes me, but she's nice to me, and that's all I can hope for from most people, so...there's that.

After getting the movements down, and the umpteenth time of lip-syncing "I've come for your daughter, Chuck, Ah-ha-ha-haa..." one night, and "Oh, no!" with his head-whipping around another night, we get the shots.

Saturday afternoon, I'm put through my paces in a big way.

For this final shot, a little girl joins us. She's dressed from the waist down to match Winona Ryder's attire so Winona will appear to-scale with the snake puppet. My wrist and arm are exactly the same slenderness as the Beetlejuice snake body. Instead of lip-syncing this time, I'll be hiding in the shot behind the snake — with only millimeters to spare.

I lay on the floor, cradle the head in my hand, and keep the snake body balanced along my arm as I move the puppet between the girl's feet. It's an awkward position, but knowing I'm the only one in the room that fits the position gives me a feeling of importance that I can only hope Steve and Diana appreciate. Their opinions shouldn't matter, but to me, they do. They're the cool kids, and I desperately need their approval — or at least for them not to hate me.

It doesn't take many shots to get a clean scene, and just like that, the filming is done. And in seconds, I return to being just that friend on the fringe of the creature effects world, the one making toy prototypes.

A few days later, I return Geena and Alec's wardrobe sets to Tim, and that incredibly awesome job is gone.

So, this is what it feels like to be a freelance effects artist. The job comes; the thrill grows; then suddenly, you're left with nothing but the exhaustion — and the glory of having created something nobody has done exactly the same before — and I'm hooked. I want more of it. A lot more.

The creature effects people know who I am, even though I've not worked directly with most of them. I mingle regularly with the people who work for the royalty of the creature effects industry — people who worked with Rick Baker on *American Werewolf in London* and Disney's *Captain EO*, and Greg Cannom on *Cocoon* and *The Lost Boys*. They work with John Buechler on *Ghoulies*, Tom Savini on *Creepshow* and *Dawn of the Dead*, and Stan Winston on *Alien* and *Invaders from Mars*. I know what's coming out before it has even finished filming. I know who's working for whom, who's working *with* whom, who's hiring, and who's looking for work. But I have to pay the bills, and Teddy is my lifeline. So, until I get more job offers than these few random ones I can do in the evenings and over weekends, a toymaker I must stay.

CUT TO:

24. Reseda, California — Alchemy II

With Linda now in charge of Human Resources at Alchemy II and Arden heading the fabrication department, Arden uses her authority to redesign the Teddy walkaround bodies from laminated disasters to lightweight, washable suits like the ones she built at Shafton. I don't work directly on Teddy's body pods, but instead, after training me to cover heads with David Raccoon, she puts me in charge of the covering and detail work on all of Teddy's costume heads.

Teddy Ruxpin and I stay close. I move my workspace to a table in a storage room — a room I cleaned, organized, and labeled boxes in with such detail that I could navigate others to find things without even being in the building. It's just Teddy, me, and my Walkman of music.

I go for days without engaging with anyone from the fabrication department — or anyone else, for that matter. I spend my hours obsessing with making sure every head is covered identically, so that no kid who ever sees two Teddy Ruxpins at different times will ever know there is more than one Teddy Ruxpin.

One day bleeds into another, until one particular morning while getting ready to spend another day with Teddy, I discover a hanger with a black and white flannel shirt and red T-shirt tucked behind my clothes — *Beetlejuice* wardrobe. I missed a set.

They're going to think I stole it. I don't know who to call.

I leave the shirt set deep in the back of my closet, like a hidden body that'll get me sent away for life if ever found.

At work, I sew the fur pieces for Teddy's heads together in the same order. I cover each one with the same steps, in the same order, starting with the same eye, the same spot on the nose, and the same mouth corner every time. I never change my process and never skip a step. It's not tedious; it's from my heart.

To me, Ken Forsse and Teddy Ruxpin are interchangeable. What I do for Teddy, I do for Ken. So, I will take care of Teddy with the respect he has given me. Ken Forsse, Teddy, and the entire Alchemy II family gave me a chance when

I had almost nothing to show to prove my worth. They gave me the time and the stability to gain my footing and make enough friends in the industry to be able to know I'll be staying in Hollywood — though I still feel like they see me as a weird outsider because I'm still a generic brown-hair, average-looking girl from the Midwest.

Still, the shirts haunt me. Nobody has asked about the shirts, yet my head keeps telling me that when my secret is discovered, I'll be labeled a thief, and if that happens, my first significant film contribution will also be my last.

Every day, I obsess over the hidden shirts. They remind me I've stolen something. They remind me I have a secret — I have of piece of Hollywood history. They remind me I worked on a real movie — and I loved it. They remind me of my dream. They remind me that somehow, I'll have to figure out how to leave Teddy — Ken.

I don't know how that's going to happen, but I know it's going to hurt.

CUT TO:

25. North Hollywood, California — MMI

Alchemy II is winding down.

Worlds of Wonder is no longer playing completely clean with Ken Forsse. The WoW stock I bought is dropping, and as far as I can see, it will continue to fall — and I'll cheer it all the way to zero for what they're doing to Ken and Alchemy II. But this also means my job won't be stable for much longer. This Chain is breaking. To not fail, I need to become a link in a stronger Chain — and I need to do it before the rest of the crew starts job hunting, so I'm not second fiddle to their resumes.

Not long after I put out the word among my friends that I want to start freelancing, Ken Hall calls. He's heading John Buechler's shop, MMI (Mechanical and Makeup Imageries) while John is in Italy for the filming of *Ghoulies II*. "We need someone to build a suit of one of the Ghoulie hand puppets, so they can get shots of it running without a hand up its ass."

"I don't know how to build — "

"That's okay. I'll teach you. It's only going to be used for a couple of insert shots. It doesn't have to be perfect. If it stays together for a day or two, it'll be fine."

I give Linda my two-week notice, but she won't accept it.

"How about a one-dollar-an-hour raise with a two-week leave of absence? Go have fun and we'll see you when you get back."

Considering I'd otherwise be unemployed after I finish the suit, this sounds like a much better deal.

MMI is hot and smells of plaster dust and stale foam latex, but mostly plaster dust. Every shop I've visited seems to have its own odor. Some favor the smell of oil clay, others fiberglass, Barge rubber cement, or hot machinery. This one smells like plaster dust.

Ken shows me a complete body form of Tom Floutz cast in fiberglass, one of the mechanics who will ultimately wear the suit. He points to a pile of sheets of mattress foam. "Just build up the muscles on a body stocking over this form until it looks like this." He hands me a polyfoam pull of the notorious Toilet Ghoulie featured on the first film's posters. "Once you've built that, we'll cover it with latex skins, so don't worry if you have to piece anything together."

A Toilet Ghoulie.

The bathroom in this place is scary enough without adding the threat of Ghoulies coming out of the toilet. With the shop being one hundred percent male-populated, the bathroom has been decorated by *Playboy* and *Jugs*, and is apparently being maintained by the Not-me Ghost. I've always had issues with bathrooms — more than I'd like to admit.

FLASHBACK:

26. Houston, Texas — Summer Between College Years

The summer between my first and second years of college, while the receptionist is on a vacation for a week, I fill in at the company where Daddy works. It's a week filled with firsts. It's my first time answering a phone and talking to normal professionals, first time typing a letter for someone else — thank you high school typing class and college business course.

Sitting straight-backed at the front desk, dressed like in a blouse and skinny tie, skirt and high heels, and Normal Receptionist Mask that's based strictly on what I've seen on TV — since I'm realizing how little I paid attention to receptionists as a kid — I have absolutely no idea what I'm doing.

Two men enter, laughing as they hurry into the offices behind me. Soon, another guy hurries out, only to return a minute later laughing.

I sit, watching adult after adult walk briskly by, only to come back laughing.

I tell myself they aren't laughing at me. But it hurts that I don't matter enough for them to include me in whatever is going on, and I feel my confidence fade.

Instantly, my head starts screaming *They don't like you. They don't want you here.*

When the next one walks through the door, I perk up and smile, trying extra hard to push off back Cloak of Invisibility.

They don't even acknowledge that I'm sitting there as they scurry on by.

You don't matter, my head tells me.

My dad goes out without slowing down — *He's embarrassed by you* — but when he returns, he stops. "Go in the bathroom and look at the toilet."

I don't want to go. I don't want to be the butt of their prank.

My thoughts must be showing — I need to be more careful in the future — so my dad adds, "Really. Just go look at the toilet. You'll see."

I push open the bathroom door, and then the stall door.

The toilet looks fine.

I step closer.

The water in the bowl is swishing in a lopsided loop, even though the commode isn't running. As I watch, the water keeps up its continuous swish, swish, swish. It doesn't vary. It doesn't stop.

Now, among my many (and I do mean *many*) secret obsessive bathroom Rules, including nobody can hear me pee, no more than three breaths in a single public bathroom, and flush with my foot, one of the big ones is: I cannot be in a bathroom when the toilet completes its flush. When I was four years old, Julianne clogged the toilet, and it overflowed. While my mom worked to stop the rushing water, Julianne stood crying and kept repeating, "We're going to drown! We're going to drown!" Visions of overflowing toilets have terrorized me ever since.

This swirling toilet bowl is not helping my situation at all. Slowly, I back away from the toilet, until I can no longer see it. Then I dash out of the bathroom.

Hurricane Alicia is due to hit New Orleans in seventeen hours.

"It's the hurricane, messing with the water pressure from the Gulf of Mexico," one of the guys says.

The toilet is doing magic tricks on the twelfth floor of an office building fifty miles away from the gulf.

No matter how badly I need to use the bathroom, I won't go back in for the rest of the day. By five o'clock, I'm sweating, and my bladder and head have been in a screaming match for over an hour — but the staff let me in on the conversation. They accepted me.

DISSOLVE BACK TO:

27. North Hollywood, California — Back to MMI

A Toilet Ghoulie …built by a girl with bathroom issues …in a shop run like a boy's club. Can this job get any scarier? If these guys figure out how weird I am, I'll never work here again once this job is done.

"So, where's this *Tom* who'll wear the suit?"

"He's already in Italy." Ken's jaded chuckle says it all. "There won't be any fittings. We'll box it up and send it over for them to deal with."

Yes, the job *can* get scarier.

I get to work measuring parts of the Ghoulie — which I learn, thankfully, is actually called the Fish Ghoulie. Reversing the process I used to create the miniature clothes for Beetlejuice, I calculate the Ghoulie's enlargement percentage based on its estimated finished suit height compared to the puppet's height.

Whether it's nerves or from the heat, I'm sweating from practically the minute I arrive until I go home. Giant fans blow through the open roll-up door, but the San Fernando Valley summer heat coming off the cracked black-top parking lot surface is the same temperature as the shop interior, so all the fan does is stir the air, sticking a hearty layer of dust to my sweat.

I wasn't sure how to dress this morning. I've heard plenty of stories of girls becoming "shop bunnies" — meaning all looks and no talent — and Hollywood is full of stories of couch casting and people sleeping their way to the top. I don't want to get a reputation of being a tease around the shop of loaded with Peter Pans. But the place is so unbelievably hot. Most of the guys wear shorts and t-shirts with the sleeves cut off. Some of their shirts are more armholes than shirts — definitely can't wear that.

The next day, I try wearing a t-shirt, but by lunchtime, I feel dipped and floured chicken ready for the oven.

Day three, I decide to hell with it and resolve that my shop uniform will be shorts and tank tops or cropped t-shirts, with shoes from my ugly shoe collection as Ken calls it, and not once do any of the guys shame me or give me any flack about being the only female in the shop.

I'm safe here. Most of my friends growing up were guys ranging from handsome to dorky, and now I'm working with guys that fit that same range. Just like my Dungeons and Dragons gang, these guys more focused on their monsters than me — and I love it. Not only do I feel safe with these guys, I feel like I'm home.

By the end of the week, I have momentum and my confidence grows. Ken gives me a set of giant polyfoam hands and feet for my suit, and finally the head John Criswell mechanized. He shows me how to cut out the fin silhouette in L200 for me to use to build the back and tail over, hiding the zipper beneath the huge spine. I'm going to have to work even faster.

Monday, I dive in, knowing I need to finish the build-up by the end of the day, when Ken starts delivering the beginnings of the pile of scale-textured skins, made by brushing in liquid latex into an open mold that's a negative of the final skin texture. He shows me how to cut and interlock them, so the scales appear continuous and how brushing more liquid latex over the skin seams binds them together permanently.

No matter how many skins I cut up, the pile grows as fast as I use them. The pace is merciless, but I keep up. Other than Ken's brief lessons, I'm working completely solo, because he's busy painting eyeballs, answering the phone, and taking advantage of being the boss to work in the only room with air conditioning — I can't blame him for that. If I could fit this enormous body through the door, I'd work in that room, too.

Nearing the end of my second week, the idea of returning to work at Alchemy II isn't any more appealing. I've gotten a taste of the freelance world, and I'm obsessed. Building this suit is dirty and sweaty and challenging and freeing, and these guys make me feel so worthwhile.

They appreciate my work and openly praise me. They've adopted me. I don't know how I'll be treated in other shops, but working for MMI, I feel welcome. Building this suit, I'm not just one of many sewing multiple copies of the same thing. I'm making something utterly unique — and I want to do more.

A few weeks later, Ken calls to tell me how much Production loved the suit. "They rewrote the ending to use it more. They're no longer using it just for a couple of shots. It's become the Ghoulie God.

"To destroy the god, they wrote that it had to blow up. They stuffed the suit full of explosives, but when they detonated it, it just stood there propped on the post. They rigged it a second time and set it off. Still, nothing happened." He laughs. "Lynette, you built that suit so well, they couldn't even blow it up! They're going to have to Rotoscope the explosion over it."

Working on one of Charlie Band's Full Moon Production movies isn't held in the highest regard among the creature effects people. However, I remember standing in Tim's apartment at that first party and hearing about other's B-movie projects. Everybody who succeeds in this industry is going to have a few of those projects they don't often admit to on their resume — and many of those projects are through Full Mood Productions and MMI. I have been initiated. And in the process, I earned my first hat-tip from a bunch of guys who aren't used to having females in their clubhouse.

FADE TO:

28. North Hollywood, California — A Few Doors Down from MMI

I finally do it. I quit Alchemy II. Linda offers me another dollar-an-hour raise and another leave of absence, but I don't accept it.

"It wouldn't be right. Even if I take the raise, I'll be right back in here, in a matter of months, giving notice again anyway. I need to go."

She wishes me well, tells me I can have my job back if I change my mind, and I walk out, leaving Teddy behind.

I'm leaving a job I've had for a year and eight months for a six-week job that will end right before Christmas, making enormous black-light puppets for *The Masters of the Universe Touring Stage Show.* Not exactly a Hollywood blockbuster, but Tim is heading the project, and Steve Sleap is the key foam fabricator. When this project is over, I'll have studied the work of the second of the three top L200 sculptors in the industry (Terri being the third.) I can't pass up this chance.

This shop is freezing. Apparently, these warehouse units aren't made to stay warm in December any better than they're made to keep cool in August. Since this isn't an actual shop but simply a temporary space set up for the project, the industrial sewing machines are rented and table space is limited, and I spend a lot of my time crawling around cutting my pieces on the stained carpet of the warehouse's office floor.

The only way to see how well puppeteering the seventeen-foot-tall soldiers and eighteen-foot-tall giraffes works is to take them outside. And the eight Jigglers — four-foot-tall birds made up of Styrofoam balls covered in hot pink spandex — take so much time we're working fifteen-hour days just to keep up.

The creme de la creme of the project for me is covering the Zebrite, a white quadruped zebra suit with stripes that light up and change colors according to its mood. Not only does this mean that while covering the Zebrite, I get a close look at Steve's methods the same way I did Bill Bryan's, but since I'm the same size as the performer, I get to climb inside and test out the suit.

L200 is strangely loud on the inside. I can hear myself breathe. And I'm not cold anymore — actually, it's downright hot in here — and my vision is limited to whatever I can see peering out a one-inch by three-inch hole in the bottom of the Zebrite's neck.

The limited vision takes a little getting used to, but thanks to my dance training, soon my body becomes the Zebrite, and I'm able to move the head and keep all four legs walking in proper opposition, anticipating distances and interacting with the shoed legs visible through the neck hole. Thank goodness nobody can see the real me in here because the more my body becomes the Zebrite, so does my face. As the lights change colors from sad green to shy red to happy blue, I go from almost crying to big-eyed and desperately hopeful to smiling and bouncing like an overjoyed idiot.

It's so freeing that when Tim unzips the belly to turn me back into my shell of a normal person, I only come out because I have to.

I emerge to see the delight my performance gave the crew and my chest swells with that same feeling of importance I felt puppeteering the Beetlejuice snake. Until this very moment, I thought I couldn't be an actor. Now I know being a character doesn't transform me; the Masks do.

FADE TO:

29. Simi Valley, California — A Bigger Warehouse

In my spare time, I'm working with Terri to create Renaissance outfits for her wedding. I'm her Maid of Honor, but I don't think beading trim for velvet dresses and making doublets shows Terri whether I can puppeteer or not. Still, the word running through the effects industry is that *The Blob* remake is becoming utter chaos and the experienced puppeteers won't touch it, so she refers Howard and me for the job.

"It'll be a good opportunity for you. Just pretend you know what you're doing, and you'll be fine." That's her advice.

Because of my obsession with not disappointing people, I'll admit I've thrown myself in the deep end at times, but for the life of me, I don't understand what I do that inspires others to refer me for jobs above my skill level. It's been happening since before I got to Hollywood, starting with that receptionist job at my dad's office. But being a receptionist that couldn't type was only the beginning.

FLASHBACK:

30. Houston, Texas — Summer Between College Years

A few weeks after Hurricane Alicia bears down on Houston, Texas, and the city settles back into its routine, Dee Murr, one of the programmers from my dad's office, calls and hires me to help assemble programming manuals. It sounds boring, but I'll make five dollars an hour, which is more than I've ever made. Of course, I take it.

She steers me to the copy room and hands me a neatly labeled ring binder. "I need eighteen of these." Her manual makes the Bible look like a pamphlet. "Here's plenty of paper, covers, dividers, colored tabs, label inserts, plastic sleeves, markers, and a hole punch." She points to the machine buttons. "Start, pause, and here's where you set the quantities. Just let me know if you need anything. Make one. Then when you know you have it all figured out, you can make the rest."

Off she goes, clearly assuming I know more about running a printer I've never seen before than I do. Fact is, I've never run any printer — ever. But she trusts me to do this. I'm backed against a cliff and she'll push me off if I fail, I can't have her doubting her decision to hire me. Somehow, I have to make this work.

I don't know how to refill the paper, and whoever used the printer last only left it with a dozen sheets of paper in it. I ask the first person who passes by how to reload it — which also allows me to get printer lessons from someone other than Dee. Then, the whole thing prints backwards, so I have to re-stack all umpteen-hundred pages from back to front by hand. But after a few false starts, I manage to get one done.

From that one manual, I develop a system of hole punching and labeling while printing and sorting that takes up the entire room, that is so efficient that when I'm done, instead of hearing Dee say, "I didn't expect to have to pay you an arm and a leg for some stupid ring-bound books," I hear "You finished already?" and she hires me out of her own pocket, to continue building manuals for her.

While I'm the best manual maker in the office and actually find the multi-step organizing work surprisingly therapeutic, I'd better tell her of my college and career ambitions before she starts making long-term plans for me.

It's all I can do to confess my intentions to her, because my head is telling me, *She'll hate you forever. She's going to kick you to the curb and never hire you again, you disloyal freak.*

When I finish over-apologizing and groveling, she smiles. "I've been asked to make a Victorian suit for a friend. Do you want to do it? He's been pestering me about it for a while, and I really don't want to."

I have no experience making men's clothing whatsoever — but I got an A on that first suit.

My Hyper-drive head kicks in again. I'm not learning men's tailoring until next year — but if I can alter an existing pattern — I don't even know what a pistol pocket in a tailcoat looks like, but if he can describe that part, I should be able to figure out the rest. "Sure." I can use the money.

Miraculously, with the help of my patterning education and a store-bought McCalls pattern, I do figure it out, and Jesse is so happy that his suit becomes one of my first portfolio pieces.

DISSOLVE BACK TO:

31. Simi Valley, California — Back to that Bigger Warehouse

I know I'm in the deep end this time as I'm handed two trash bags and a roll of duct tape by someone already modeling them as the standard work uniform and told to cover up.

I don't know what's in store, but I'll trust Terri isn't trying to sink her fiancé and me, no matter how ridiculous I feel standing around in a black garbage bag skirt and shirt — the head of the Fashion Design department would be so proud of my accomplishment just now. I pop on my Confidence Mask, and I'm ready to do …something.

A slender man with notable ears introduces himself as the visual effects coordinator, Michael Fink — but we can call him Mike — and escorts us to a larger room painted black. "Troy, show them how to load the quilts, and we'll shoot the wedge after lunch.

Since nobody else is around, I guess Troy is the lead on this. He takes us to a table with China silk quilts spread out. *Quilts* is a loose term. Basically, they're pale pink China silk spatter sprayed on various shades of pink, darker pink and purple veins randomly airbrushed on it and scribbled stitching to create pockets.

Troy picks up a giant plastic syringe, similar to the ones I filled with Barge cement to glue detail areas on the Teddy Ruxpin walkaround heads, but if I used dog-size syringes on Teddy, these syringes are for elephants. He draws it full of slightly tinted pink slime from a fifty-gallon trashcan. "The goal is to find the hole in every quilt pocket and fill it until the slime starts oozing back out the hole and through the weave of the silk, turning the silk translucent.

Howard and I grab syringes and start filling. We fill a couple of smaller quilts about three feet square and one so large it could be a sleeping bag.

Surprisingly, it takes us until lunch to get them filled. Not surprisingly, my trash bag fashions are slimed outside — and in. After trying to clean up enough to look normal working at McDonald's, the stares I get from Simi Valley's tucked-shirt-and-loafer society tell me I failed horribly. I think I'll bring my lunch in the future. Going out to eat is too uncomfortable.

The three of us return to recreate the scene of the blob rushing over the theater seats. I don't know where Mike went, but we're on our own. It's just us three puppeteers, a cameraman, one grip/ gaffer, and a pile of slimy quilts.

Within minutes, we discover a problem — me. I'm too short. The miniature set we're under is built to accommodate six-foot-tall men, and I'm only five-seven. I can reach the slimy quilts covering the giant hole we're reaching up through, but I don't have any reach left to push the blob anywhere except off my face.

The grip slides a couple of wooden boxes — for some unknown reason called *apple boxes* — under my feet, matching me to Troy and Howard's heights.

From beneath the miniature set, we cram all three sets of our arms up through a hole large enough for the blob to fall in if we don't hold it up.

"Action!" the cameraman calls out.

With no monitors to see what we're doing, we start pushing and shoving, heaving and grunting, to move more than a hundred pounds of oozing, shapeless ick as it drips its slime back out of the injection holes onto our heads and suctions itself to the floor between the tiny theater seats overhead. At the same time, we blindly knead and fight to keep the Blob moving and pulsing over the tiny theater seats against its will.

Instead of pushing the blob up, I hit the edge of one of the boxes. The box flips out from under my feet, and I drop off onto the slimy floor.

I can't be the girl who was too small and weak to keep up with these two six-foot-plus tall, big men. I reset my box, cursing myself inside for ruining the shot, and get ready to go again.

By the end of the day, I'm cold and so slime-covered that slime oozes from between my fingers as I squeeze out my braided hair. My clothes are soaked, and I drive with a trash bag on my car seat to keep from destroying everything I own. The dried slime on my arms is plucking out my arm hairs one by one with every gesture I make.

This job is going to be a challenge — and I love it.

(ONE WEEK LATER)

The rest of the first week, we fight our blob quilts through that theater and a new shot that uses not only the quilts but a cable-controlled tentacle.

On Monday, when Howard and I show up for work — we're now carpooling on his motorcycle to keep from ruining my car interior — we enter to find an army of new puppeteers waiting for their trash bag fashions. I don't know exactly how many there are because the place is dimly lit, and the group is in a tight cluster — and I don't think they'd appreciate me asking them to line up so I can count their noses.

In any case, there are easily sixteen or eighteen of us now.

Shortly after Troy shows the group how to fill Blob quilts, Mike reappears. "Troy, Brent, and Lynette come into the conference room. The rest of you, keep filling quilts."

I don't know what's happening, and if Troy knows, he isn't saying. Surely, he does, though. Somebody has to — actually, with how this film has been going, maybe not.

Mike gathers us around a table, pulls out a giant ring binder, opens it up, and pulls out a few pages, handing each of us a different set. "The shoot is going too slow, and we're already behind schedule. So, we're going to use three rooms for three different sets with one of you as lead puppeteer on each set."

He says more, but my brain locks on *lead puppeteer*. What did I do last week that makes them think I can do this? Apparently, I've put on an extremely convincing Mask this time. Troy, I know, is a professional puppeteer. I think Brent may be, as well. Me...? I'm... well... just me — barely twenty-two years old, and the only other set I was ever on, I dressed little people as Bounders.

"The storyboards I just gave you show the shots you are assigned." He continues as if we're all old hat at this. "You need to get your wedge shot today so Chuck can approve it during dailies tomorrow. Then you'll come back and shoot the scene. Each shot needs to be done in two days to keep us on our new schedule." He pulls out a list of quilt and tentacle inventory. "Here's everything you have to work with. You'll need to divide it up among you. Do the same with the puppeteers out there. Depending on the shot, you'll be shuffling the crew, so don't think you're building a permanent team."

On the spot, with everyone looking, I repaint my Mask to become a lead puppeteer — which is tough, because I don't know what a *wedge* is — or *dailies*. And who is Chuck?

We negotiate the inventory and decide how many bodies we each need.

"I need at least six, but could use seven."

Brent never looks up from his pages. "I think I'll be able to get away with four."

Troy studies his shot. "I have to have seven or eight because I need three for the tentacles."

"I'll try to make five work. But I absolutely have to have that giant quilt then because I won't have any extra hands to keep edges from separating."

"I can do mine with small quilts."

"Done."

As soon as we return to the group still filling quilts, without knowing anyone's skill level — or at least I don't — we pick out teams like we did back in gym class. There are two other girls; the rest are guys ranging from shorter than me to seven feet tall, thin and thick, short-haired teen jock-looking types to long-haired rockers. The only thing we have in common is our ability to wear black trash bags and duct tape with flair.

With our teams set, we join them in the quilt-filling ritual. While some of the newbies are new to this film, most have considerably more experience than me. Not all of them are puppeteers; many of them are generally PAs (Production Assistants) working their way up the white-collar side of the industry.

I'm faking being the boss of a crew that knows more than me. If I'm to get this job done — and done well — I'll have to think hard, learn fast, and pretend better than I've ever done before. This will make for an interesting time, for sure, but I cannot fail — which means I'd better ask Troy what a *wedge* is.

(TWO WEEKS LATER)

I now know a *wedge* is footage shot to test the light levels, and *dailies* are the previous day's footage we show to Chuck for approval or input. *Chuck* is the director who is so far behind on the first unit he'll probably never step foot on our stages. And so far, I'm wearing my Lead Puppeteer Mask with style.

At dailies, Chuck always approves the rehearsal footage my team shot while doing the *wedges*, so we're on schedule, and after I figure out what *over-cranking* and *under-cranking* means and which one causes the scene to speed up versus which one creates slow motion, I can plan the shot alongside my cameraman like a pro. Most importantly, the crew likes me and follows my decisions without question. Maybe they don't know what else to do, or maybe it's because I don't pull rank and still fill quilts with them.

With no directors of any sort, or even Mike around, every shot is my design, set up by the cameraman and directed by us together. I'm twenty-two years old and playing the second unit director role. If I had interviewed for the job, I never would've gotten it, but my Confident Leader Mask is holding, and I am on a roll.

This morning, Mike assigned me a heavy scene — part of the sewer attack. This one demands a big crew, all of the biggest quilts, and a lot of muscle.

By lunchtime, we've dry-rehearsed the action and set the camera and lighting.

Howard and two other puppeteers stay in and eat lunch with me. I eat fast and pull out the trim for my maid of honor dress to get another six or eight inches of beading done, putting my Fashion Design degree to use in a more direct way for once. By my calculations, it'll take eleven thousand glass beads and pearls, so if I'm awake and not working, I'm beading.

Seven and a half inches done. I check my watch. *Twelve-fifty-four.* Six minutes left. Perfect. I tuck the beading safely back into its trash bag, hurry to the bathroom, and make it back to the stage by twelve-fifty-nine.

One-o'clock. Still, only four of us. Nobody else. The cameraman and our grip/gaffer know they have at least an hour before we'll have the quilts filled. But where's my team?

Howard and one other take the fifty-gallon trash can to mix up a fresh batch of slime while we two spread the quilts out on our plywood and sawhorse table and don new trash bag fashions. This time, I tuck my top bag into my bottom one and tape them together before using more duct tape to add overall straps and false pocket trim.

With our new bucket of slime back, we start the injection process. Surely, the rest of the crew will be back any minute.

After twenty minutes, we're still an abbreviated crew — and I'm pissed.

Thirty minutes. Still short. The anger radiating in my bones has to be on the verge of turning the slime to froth.

I start filling faster. "If we can, I want these quilts filled before they return."

"Shouldn't we slow down and make them help?"

"Nope."

Every morning for dailies, when we three head puppeteers join Chuck, Mike, three cameramen, producers, and whoever else is there I'll never be introduced to are there, I know Troy and Brent are rolling their eyes at my amateur attempt at directing.

Troy and Brent get assigned more of the specialty scenes involving more tentacles and smaller crews, while I'm getting mostly the brute strength massive blob shots, and — regardless of what we were told at the start — our puppeteer teams are mostly set. I have the ones neither of them want, along with the girls. I've built a kick-ass team from their rejects, a team delivering every single time.

But each day is a new chance to fail. Every morning, a new threat waits in the dark screening room. Every time, I wait to hear Chuck tell me how I failed to deliver an acceptable wedge or a clean final scene. Before each new assignment, I wait to hear they're replacing me with someone more competent.

I don't simply worry that I'll get found out. Being *found out* is not automatic failure. I was *found out* in kindergarten when I used to fake that I could read entire books by making up stories that synced with the pictures. Being called out by Tommy didn't embarrass me because my audience cut him off, informing him that they liked my story better than *T'was the night before Christmas and all through the house...*

I absolutely cannot fail. Not my parents, who know I'm working on this movie. Not Terri, who put her reputation on the line by recommending me. Not my dream, or I'll have to explain the everyone I see from this day forward how I failed. I am the lead puppeteer on a Hollywood monster movie. I will not allow myself to fail — and I certainly won't let a bunch of irresponsible idiots who seem to live by no rules at all sink me.

I jam my syringe into the quilt and plunge the entire contents into the pocket, watching the silk turn translucent, leaving only the pink splatter and blue veins, proving that there's anything structural there. "If they help, they won't feel like getting back late is that big of a deal. If we're done filling, they'll be able to see just how late they are and how close they are to being replaced."

The other three look at each other and smile — and start drawing slime into their syringes and plunging it out faster. Soon, we're paired up, two filling syringes and two injecting. We catch our rhythm, getting better synced and quicker as we go. Smiles grow, and we see the finish line.

Thirty gallons in last fifteen minutes. The rest of the team strolls in, laughing and chattering as if they have all the time in the world.

We are so nearly finished we downplay the few empty pockets.

I take a step back and turn to the tea party bunch. "It's about time."

Their cutting up doesn't even waver, and I will *not* be ignored, not with my success in their hands.

"Lunch was over forty-five minutes ago." That's how the statement runs in my head, but when it comes out of my mouth, it starts with "Lunch was over" but finishes with "FORTY-FIVE MINUTES AGO!"

Everybody freezes as my voice smacks against the walls.

"We have a shot to get today, people, and I will NOT allow this stage to fail. I will NOT allow you to get fired because you couldn't figure out how to tell time. You are not children. You are grown adults who are EXPECTED to be professionals." I look from one giant set of eyes to another as I gain steam. "You are part of a TEAM. But instead of acting like you care about anybody besides yourself, you come strutting in here like a bunch of spoiled brats who expect us to cover your asses by doing all the work for you." I point behind me. "Well, these three people DID cover your ass, and you'd better thank them. If it weren't for them, we'd all be fired before the day is out — and I will NOT allow YOU to decide MY FATE!"

I have no idea what else I bellow, but I have no doubt the stage next door is listening to every word. I'm off the rails and I don't care. I attack without mercy, hoping to bring at least one of them to tears. I want their submission, and I want them to feel the fear I feel when *The Chain* Rule is broken. I want them to fear my authority, so they'll never sabotage my Rules again. But more than anything, I want to scream.

My lifelong panic floods the room. All my frustrations, I target them.

I hate their casual attitude over something I think is important — and I think everything is important. I hate their lack of respect toward the team — and me — because I see blatant disrespect as a crushing personal attack. I hate irresponsibility. I hate deliberate ignorance when the answers are obvious. I hate excuses — because excuses are just a pathetic attempt to cover failure. I hate imperfection. I hate hate hate that I am not perfect and never will be, no matter how hard I try — and I try so very hard. I hate their entitlement attitude. I am not entitled to anything I don't work hard to earn, and neither is anybody else. I hate losing control — and while I am out of control now, I'm referring to having to submit my career to the hands of these fools who don't care. And I hate people who don't care — because I care so very, very much.

I throw open the door to my Fear Room, shove them in, and slam the door shut, leaning against it so they can't escape. I need them — anybody — to feel my fear, understand it — understand me — so I won't have to be afraid alone.

I stop.

I scan the faces of the people, their feet still glued in place.

They hate me now. I should apologize, but it's too late. Ajar though it may be, I said all that while still wearing my Confident Leader Mask. All I can do is continue playing my role.

I just alienated my entire crew — save maybe the three who filled the quilts with me — and now I have to figure out how to get this shot done with a shattered pile of chain links that probably everyone in the building heard me break.

I settle my Mask back into place to hide my failure as a leader, lift my chin, and turn back to the quilt to finish those last few pockets.

I am alone. Am I really so different? Is caring really so horrible?

One by one, my crew drifts closer, quietly resuming their duties. They stay, but I'm alone. I'm always alone.

Quietly, I slip through the door leading to Dark Abandonment — but right before the last rivet locks me in, I hear *I'm sorry.*

Over the next hour, I will hear I'm sorry from four of my five tardy team members.

I make a mental note. I won't use that fifth one on my team again, not because he didn't apologize to me — I'm used to being forgotten. I won't use him because he doesn't care enough about the job or the team to apologize to *them.*

RETURN TO:

32. Van Nuys, California — Stan Winston Studio

As much as I try, I can't fix everything.

I haven't worked directly with Kathy yet — we haven't even spent much time in the same room — but she still resents me being here, though I've been here for months now. *Jurassic Park: The Lost World* is my second project at Stan's, and while Kathy stays cordial, she isn't as good at wearing masks as I am. She doesn't stifle her frigid vibe very well.

That's going to have to stay her problem, though. Raptor self-destructive seizures aside, I love working here, especially at times like these — the wee morning hours. All of us quietly progressing on the Alpha repairs in perfect sync, listening to The Smashing Pumpkins — which personally, I could do without. Nobody telling anyone how to do their jobs... We simply *do*.

Chris grabs my scissors to cut ...who knows what with him, but if he ruins my good scissors by cutting —

"Oh." He drops them like they're hot. "You and your lefties. I hate those things."

Being a lefty has saved my scissors from being the victim of kidnapping more times than I can count.

He wanders off to find right-handed scissors, and The Smashing Pumpkins takes over the atmosphere in the otherwise quiet shop once again.

Stan doesn't usually approve of people working all night, but in this case, logistics demand it. The mechanics and electronics departments need access to Alpha during the day, so we're tagging off access to her by working from eleven p.m. to eight-thirty a.m. for a couple of nights, giving us an hour of overlap with the crew coming in to keep communications smooth.

I knot off my thread, cut off the excess, re-thread my needle, and start anchoring the wrinkle just to the side of her throat fold. After trimming skins, patching air bubbles in the foam, and troubleshooting where best to anchor the skins for the best movement, I'm as familiar with the wrinkles on these Raptor skins as I the streets in my neighborhood, especially the ones I added while we were patching — the ones that spell out my first name in front of her right haunch.

Chris disappears up the ramp to the mold-making room, bringing back one of the carts so we can move a few other Raptor body parts out of our workspace. As we heft legs and arms onto the cart, David mentions he's hungry.

The clock on the wall says three-fifty. Ten minutes to our version of lunchtime.

Since we can't order delivery or go through a drive-thru at this hour, we'll just take a half-hour break and keep going.

Chris takes the cart back up the ramp, but when he reaches the top, instead of tucking it away, he rides it back down, gliding clear down the ramp and halfway across the main shop floor.

David takes a turn riding the cart down the ramp. Then it's my turn. I fly down the ramp, praying someone will stop me before I collide with Alpha and break her again —

There are security cameras.

Stan can see us any time he checks the feed. If I were him and had just a few bodies loose in this building — as we are — I would.

David catches me and the cart at the bottom, takes it to the top, and whizzes past me again.

We're breaking a rule — *I* broke a rule.

Chris retrieves the cart. "Want to take one last ride before I put the cart away?"

The nagging in my head never stops, and I have to live with myself. "No. I'm good." I so want Chris and Dave to keep me on their crazy little team — but now I'm the spoilsport.

I'm growing used to feeling not liked — unwanted. I hate it, but after millions of times my head has said it, it's just the way things are. Most of the time, the feeling comes from inside myself. I'm trying more and more to argue with it, to back it up with counterpoints. But with Kathy, the worry is legitimate.

Enough others are saying things to know that none of the fabricators here are all that thrilled with me being here. Either that, or there's a huge conspiracy created by an entire group of people to make me paranoid. With the number of comments, I've gotten from such a wide range of personalities, I'm confident it's the former.

Knowing Kathy's resentment is a fact earns my head the victory almost every single time.

I can't confront her. While we're not working directly together, she's still in charge of the department. More importantly, I'll hurt her feelings. Any time I stand in the room of What's Right, I stand in the dead center with my feet sunk so deep into the floor that the only way out for me is my own destruction. If I open my mouth, she will deny the undeniable, and I'll tear into her the way I tore into the crew on *The Blob*.

I still haven't forgiven myself for scolding my brother for dulling the tip on the pink crayon that I had rubbed to a sharp point for my sister's princess's lips on her coloring book page. Every time I replay that pink crayon scene in my head, I feel terrible all over again. The older I get, the more I'm able to feel the confusion in that little boy's eyes. It doesn't matter that my brother doesn't remember the incident. Every time I replay how I made him feel in that moment, guilt tears me up. And I can still recall the kid on the motorcycle who hurt my friend's feelings, so I left him in tears. And when my sister yelled at me, and I attacked with such ugly words she ran from the room in tears. And all the other times I can recall — and feel — as if I'm in that moment.

I never forgive myself for attacking the way I know I can, so I can't confront her and plant another ever-haunting scar on my brain.

My whole life, I've worked every second to be worthy of acceptance, yet still, in the fabrication room, I'm not worthy — and it hurts.

I don't know what I can do to change Kathy's mind, but I have to do something to fix this. I don't know what that *something* can be, but there must be something.

Meanwhile, at least I have Chris, David, and most of the rest of Stan's shop backing me up. The many should be enough to offset the feelings of the few — but it never is.

FADE TO:

33. Burbank, California — A Small Warehouse Near Toys R Us

I'm always certain that the last time I work with anyone it'll be the last time I hear from them, so after working with Bill on the Wooly Whats-it, I didn't expect someone of his caliber to call me to work with him again.

When I answer the phone to hear him ask me to partner with him on the giant shoes for *Honey, I Blew Up the Kid*, while *the kid* might be blown up, I'm blown away.

Despite the movie being a Disney production, Bill gives me directions to a warehouse with a roll-up garage door, just a few doors down from Foam Mart — one of the leading foam suppliers for the industry (then and still today). I've figured out that these warehouse units house most creature effects shops. Sometimes, they're permanent enough to have posters on the walls and shelves of molds from previous projects. Many others, like this one, are as temporary as the one for *Masters of the Universe*, with the barest of tools and rented equipment. They're always either too hot or too cold and dusty, but there's plenty of space, and that's what matters.

Bill greets me with a "Hi, how ya doing?" introduces me to the project coordinator, and starts right in talking about the project.

As with the other freelance jobs I've gotten so far, I've never been interviewed and have never shown anyone my portfolio. That's fine with me. I've never gotten around to polishing that Mask.

FLASHBACK

34. Seventeen Months Later — Dallas, Texas

To graduate from Bauder Fashion College, during our final year, all students must go on at least three interviews before taking one of the jobs for their internship. The list of pre-approved companies includes ready-to-wear manufacturers, furriers, milliners, theaters, and design houses in Fort Worth and Dallas. I target the theaters and costume houses.

The Cordoba my parents are loaning me is under repair, so for my first interview, I carpool with another kid whose interview backs up to mine. Halfway there, his Toyota gets a flat tire. We change the tire — actually, he changes the tire following my instructions because his chauffeur always changes their tires, but I'm wearing my grade-A white suit — and lower the car off the jack. The rim sinks all the way to the pavement, the spare tire every bit as flat as the one we just took off.

After rolling the first tire up the exit ramp to the gas station, we refill the tire, hoping it'll hold air long enough to get us back to the dorms. Then we call our instructor, asking her to relay to the company that we're going to miss our interviews.

After she chews us out for calling her instead of the company, and I hear how dumb I am, I can't reschedule that interview and face my shame.

With very few costume houses on the list, I can't blow anymore, or I won't have three to interview with, and I'll have to talk to *normal* people at *normal* design companies — a thought too terrifying for me to accept.

I manage to set up interview number two with a costume house called Magic To Do.

For the sake of reliable transportation, my parents loan me my mom's white 1964 T-bird with turquoise interior to drive until the Cordoba is fixed.

Dressed again in my grade-A suit, but this time, I've added my best Calm Mask to the outfit, I'm able to hide my desperation pretty well — I think. Maybe I should have worn my Cool Mask, or my Confidence Mask, but it's too late to change now without coming across as neurotic.

Somehow, Mark, the guy interviewing me, winds up talking about cars, and I tell him about the T-bird I'm driving. He leads me to the door. "I have to see it."

I don't know whether my resume, my Mask, or personality gets me the job — or whether it's the car. Frankly, I don't care. I get the job, and I never do go on those other two interviews. Job interviews are rejection quests. I don't think I'd survive three of them.

While my classmates tell stories of gluing cherries on hats and other mind-numbing tasks for no pay, I'm working for five dollars an hour, sewing Peter Pan and Alice in Wonderland costumes for Disney parks.

Before I've even been there two weeks, Magic To Do wins a contract to make dancing potato chip bags for a Ruffles-Frito Lay commercial. While I'm not working on those chip bags beyond holding this here or assisting Mark there, I watch those two giant chip bags come to life with total fascination — and envy. But when I compare what I'm doing with my friends, I can't complain.

Mark smiles. "Don't get any ideas. When you finish your hours, we'll be letting you go. We're not looking for another employee."

Every day, I come to work feeling like I'm a person with a death sentence, watching my final hours of life tick away.

I tally my hours, calculating them against the chip bags deadline. I'm going to miss seeing them finished by six shifts — twenty-four hours. With pencil in hand, I stare at my time sheet. If I under report my work by a half hour, I won't get paid for that half hour. But if I do that each shift for a few weeks, I'll be in the shop until the chip bags are complete.

I watch my hours, continuing to delete a half an hour here or an hour there. I think Mark knows what I'm doing but since my staying isn't costing them money, he doesn't say anything until his partner catches on that I should've been gone a good two weeks earlier.

"This is going to have to be your last week," he tells me when I come in on Monday — but that's okay. I've timed it well.

Before I go, I legitimately help complete those potato chip bags, by assisting in laminating clear plastic over the silk-screened artwork, fighting the massive sheeting to assure no air bubbles stay trapped. I get my first real taste of a foam, fabric and spray glue project — and it's a blast.

DISSOLVE BACK TO:

35. Burbank, California — Back to the Warehouse Near Toys R Us

I never could've guessed that one failed interview and an afternoon with giant potato chip bags would eventually lead me to work with the Marshmallow Man — no interview necessary — yet here I am.

Bill holds up one cute red and white toddler-sized Adidas high-top tennis shoe barely bigger than his palm. "We need to make a pair of shoes to match this, but scaled up to sixteen feet from heel to toe." He pauses for a few seconds, giving my head time to start running.

How are we going to do this? — How much time do we have? — Just the two of us? — How do we match those shoe-strings? — The logo? — The —

"…and a single shoe, eight feet long, complete with tread on the bottom."

It's all I can do to keep from laughing, but I hold tight to my Professional Mask and don't blink. "Anything else?"

"And while a toddler's foot doesn't bend much when it walks, we need to make sure the shoes can bend a little, so they don't move like blocks when they're puppeteered by crane."

By crane. Now I do laugh. "Of course." This is going to be one big marionette.

We settle at the one folding table with two folding metal chairs in what should be an office — with the only air conditioning in the place — to calculate the scale, the layers of construction, and the materials shopping list.

The second day, Ron, the project coordinator stops by. "When are you going to get started?" — as if we haven't been doing anything.

"I need to see progress when I come in."

Suddenly, I feel like I'm back in Ms. Sisti's sixth-grade English class, getting chewed out for not getting an *A* on the vocabulary test. "If you'd just take the time to study…" sounds the same as … "if you'd just do something…" I *did* study for those vocabulary tests — my mom even quizzed me the night before. But with my head — insisting on fairness and diplomacy — I could fit several definitions to several different words, which only served to stick me with another humiliating Monday morning, teary-eyed lecture out in the hallway.

With nothing but a pocket calculator, a tape measure and a ruler, there's only so fast we can go. Still, Ron's the one in charge, so he gets to be right…as long as he's in the room.

"I ordered some Styrofoam for the core," he says. It'll be here in the morning. You can get started carving the feet. That will keep things moving until the rest of your materials arrive."

Bill sneaks a glance in my direction before answering Ron. "The feet?"

We wind up spending way more time than necessary on these feet because Ron insists they have to have toes, ankle bones, arches …the works. Neither Bill nor I know why we need to start with bare feet to make these tennis shoes (to this day, I don't know why), but Ron is the boss, so bare feet he'll get.

With Bill wielding a chainsaw and me buzzing away with a belt sander, we make a decent pair of enormous Styrofoam feet in about a week.

After adding thick foam spacers to give us the interior of the shoe form and laminating vinyl to mattress foam to make the vinyl the appropriately scaled thickness, we build the red and white shoes and the one small version — if you can call an eight-foot sneaker *small*.

As we build, the crew grows from just Bill and me to Bill, me, and several more who bounce between helping us heft and throw the massive sheets for the shoes, sewing the scaled-up corduroy pant legs, and weaving the shoestrings.

Almost done. I take a few steps back and hold up the original toddler shoe. Our shoes are almost a dead match for the little one. That word — *almost* — is killing me. There's a slight discrepancy between the two profiles in the toe area. Part of it is because we have to leave a hollow area to accommodate the bend. The reason doesn't matter to me. It's not perfect. If Ron catches the error, we — I — have failed.

Bill has been assuring me the whole time that it won't read on camera, but I'm not looking at it on camera — and neither will the client.

It's not perfect, and it's too late to fix it.

The phone rings, and Bill disappears into the office.

He isn't gone long. When he comes back, he stands beside me, admiring our work. "I promise. That few inches is never going to show. They're not going to hold still on it long enough for anybody to see it."

He may be right, but it doesn't help me let it go.

"Do you want to hear what they *do* want to see?"

I turn to him.

"The tops of the shoes have to come off."

"They what?"

"On the flatbed trailer, they won't fit under the power lines to get onto the Las Vegas Strip. We're going to have to figure out how to decapitate them and then reassemble them in Las Vegas."

They've lost their minds.

"And then disassemble again to get transported back to Burbank to finish filming."

I don't know whether to laugh or cry. He's right about one thing. That couple of inches isn't what the client is going to be looking at. They're going to be looking to see if we can create a miracle — overnight.

With a bit of ingenuity and a lot of praying, we dissect our shoes with electric carving knives and slice them up as cleanly as a chef with a turkey on Thanksgiving.

The payoff: The shoes can't be reassembled without us, so I get to go to Las Vegas. I also get my first experience in a complete brown-out dust storm, and my first time at a blackjack table, all compliments of Honey I Blew Up the Kid and a big pair of baby shoes.

And just as Bill said, the clients never notice that couple of inches. So, while I'll always know the shoes weren't perfect, I learn that not every flaw I see matters.

FADE TO BLACK.

36. Burbank, California — NBC Studios

When I return from Las Vegas, I have my next job lined up before we reassemble the giant shoes for the final time. Lisa, a friend of Tim's, calls me from NBC Studios to work on *The Thunder Cats Touring Stage Show*. Finally, I'll be working in a big shop with air conditioning and everything.

I park my little Honda hatchback — the one I bought shortly after a hit-and-run driver totaled the big yellow Cordoba — in the lot across the street. I pass through the main gate and walk right past Johnny Carson's convertible parked nearest the doors.

The guard directs me to the costume department, a beautifully clean, brightly lit pair of rooms with flecked white linoleum filled with partially constructed beaded gowns and tailored suits on mannequins. The hum of the sewing machines and thump of the riveters create a rhythm that fills me with excitement.

Jonathan, the head of the costume department, meets me in the front area. "There isn't space for you in here, so we've cleared an area for you to work upstairs." He leads me out into the main storage area, an area large enough to shame most factories.

Against the wall, a set of wooden stairs not much better than a ladder with a railing lead to a balcony. As we ascend, the heat builds — so much for the glamor of working at a cushy studio.

The work area is barely big enough for two worktables because of all the boxes and metal closets lining the only two walls. With the elite atmosphere from only three of us up here — Lisa, someone named Donna, and me — it isn't without a certain amount of coolness, as long as the word *cool* isn't referring to the temperature.

Directly below the two-by-four railing overlooking the enormous expanse, NBC's Wheel of Fortune wheel sits in off-season storage. Seeing it in person for the first time, I'm surprised to see the wheel is made of the same materials and looks no better than the set from my high school play *Anything Goes* — plywood, paint, and glittery laminates.

After I hear tour guides stop groups time after time to say, "Yes, this is the real wheel used on Wheel of Fortune!" followed by oohs and awes as the groups continue down the hall to look in the viewing window to the actual costume room, any glamor working in a storage balcony at NBC falls away by the afternoon of day two.

The first thing I build for the touring show is a panda bear suit. The wearer will be doing acrobatics during the performance, but since it's too big to do padding like I did for the children's video monster, I use the beanbag method I learned while rebuilding the Wooly Whatsit.

I make a cotton jumpsuit interior and a final shape exterior shape and then sew baffle spacers between the two to keep the bean bag pellets from sinking to the bottom. Once covered, the fur stifles the swishing sound of the pellets enough to keep the sound from carrying to the audience.

When Kurt, the project coordinator pops by, he assigns Donna a *Karate Kat* character named Big Mama, me Cat Gut, and Lisa takes *Tiger Sharks'* Octavia. I remind myself it's not what I've *done* but what I *know* I can do that matters, so I put on my Confidence Mask, and without blinking, I say, "Okay," even though I've never built a head to match artwork before.

Quickly, I pick up on Lisa's technique. I mimic her, and my confidence grows. I get into a flow, matching her steps — head, nose, brow, chin… I don't know where we're going on these heads, but I am certain that my Cat Gut head will look like it pairs with her head well enough to keep people from questioning who made which head. But as the day goes on, my confidence turns to frustration. Everything I try only makes the head look like a feline Mr. Potato Head, but then, so does hers. They aren't cute. They don't look anything like the artwork. In fact, they look ridiculous.

I detour from Lisa's process and try to fix Cat Gut to look more like his art, adding here and there to build up more detail. Now, it looks like a detailed feline Mr. Potato Head.

I'm failing.

That evening, I call Terri and tell her what happened to my head.

Her tone changes, and I can hear the eye roll in her voice. "That girl has no idea how to foam sculpt. She's a puppeteer who mainly does marionettes and stage productions. Trust me. I've worked with her. Don't listen to her unless you want to learn to do something wrong."

"Now what? I have to make this head, and I have no idea what I'm doing. I certainly don't want to leave all the heads to her and get stuck working on a project that'll look so bad that we become the laughingstock of NBC."

"Here's my advice. Start with the nose."

"That's it? Start with the nose?"

"Yep. Lynette, you can do this. You just started in the wrong place. Always start with the nose."

I throw away yesterday's prototyped head and dive in again, starting with the nose. The head goes together so quickly that I have it done and covered in just a couple of days. When Kurt stops in, he gives Donna a few suggestions and loves my Cat Gut as-is — not so much with Lisa's Octavia. He suggests to her how she can tweak this and adjust that, and I can feel her regret for hiring me. She was supposed to be the queen bee, and because of Terri's advice, she's falling out of favor.

Next, Kurt hands Lisa a set of drawings, and she distributes them, giving me the art for WilyKat, a human/cat cross boy in *Thundercats*, and herself, Cheetara. For my life, I can't figure out why she doesn't assign all of one set of characters to each of us, so the different art styles aren't so apparent. It's like she's trying to create a contest among us — and I hate it.

She got me this job. She's in charge. If I match her ugly work, I look like an idiot to Kurt — and Jonathan. If I follow Terri's advice, I can make great-looking heads in comparatively very little time, but I will make the person who can recommend me for work in the future hate me. I'm doomed either way.

The perpetually nay-saying voices in my head bicker on. One of them will have to lose, so I might as well decide which decision will cause me the least professional damage.

I shut down the voices.

With WilyKat being half-human, this head holds a whole new set of challenges.

Again, I watch Lisa build Cheetara's head, to see if I can glean any tips or at least try to create some relationship between our two styles. But she's soft sculpting the facial features on a batting-covered egg. There's absolutely nothing I can do that can make my head resemble hers unless I'm willing to utterly disregard the character designs and turn my Thundercat into a Cabbage Patch doll.

I can see the geometry of the face in the drawings. It's obvious to me.

I slide down my table, positioning myself directly behind Lisa so I can't see her work, nor can she see mine.

Starting with the nose, I have WilyKat's face figured out in hours. I'm sure years from now, if I were to rebuild him, he'd look better, but since he's for a stage show and will never be seen close up for a first shot, I'm pleased — and at the very least, he looks a lot better than the Cabbage Patch head at the next table.

The next day, Kurt drops in to check our progress, and he loves my WilyKat just as much as he loves my other pieces, but even he comments on the lack of artistic continuity in the show's pieces. It's evident some sort of passive-aggressive battle is going on in our little balcony. At least the project is near the end.

Marc Tyler called me two days ago, asking me when I was available. The day after I finish here, I'm going to work for Sid and Marty Krofft on a new TV show called *D.C. Follies*. Donna congratulated me. Lisa did, too, but something in her tone tells me she's irked she wasn't offered the job.

This morning, I have a dentist appointment. I scheduled it weeks ago, so I have to go. If there were any way to reschedule, I would. I hate missing work.

Since I was little, I haven't been able to stand missing anything. I didn't have to get up for school until an hour after my older siblings, yet I got up before them just in case I missed something — like which breakfast cereal was poisoned. Now, the only way I can assure nobody is talking hate about me is always to be around. I can't help the thought anymore and can skip the dental appointment.

I return to work midmorning to find the white fur on my panda painted with a can of black spray paint. "What the hell happened?" — probably not the most tactful wording, but it's too late now.

"The color change between the black and the white was too abrupt," Lisa says — as if pandas don't have pretty distinct lines between their black and white markings.

"It's my suit. You could have just said something, and I would've fixed it."

The acrylic spray paint isn't necessarily the wrong answer — even from a spray can — but she stood so far back that my panda bear looks like it rolled in a coal pile.

"It looks filthy" — she's ruined it. "And there's no way to fix it."

Kurt pops up the stairs while I'm still shell-shocked. "Hello, everybody. How's it going today?" He's always so cheerful, and he is this time, too — until he sees my panda. "What happened?"

That's what I should've said. Funny how we both said almost the same thing, but his not-quite-gone smile versus my tight-pinch choke and bug eyes makes all the difference.

I'm both embarrassed and crushed. Any second now, I'm in for my *Jody Attack*. I feel myself leaning away from the man to save my ears from his deserved verbal assault.

Lisa struts over, puts on an air of authority, and proudly explains her decision.

The man steps closer. "That's not coming off. Is it?" He says it quietly enough that I can tell he's talking to me — only me.

I can't even speak. He rubs the fur. "Anything you try is probably going to smear it, huh?"

I want to cry — but that's not allowed. My feelings can't matter. I nod.

He accepts the fact that his panda in the show will be an acrobat who moonlights as a coal miner, and life goes on.

I'm mute that day, and the few days left on the job. If I speak beyond the minimum required words of professionalism, I will explode. We are a bunch of fools in Kurt's eyes, and I'm sure in the eyes of Jonathan, too.

No matter the reason, I am a failure.

FADE TO:

37. Sun Valley, California — Sid and Marty Krofft's Shop

Coming off last week's failure, when Randy, the head of Krofft's puppet-making department, sets me up with an enlarged front view and profile to-scale caricature drawings of Nancy Reagan as my first puppet assignment, I'm not sure I have a Mask thick enough to be able to survive this job.

I'm supposed to relief carve her head out of a solid block of mattress foam using an Exacto knife, carving knife, and a sanding wheel the size of a quarter on a Dremel. If I carve too far, if I nick too deep, if I angle my Exacto knife when I cut the eye sockets, I have to start over. The process is entirely foreign, but at least this time, it's supposed to be. This is a technique of Randy's making, so everyone comes in blind.

Precision... I love it. But with my confidence at a new low, the foam block might as well be wired with electricity ready to zap me with every cut. Craig, the other guy who also started today, has already started over.

Randy carves almost half his heads with a pneumatic sander, which has a four-inch sanding disc on it and carves a lot faster — meaning he can massacre a head faster, too. When he gets to the Dremel part, he calls me over. "Now, watch."

I study every stroke, every angle of his hands, every measurement he references.

Three days later, Nancy is completely dug out of that foam block. Surviving one head doesn't have me convinced I can do this, and with Craig starting over again — his third attempt at his first head — the confidence is no higher now than it was on day one.

I use Rit dye to turn Nancy's white foam peach and some sheet foam brown for her hair. While I cut strips of the still-damp foam for her hair to start her hairdo, Craig gives up and quits.

I almost envy him. The demand for perfection is so high. We can't ignore a flaw like Bill and I did on *Honey, I Blew Up the Kid*, or accept a mistake the way

Kurt did on my coal-mining Panda. We're making caricatures of famous people. Mismeasuring will make them unrecognizable, and unrepairable mistakes make them trash. My Rules won't allow me to quit — if they did, I never would've made it to Hollywood in the first place.

At this point, my Fear Room has a revolving door on it.

I push through my fear, finishing Nancy's hair, making her teeth, painting her face, and finishing her puppet body, palette, arms, and rigging, and off to set she goes for the next week's filming.

After the *Thundercats* disaster, I need this win. As long as Lisa keeps the fiasco quiet, maybe I'll survive, but the threat is real. The effects industry is even smaller than I imagined. Almost everybody really does know almost everybody. The old saying "You'll never work in this town again" can become true in a heartbeat, and because of Lisa, that heartbeat now lives in my throat.

The following week, Randy assigns me Sean Penn. He picks and pokes at my attempt, and a *Thundercats* storm cloud begins to hover over me. Randy knows Lisa. I don't know if they've spoken, but I can't take much more of this. He needs to fire me if he doesn't like my work.

But he doesn't fire me. Instead, he picks at me all the way through my Sean Penn and my next week's Tammy Faye Baker.

He calls me back to his table again, telling me to bring my head of the week. "You're close." He pushes the mouth corners deeper with his thumbs. "Just take it all about a half inch deeper."

I return to my table and carve the profile deeper, then return to his table again.

He turns the foam back and forth and pushes the foam here and there. "Here…" He picks up his Dremel and sands the mouth corners even further.

This is my fourth head, and I'm still not good enough. "Why do you keep me on? You haven't been happy with any head I've made yet."

He turns to me, still smiling. "What do you mean?"

"You didn't pick on Craig like this, and he never did get a head done."

His smile doesn't fade. "I'm not picking on you. I didn't help him because he wasn't going to get any better than he already was. You're worth teaching."

I'm *worth teaching*. Randy is ridiculously talented. He was a rocket scientist before he started working in the industry. He can conceive something, draw up the design for it, then sculpt it, mold it, build the mechanics and electronics for it before he paints and figure finishes it, and even sew the clothes for it. He can do everything — and he considers *me* worth teaching.

I thought Ed Parrish was picking on me, so I quit being his student. I let Ed down.

I won't let Randy down. I'll stay and let Randy pick at my work as much as he wants. I will learn and I will get better.

Marc stays most of the first season, but when he gets an offer on another job, he makes his getaway, saying he doesn't enjoy the pressure. Three others try their hand at foam carving and voluntarily quit within a week or two.

The puppet team settles into just Randy and me making every puppet.

The Kroffts up the weekly order from three puppets a week to five or six. I take over making all the bodies, dying the foam, creating the hairstyles, and doing most of the finishing work and coloring, while Randy carves the heads — because he can now carve one in about six hours, while I still take almost double that.

I may not be as good of a carver as Randy, but we make a good team, just the two of us... for three full seasons ...with my Confidence Mask sitting nearby, in case my Normal Mask isn't enough someday.

FADE TO:

38. Houston, Texas — Summer after Graduation

I'm feeling the pressure. I graduated from college with an Associate of Arts degree in Fashion Design and an award for my tailoring, and I'm nineteen years old. I have one year to make it to Hollywood or fail. That'll make me a lifelong liar, and nobody will want me anymore.

I can put off going a little longer because I don't have a car. A week later, Daddy co-signs a loan for me to buy a 1959 Ford Custom. Not necessarily the most practical vehicle, but it gets surprisingly decent mileage and is as safe as driving a tank.

College, age, a car… My excuses are running out. There's one more reason left before I have to make the jump — ready or not; I need to pay off the car and build a savings account. Within days, besides my job at Lord and Taylor, the same guy who hired me last summer to make him a suit calls again. This time, for a full suit with a frock coat.

When he comes to pick up the second suit, he offers to spread my name through his Victorian reenactment group. "You could make a living doing not just suits, but dresses, petticoats, corsets …the whole nine yards."

Not wanting to be a seamstress nor hurt his feelings, I latch onto the storm cloud over my head — and in it, too. "That would be great, except I'm moving to Hollywood soon."

At this point, the very idea scares me, so I have to keep proclaiming my goal loud and often to keep from chickening out.

"Oh yeah?" he says with a tone that makes it sound like he's impressed.

It's October. I turn twenty next month. I'm running out of time — and excuses. "Yeah, I want to take a shot at costuming."

"That's great. You're good. When are you leaving?"

I'm not ready to proclaim a date just yet. "Hopefully, in the next few months. I'm building up my savings right now."

"I have a brother who lives in Van Nuys, California. He's a comic book illustrator." He jots his brother's phone number on a scrap of paper. "I'll let him know you're going to call. Maybe he can answer some questions for you."

His brother tells me he has friends who work in film. "The industry is slow right after New Year's. February is when things really get going." He also informs me that to find relatively affordable apartments in a pretty safe area, stay south of Sherman Way, north of Riverside Drive, east of Van Nuys Boulevard, and west of Lankershim.

I don't know what those street names mean, but I'll take his word for it and mark the area on the Los Angeles County map I picked up at AAA.

February it will be …I guess.

I'll pay off my car and have three months of survival money to live on.

I make February twentieth my official date. I announce to everyone I can. I start remodeling my Fear Room to make it comfortable to live in. With no way left to back out now, I'm going to be spending a lot of time there.

DISSOLVE BACK TO:

39. North Hollywood, California — My Chandler Apartment

Between seasons of *DC Follies*, I still have bills to pay. Luckily, the phone keeps ringing, the answering machine keeps recording job offers, and I keep saying *yes* to as many projects as I can handle at once to keep from being forgotten. The message I didn't expect to hear is the one from Jonathan, the costume department head at NBC Studios.

I don't know if the tour is still going on, but if it is, this isn't going to be a fun call to return. It'll be a *Jody Attack* because of how incompetent the suits were, and how he'll expect me to fix them for free, and how ugly they are, and how the client has never been happy with any of it... Still, I have to return the call. That's the Rule.

I dial the number that will go directly to his desk.

The phone rings — and my hand starts shaking. My whole body shivers as I enter my Fear Room. I grip the phone tighter and begin pacing to burn off the adrenaline.

Pacing during phone calls is typical for me. I walk miles around my living room, forcing myself to control the energy enough for the person on the other end of the line to think they're talking to a normal person. I won't slow down until I start getting winded. Then, I'll decelerate just enough to keep the listener from realizing I'm not calmly sitting in a chair.

"This is Jonathan."

I cringe. "Hi, Jonathan. It's Lynette. I'm returning your call."

"Yes! Great to hear from you. How's it going?"

Most free-lance conversations start with *How's it going?* It's a weighted question. My answer will tell Jonathan if he wants to offer me the job or whether they've made a mistake in calling me after all.

"Good." Do I feign busy so I can't repair the suits, or do I play nice and hope he will, too? My Rules require me to do the latter — dammit. "I just finished the first season on a T.V. show." As I make my billionth lap past my white wicker fan back chair, I pause long enough to straighten the cushion before walking on, keeping my voice as cheerful as possible. "Whatcha got?"

"We're making the costumes for the Olympic Ice Dancing team. We have a set that needs red, white, and blue flames airbrushed on them. You do that sort of thing, don't you?

He's not calling about the tour disaster. He doesn't hate me yet.

"Sure" — not really, but I have an airbrush, so I'll figure it out. I'll call Terri to work on it with me. She'll keep me from jumping out of a window.

I'm not worried about not delivering a good, finished product — that worry comes when I hand over the finished project. I'm not even concerned about what he's offering to pay for the work. For now, all I hear in this job offer is *I'm calling you, not Lisa.*

I forgive myself.

FADE TO:

40. North Hollywood, California — My Chandler Apartment

Terri's amusement over the number of times she's been called to rebuild something Lisa made starts wearing off on me, and it's a good thing because this time, we're giving up our weekend to strip down and rework an elephant walkaround head she made for Shafton, Inc.

Since Steve Sleap passed away after losing his battle with AIDS, Shafton has been on a never-ending hunt for his equal, but there are so few sheet foam sculptors who are proficient with L200 that they've had to use whoever's available. In this case, it was Lisa, who isn't as proficient as she thinks.

"I don't know how that woman still gets work," Terri laughs. "Everything she builds has to be rebuilt. You might as well reap the rewards, too."

Not long after we save that elephant from looking like it was poached and harvested by Dr. Frankenstein, I get another call from another shop I've never worked in before.

It's Sunday morning when the phone rings. I'm sure it's Ken Hall letting me know the gang is getting together at the Copper Penny for brunch. He'll be pleased — and surprised — to hear I'm not repainting my relining drawers or kitchen cabinets like he caught me doing the last time he called with a brunch invitation. Instead of Ken, it's someone I don't know named Rick Lazzarini.

He tells me he owns a shop called The Character Shop. "I have a puppet that I need for a commercial shoot, and the person I hired screwed it up and can't fix it. I called Randy Simper to see if he could save me, and he recommended you. Can you come in?"

"Do you want to see my portfolio?"

"I don't have time for all that. Randy says I can trust you, so I'm trusting you. How soon can you get here?"

He means *today* — like right now. I throw on my shoes, grab my purse, and drive the twenty-five minutes to be there in thirty.

He leads me to a table where a hideous gopher puppet sits, looking more like roadkill than something ready to sell Wilson golf balls. "This is supposed to shoot tomorrow morning." At first, he hesitates to tell me who made this mess, but it isn't long before he's panicked. "You know what? Screw it. I don't owe her anything."

Yep. Lisa has struck again.

"Can you strip it down and recover it today? You don't have to do the eyes. They're mechanical. We'll install them tonight after you finish."

Hyper-drive time. Two small rabbit pelts and one yard of fake fur — She mutilated the fake fur by randomly chopping pieces out of the middle — Just scraps — It's already eleven o'clock — No time to hand-sew a patchwork of fur bits — No time to drive into downtown Los Angeles in the hopes of magically finding a store open on a Sunday that just happens to have fake fur yardage that will be a perfect match for a realistic gopher. I can only use the two rabbit pelts to give Rick something better than he has right now.

I'm tired of being the discount clean-up crew once the time and money are gone. If I can tear this thing apart and improve a puppet by Lisa — who so many treat as my superior — maybe, at the very least, I can become her equal.

I don't know what Randy told Rick about me, but Rick trusts me enough to leave me to destroy the only thing he has to deliver to his clients in less than twenty hours.

I will not — no — the Rule is: I cannot fail …him or Randy.

Thanks to Rick bringing in pizzas, I don't have to stop for dinner, and I get the gopher done early enough for him and his mechanics to be able to install the eyes and still get a reasonable night's sleep before heading to set in the morning.

The puppet still doesn't look great, but he says he's happy with my work — he doesn't really have much choice under the circumstances. All I can do is leave and hope he doesn't grow to hate it once he's rested.

FADE TO:

41. North Hollywood, California — My Little Back Bedroom Shop

Terri stops by after she gets off work at Walt Disney Imagineering to tell me she has a job she thinks we need to do together.

Pain tries to follow us as we go into the back room to work, so I pick him up and sling him around my waist to keep him from getting left behind.

"A lady named Nancy Tokos approached me at work. Something about building some hand puppets for one of the restaurants Disney is opening in Tokyo Disneyland called the Pan Galactic Pizza Parlor." She plops down in a chair with a piece of the micro sweater I sub-contracted her to knit on hatpins for Ted Rae's stop-motion miniature Freddy Kruger for *Nightmare on Elm Street: The Dream Child*. "I can't take the job because I already work for Disney, and, for whatever reason, this is considered a conflict of interest. But if you take the job, you can work on it full-time, and I can still work part-time without getting in trouble because I can do freelance work — just not for Disney."

"That's about the dumbest thing I've ever heard." I drag Pain's tail from between the blades of my Exacto knife and keep cutting the pattern for Lisa Wilcox's blue and white shirt.

"I know, but that's the Disney way."

A few days later, Nancy Tokos calls me. I meet her at her office along with the rest of her team. She needs ten puppets, one with random facial features and costume pieces, to become four puppets. She hands me two pieces of paper.

All the drawings fit on two pieces of printer paper. No front or side views. Just loose little thumbnail concept sketches.

"Can you give me a bid and get back to me by the end of the week?"

"When will I get the final art?"

"These drawings are fine."

I've heard for years from everybody who's ever worked for Disney that they micro-manage to the nth. I can't even get the idea of building puppets for Disney with this little bit of information to compute.

Terri and I work up a bid. I call Nancy's with the numbers, and the next day, she has a courier drop off a check to get me started.

The puppet designs inspire me to think out of the box and collect odd bits from dollar stores and thrift shops. I used model kit parts for knobs and buttons, the hose from a 1960s hairdryer for a long nose, Legg's pantyhose eggs for eyeballs, and curtain rod rings for earrings. Who knew the alligators I made out of egg cartons and my first paid job duplicating an ostrich marionette I made for myself out of Styrofoam balls, feathers, and dingle ball fringe would train me for my first job with Disney?

The deadline is tight enough that even with Terri working the evenings with me, we won't be able to finish without more help. So, I hire two others to work with me full-time in my little bedroom shop.

One week into the project, I set up a *dog and pony show* in my shop, which is the industry term for when the bigwigs come to check the progress of their project. Nancy shows up with two others. None seem fazed by the idea that puppets for a Disney theme park are being made in some girl's apartment bedroom, nor that I'm constructing them out of dime-store junk.

Nancy and the others look over the puppets for fifteen minutes before Nancy says, "They look fine. We'll see you on set."

That's it? *We'll see you on set.* She doesn't feel the need to critique me, correct anything, or even oversee the construction of these puppets at all? This is definitely not the way I've heard that Disney works from any Disney employee — including Terri.

Shortly after, Nancy calls, asking me to bring the puppets into the office to show the mucky-mucks — there it is.

Here's the left turn I've been waiting for.

But it isn't. Everybody is ecstatic with these unbridled Disney puppets.

Terri, Howard, and I take the puppets to their first day on set two weeks later. When we start unveiling the puppets from beneath their trash bag covers, Nancy stops us. "Hold on a second. I need to go get someone."

Okay. *Now* it's coming. She's seen the first couple of puppets, and she's gone to get her superior to show them why the shoot will have to be postponed.

She returns a few minutes later with a man named David — and I brace for the Jody Attack. "Aren't these perfect?" She grabs the nearest one — an ugly green character known for eating the pizza delivery guys. "You need to talk to them about making your Calamari Alien."

It turns out that David needs someone to build a hand puppet of Admiral Akbar from Star Wars to be filmed for Tokyo Disneyland's Star Tours. "It needs to have blinking eyes, too. Is this something you think you can do?"

Hyper-drive… Go. The body, no problem — I have no idea how to do the latex skin — Terri sculpts — Talk to Randy about the eyes — Between us, can we figure this out? I look at her, trying to code-talk to her before committing.

I give a cautious nod, and she nods back. "Sure, I think we can do that."

"Great! Get me your bid sometime this week. I need to get going on this soon."

David and Nancy leave Terri and me to finish prepping the Pan Galactic puppets. The minute they're out of earshot, Terri leans in. "How are we going to do that puppet?"

"I don't know. You were nodding, so I thought you had a plan."

She laughs. "I nodded because you were nodding. I thought you knew."

Talk about funny-not-funny. Claiming skills I don't have is always a bad idea. I can't allow myself to become like Lisa, nor will I allow myself to be embarrassed by retracting what I said to David not five minutes ago. I have faith in Terri. If we get the contract, we'll figure out how to make Admiral Akbar — we have to! And we'll make him great — he has to be.

That potential fiasco will have to wait, though. Right now, we have to impress *this* client.

Our Pan Galactic characters are being filmed so the video can play in a loop synced with other animatronic figures to entertain people standing in line at the pizza parlor. The dialog is prerecorded, so all Terri and I have to do is lip-sync to the recording — in Japanese. Maybe Nancy should've mentioned this earlier. I don't know Japanese.

"I do," Terri says as if it's no big deal. While she may not be completely fluent, she studied enough to get the gist of what they were saying so we could give the characters the right attitudes and reactions.

After a few days in the studio, we all rendezvous down at Disneyland for one final day of location filming.

It's Thursday. Thursdays are always light in the park with short lines — so short, in fact, that we have to ask people to wait to go onto the ride so we can create a line for the characters to stand in. Then, after Terri and I spend a couple of hours in a Disney dumpster with another puppet, the Pan Galactic pizza parlor puppet shoot is a wrap.

The very next morning, I win the Star Tours contract, and David drops off a polyfoam pull of the real Admiral Akbar for reference. I see why he needs a hand puppet. The head is enormous! And without access to the actual head from the film, reproducing the character using a skull this size, my entire bid wouldn't even get them an eye-blink mechanism.

For the budget and tight schedule, Terri and I will foam fabricate the entire puppet — no sculpting or molding, and no foam latex like the real Admiral Akbar. After talking to Tim, we'll use SC89 for our skin instead. It'll keep all the detail and have plenty of mobility for the eye blink I subcontract to Randy Simper.

Terri creates Akbar's skull while I build his torso and shirt. Then, after I make his soft throat, soldering iron wrinkles into his foam, and mount his eyes while Terri is a WDI on her day job, Terri adds bits of details while I create his patch, and he's downstairs to Tim's garage shop space for skinning.

Wearing respirators, I spray tinted SC89 through a paint gun, creating layer after layer of delicate cobwebs that bridge the foam pores and smooth Akbar's surface while Terri breaks swagging micro-webs that threaten to erase his skin creases and bind up his eyelid folds.

After two nights of tedious final coating and airbrushing, Admiral Akbar is ready for his shoot.

By the time we finish lip-syncing the Japanese lines for Akbar, I'm able to lock down how much Terri and I made per hour. We made almost double our hourly rate. I'm thrilled — until David walks me to my car when I go in to pick up our final payment.

"Just so you know," he starts, "the next closest bid to yours was just over double your quote. You need to bid higher in the future."

Okay. Maybe I still have a lot to learn about bidding projects, but Terri and I made more than our standard rate, delivered on my promise, and had tons of fun.

I'm happy — and so is my client. That's how it's supposed to be.

I can breathe again.

FLASHBACK:

42. I Made it to Hollywood, Y'all!

I inhale the warm air of California in February. I'm happy, overwhelmed, excited, nervous. I'm…everything. But I'm chasing my dream. I'm actually doing it.

Moving halfway across the country is scary enough without doing it with no job and no place to stay, but I have to start somewhere. Following the Rule of the one person I know who lives here, I start my apartment hunt within the Sherman Way/Riverside Drive/Van Nuys Boulevard/Lankershim radius.

I finally find an affordable semi-furnished studio apartment with a manager willing to let me go month-to-month, if I pay the first three upfront.

I put Cecil, the giant rabbit, on the second daybed and Tracy, the limbless mannequin, on the corner of the desk, and I'm home. A giant melted-eyed rabbit and a quadriplegic mannequin. Their weirdities are more obvious than mine, but I think they get me. It's too bad I never found Tracy any arms or legs. Still, she looks quite fashionable in my blue sweater and gold necklace — and her bald head wears my straw hat well.

The place isn't pretty, and it definitely isn't quiet, but it's clean and it's safe — and as a single twenty-year-old who's never lived on her own, that's all I need.

The next morning, I meet the comic book illustrator for breakfast at Denny's.

"Get a Thomas Guide," he says. "You can't live here without one."

I don't know what a Thomas Guide is, but I assure him I'll get one.

Then he tells me about a party he was going to that Saturday. "You should go, too," he says. "Maybe you'll make some connections. At the very least, you'll make some friends."

We split the bill and, on the way, out the door, he tells me he'll pick me up at 7:30 Saturday.

And because I dare to go out on what turns into one mind-blowing evening, I meet up with someone who knows someone who knows someone who hires me, starting a ripple that carries me all the way to Stan Winston Studio.

RETURN TO:

43. Van Nuys, California — Stan Winston Studio

I taught the rest of the fabricators the processes we're using on the Raptors so they can use them on the Stegosaurus, Pachycephalosaurus, and, to a certain extent, the Baby T-Rex. Kathy is assigned Baby T-Rex, and she likes to do things her way.

There's more than one way to get a job done, so if it works for her, far be it for me to criticize. But I wonder whether she's varying the process out of necessity or lack of trust in my techniques — like me with Lisa — or whether she simply doesn't want to feel like she's following me.

She's the boss. I feel tension from the others in the department too, keeping me on the outside. We all get along well on a superficial level. I've even hawked trifles at Beth's booth at the Renaissance Faire. We had a blast — or at least I did. Still, at work, I'm an outsider in the fabrication room.

So, I work out on the main floor with the guys, troubleshooting and designing the best I can, where I don't feel judged, where I'm just a co-worker, and I can almost relax.

I developed my jointed-shell theory earlier on *The Relic*, and my muscle theory started with *Dinosaur City*.

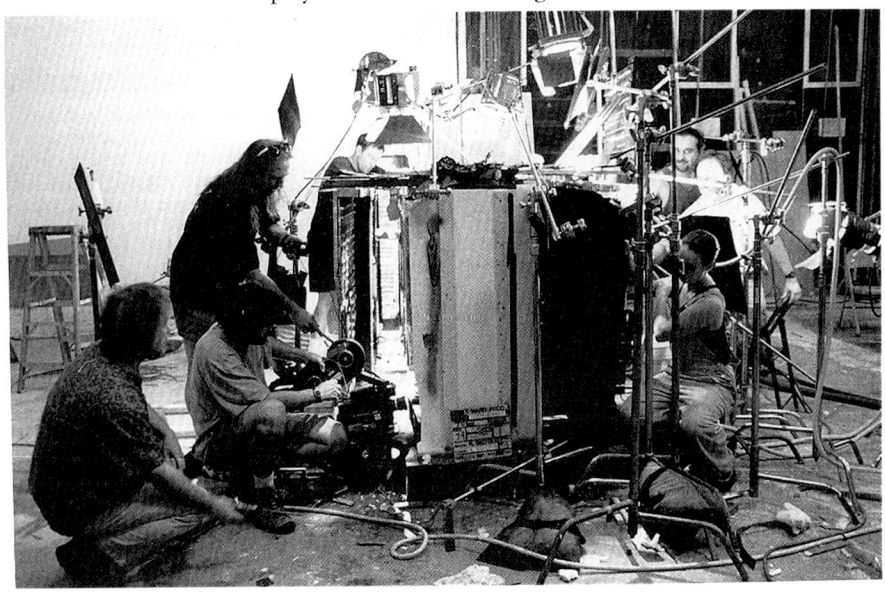

Hired by Ted Rae, I made costumes for three demons for *Days of Our Lives* and played the demon chasing Marlena

Working for Stan Winston Studio, I'm on the right (in overalls) puppeteering the mouse for *Mouse Hunt*

Working for MMI, my first movie monster under construction, the Ghoulie God for *Ghoulies II*

Getting the giant tennis shoes for *Honey, I Blew Up the Kid* ready to travel to Las Vegas for location filming (I'm squatted down, on the edge of the right frame)

After being part of the crew to make the Sil suit or Species at XFX,
I maintained Dana Hee on set and doubled for her on three occasions

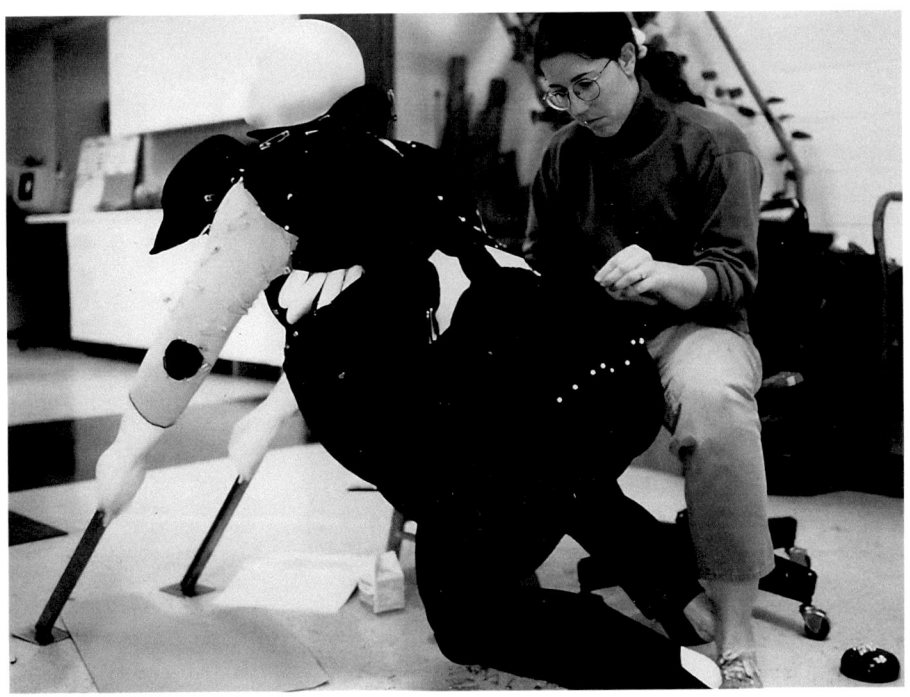

During my time at Stan Winston Studios, building gorilla suits for the movie, *Instinct*, utmost realism was the goal

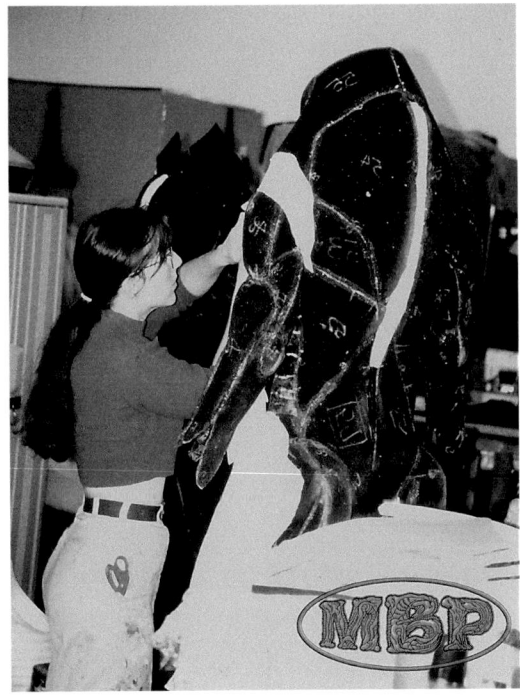

Working on the Keep Hound for *White Dwarf*, I would drop by the shop long enough to pattern, and do the actual sewing in my apartment

My first job as a full-fledged free-lancer, we worked past midnight on Christmas Eve to get the *Masters of the Universe* traveling show to meet the deadline

Teddy Ruxpin became the spokesperson for Missing & Exploited Children for several years. I always hoped the heads I figure-finished helped save lives

Painting three layers of paint on fifty Cheshire Cat stripes for one of Terri Hardin's Limited Edition Collectible Sets was definitely a sanity test

Ultraman Kaiju onset in the heat of the Hollywood summer, Durago was one of the easier suits to maintain in those conditions

Kathoga, for *The Relic*, was my first job at Stan Winston Studio and my favorite creature. I think this design by Mark "Crash" McCreery, is beautiful

FADE TO:

44. Van Nuys, California — Mike McCracken's Studio

Working on *The Adventures of Dinosaur City* will be my second time working with John Criswell. My first was while he built the mechanics for my suit for *Ghoulie's II* at MMI.

Unless you're a shop owner, most effects people take turns switching between the roles of employee and employer, depending on who wins the contract. This time, John and I won't just be working with each other; he'll be my boss.

He's renting space at Mike McCracken's studio to make dinosaurs for this low-budget movie. The McCracken father and son team will do the sculptures for the hands, heads, and feet while John builds the mechanics, and he wants me to build the dino-human suits. I did muscle-shaped build-up for the Ghoulie God, but this will be my first actual muscle suit, where the muscles will stay soft and pliable under clothing, something I've only ever seen — when I shouldn't have seen it.

Tim Lawrence smuggled me drawings he did of Harry's muscle suits for *Harry and the Hendersons* and then took me to visit the set to see the suits in person.

After Kevin Peter Hall was dressed in the Harry suit and everyone headed to set, he pulled out one of the spare suits for me to see while nobody was looking. Seeing and touching suits of this caliber made by Camilla Henneman and Juliann Smith was a privilege — one I didn't deserve. I doubt either would appreciate knowing I was given a chance to dissect their work.

Very quickly, I learned that competition for positions in this industry is considerably more vicious among the females than among males. Being a male-dominated industry, I came in thinking females would support each other, but I've been cold-shouldered, pushed into the shadows, lied about, and sabotaged by the very few females I've encountered, while the guys have treated me like just another one of the guys. Sure, there are usually titty girl pictures in the bathrooms, and I have to deal with the silly boy-talk guys do when they forget there's that lone girl around, but they've never targeted me. If the talk starts getting out of hand, one of them usually cools it down for me before I even open my mouth. *I* am the foreigner in their Peter Pan world, and while I won't join their boy-club talk, if I were to force them all to change for just me, I'd probably find myself back on the outside. At least, right now, I'm only dealing with a typical amount of competitive hate. I'd rather not add Camilla and Juliann to the list of females who hate me.

It's probably too late for that, though. I'm already a dork in their eyes, I think.

Carrying the guilt of promoted sneaking forever haunting me, I can't look them in the eye any more than a lone dog can look at a pair of wolves. Even that night on set, after Tim told me he was leaving me alone to check out the suits so nobody would come back to the trailer looking for him, I took no photos and only touched the suits for about two minutes before the guilt chased me out. I spent the rest of my evening wandering the Universal Studios back lot, watching the raccoons roaming in and out of the small town made of facades.

I can't help having an obsessive memory, though. I can't unsee what I saw of those muscle suits.

The suits for *The Adventures of Dinosaur City* will have to be constructed differently — because I refuse to blatantly steal from Camilla and Juliann. Besides, I won't have a body sculpted and molded by someone else, so I will have to foam fabricate all of my own muscles. I'm not the first person to do this, but it's rare and the first time I'll have done it.

Based on what I remember from high school biology class, I have some ideas of my own I want to try. The theories are already clear in my head. This will be the perfect job to test them. I'm sure I'll improve my techniques further over time, but the theories I use on these basic muscle suits will become my springboard for my muscle suits from now on.

Learning new skills and then taking those new skills to a new level is my new obsession. I can't leave anything alone. I have to improve something every project. It'll keep me from becoming redundant.

John tucks me away in what should be a front office, but instead, it's just an empty room with a folding table and a sewing machine. Working alone, away from all judging eyes — male and female alike — I'm free to put on my Walkman, play Wilson Phillips on a loop, and safely let my mind design techniques of my very own.

(Somewhere I still have those drawings Tim did of the Harry suit. Throwing them away would be throwing away a bit of Hollywood history. But to this day, I still have not studied them for fear of letting them influence my methods. I can't do that to Camilla. My Rules won't allow it.)

FADE TO:

45. North Hollywood, California — My Apartment

At work and at home, I'm alone a lot. I have friends, but no special person in my life. I've dated a few different guys for various lengths of time, but being in an industry so small that working with exes becomes an obligation, breakups are generally easier for the guy than the girl. I won't have exes taking down my career, and the easiest way to do that is not to create exes. After all, how many exes do you want to work with before the cobweb gets too tangled? It's best just to live a lonely life.

My snake was the most faithful male in my life — until he died about a year ago. The landlady never discovered Pain — even when he was swagged from the main curtain rod in the living room directly behind her. Nor has she discovered my new pet — a water dragon — who has taken up residence on that same curtain rod. But he's more independent than Pain was. It's just not the same. The place feels emptier with nobody greeting me at the door — even if it was a Burmese python that had grown to eight-and-a-half feet long. It was somebody.

Now, there's nobody. I miss Pain.

As I stand on the apartment's communal balcony, trying to hear if the washer is done with the final spin on my load of laundry without going all the way downstairs to check, something black scurries across the paved area under the clotheslines. It disappears behind the edge of the cinder block wall dividing the laundry area from the small grass courtyard before I catch what it is, but it's small and definitely alive.

I wait.

"Megan?" the new apartment manager calls from his door right below mine.

The little black thing bounces from behind the wall, stopping long enough to sniff the Banks rose I planted to cover the cinder block, then stops again along the bed of my miniature rose collection in a section of the yard the landlord offered up for my personal amusement.

It's a black cocker spaniel puppy.

A puppy is living in the building — not just anywhere. It lives in the manager's apartment right below mine. We are officially no longer a no-pets complex.

I'm getting a dog!

I drive to a used bookstore in Burbank and purchase a book of dog breeds to find the best fit for my lifestyle.

My dog is going to meet friends and clients, and go to the dog park where I meet one of the producers I do a lot of moonlighting for, who has a husky. It needs to be small for the apartment and intelligent for me. Quiet and sociable — probably not a terrier.

I need a beagle.

After calling every pound in the Los Angeles area in search of a beagle or beagle mix and finding nothing, one of the pounds gives me the number for Beagle Rescue.

"Do you have any beagles or mixes?" I ask the woman on the other end of the phone.

"I have two. The youngest one is fourteen years old."

That's not exactly what I'm looking for. I need a dog young enough to conform to my weird lifestyle.

"If you want a beagle that isn't in its last years, you'll have to go to a breeder. I don't get lost beagles. Beagles don't get lost."

I don't know what she means by that, but it doesn't matter. The part that does matter is that I will be buying my dog, and it will be a puppy.

I scan the newspaper regularly for puppy ads.

Weeks go by.

I see ads for Jack Russel terriers and try to talk myself into getting one of those instead. Thanks to the TV show *Frasier*, they're way more popular, but also, thanks to *Frasier*, they're not cheap. And they're not beagles.

I must have a beagle. That's what I've told people I'm getting, so it's a Rule.

After two months of searching, I read an ad from someone saying their beagle had nine puppies. By the time I visit the pups, there is only one left. They were going to keep her, but the female got pregnant again before they could get her fixed.

She sits between her mom and her dad, not much bigger than my two fists together. Her dad won't shut up. He barks and barks, and I wonder how long he can keep that up before he loses his voice — or the neighbors lose their minds — but this tiny puppy sits quietly by her mother, letting Dad make a racket all by himself.

If this little girl won't bark with her own father, she'll be a quiet beagle. She's *my* beagle.

I name her Daisy, and she comes home with me on the spot.

The cold feet don't start until I'm halfway home. I look at this tiny little thing, all ears and tail, her brown head shining in the sunlight. She deserves a place to be a scent-tracking, weed-wandering beagle.

What have I done? I work long hours. I'm single and carefree. She's going to require me to consider somebody besides myself.

She sits in the passenger seat as if she does it all the time — not the least bit stressed about leaving her parents. She catches me looking at her and moves closer.

She licks my hand.

I can't take her back. She's expecting me to take care of her. She hardly knows me, but she's content to let me have her life to do with what I will.

I committed the moment I took her away from her home. I won't let her down — no — I *can't* let her down. It's now a Rule.

It doesn't take long for Daisy and Megan to become buddies. The manager gives me a key to his place, so we can help each other give our puppies time in the yard throughout the day.

No longer am I coming home to a still apartment. I'm greeted by my tiny happy heart.

My keys rattle while I unlock the door, and I hear her sniffing along the floor and brace myself for her wiggling little body that can barely stay upright, as her wild tail whips her off balance. I open the door, and she bounces on my feet, across the room and back so fast, it's a wonder her flapping ears don't take out her eyes.

"There's my girl. How ya doing?" I sit my purse on the table. "Do you need to go out?"

Uh-oh.

As close to the back door as she could get it, sits a puppy-size pile of poo. It's my fault, not hers. I was supposed to be home much earlier.

I clean it up enough to save her bladder, but it's too late to save her spirit. Her bounce is gone.

As I finish getting up the last of the residue, she leans into me, whimpering, pleading for forgiveness, and no amount of cooing and petting consoles her. I toss the paper towels into the trash and turn just in time to see her puke.

She's obsessed with trying to be perfect, and no matter what I say or do, for the rest of the evening, she worries she's not good enough. I may have found my soul mate.

FADE TO:

46. Sun Valley, California — XFX

My obsession with perfection gains me statements like *You give your monsters the nicest butts.* That's what the owner of XFX, Steve Johnson, tells me when he sees Vincent Hammond in the suit I'm creating for him.

It feels good to return to shops to work for them again — yet it does nothing to shore up my ego against my head. The first time I worked for Steve was making a pair of enormous basketball shorts for a Nike commercial — thanks to Bill Bryan's referral.

Getting the call from Steve to work for him again isn't as much a surprise as it is a relief. It means that after I finished the last job and left the shop, he didn't decide I was a royal screw-up and vow never to hire me again — something I still stress about after every project ends. I've been working in Hollywood non-stop for nine years, yet I still can't break free of the ever-present reminder that I'm a barely tolerated spare tire. Always afraid I won't be able to deliver, I dread the day I fail, and my dream evaporates. So, I dig deep to gain a shoulder-pat, the pressure lifted for a few moments because my monsters *have the nicest butts.*

Freaked is the movie this time. It was going to be *Hideous Mutant Freaks,* but the producer/director — and co-star of *Bill and Ted's Big Adventure* — Alex Winter, decided that title was too long and shortened it to *Freaked.*

After making eight suits for *The Adventures of Dinosaur City* — doomed to be even cornier than its title — I've gotten pretty good at basic body shapes. The suits were just spandex slip-cover stuffed foam forms, but each character had their own unique silhouette. After that, I got a side gig making a gorilla suit for Michael Burnett. He wanted a gorilla suit he could rent out, which made good practice for me and gave Terri and me another chance to work together. With some muscle groundwork under my belt, I'm sure I can figure out how to make two seven-foot-tall, hump-backed, long-armed, giant-necked freaks.

"You'll be onset with us to dress these guys, right?" Steve looks so tiny standing next to Vincent in his freak suit.

"Uh" — I'll get to go to set? "Sure." I haven't been on a set with known actors yet, and this movie is loaded.

Monday, instead of going to the shop, I go into downtown Los Angeles, to the warehouse production is using as a soundstage. As I carry my equipment in to get set up, a guy emerges from his trailer, heading in the same direction.

"Hi," comes out of my mouth before I register who's behind that handsome face — Ted in *Bill and Ted's Excellent Adventure*, Chevalier Danceny in *Dangerous Liaison*, Matt in *River's Edge*. It's Keanu Reeves.

"Hi," he almost mutters, drops his head, and slows down so we're no longer parallel, so I hurry on.

Never in my life would I have imagined a star of his caliber to withdraw from such a simple thing as *hello*. That kind of awkwardness is usually reserved for weirdos like me. I almost slid under the makeup table when Steve became amused by the mohawk I'd made with my hair by banding up seven ponytails in a row and pointed it out to everyone in the trailer. The attention made me regret my spontaneity in front of the mirror this morning.

I wish I could tell him how well I understand, but anything I say will sound like a shallow excuse for a conversation, so I slam the door in the face of my wish for a new friend and force myself back into my emotionally sterile Professional Room.

After spending the morning on a dark stage, a buffet lunch in front of folding tables in the parking lot is a welcome sight. It's not fancy and definitely not formal, but it's comfortable. The day is warm but not hot, sunny but not blinding — therapeutic.

I walk past the first table, where Alex sits with Keanu, Brooks Shields, and Randy Quaid, feeling like it's the first day of school and I can't find any friends to sit with. I can't sit with the popular kids — it wouldn't be right — so I make my way to the next table with plenty of open seats. I don't know where the rest of the effects crew plans to sit, but hopefully, they won't leave me alone.

A plate drops down across from me. Mr. T settles in the chair, already talking, and what a character he is. Known for playing the kick-butt Clubber Lang in *Rocky III* and B.A. Baracus in *The A Team*, I brace myself for an intense lunch. But he's smiling — and laughing. I don't know where the intimidating Mr. T went, but this gold-clad man is a hoot. It turns out we both grew up in Illinois, and he's the first person I've met out here who knows where my hometown is. Stories about his childhood, his siblings and parents, how fried chicken set the status in his family, and the multiple reasons he wears so much gold fill the hour with a show of its own.

From mute Keanu to the ever-chatty Mr. T, the famous are, first and foremost, people. They have individual personalities and feelings that I must try to read and respect, as my Rule demands. But what really sinks in is that these celebrities are my co-workers. We are all fellow artists doing jobs we love. Our jobs just happen to have us making this movie together.

FADE TO:

47. North Hollywood, California — My Apartment

Movie sets aren't the only place I meet celebrities. The call I get this time comes from a referral from Jonathan at NBC. It's another live-stage project — this time for Bette Midler's upcoming *Experience the Divine* tour. She needs her infamous mermaid tail remade.

Her head costumer brings one of her original tails to my apartment, along with the materials, and a plastic box of sequins and baguettes. "Use the fluke from this one and just make a new body. And we need it fast. We leave in four days."

While it's for the Diva herself, it is just a lined-tail body. Pulling a pattern from the old tail assures it should fit. Some quick sewing, a stretch panel for added comfort, extra baguettes to cover the seams and create a randomness that doesn't exist in the sequined material, a closure in the back, attach the fluke, and blend it in with a few more baguettes. It's ready to deliver — if I got everything perfect on the first try.

I arrive at the studio where Bette and her crew are rehearsing and am led directly to her dressing room, where she waits for the fitting.

She's polite and professional, and from the speed of her speech and the energy in her movements, it's obvious that she expects our time to be brief and efficient.

As I pull the tail out of my bag, a girl enters with a big bag of her own. From the string-handle shopping back, she unfurls two gorgeous evening gowns encased in thin, dry-cleaner plastic bags. It doesn't take a genius to recognize designer quality.

"What in the world?" In less than a second, Bette goes from a pleasant professional to an appalled explosion. "I just spent hundreds of dollars having those dresses cleaned and pressed, and you bring them back wadded up like yesterday's laundry. What was the point? Do you realize how much those dresses are worth?" — my guess is eight to ten thousand a piece.

The girl gives an explanation that even I know isn't going to fly. Something about her hands being too full and… Whatever. Bette isn't the least bit consoled by her excuses. She makes a quick getaway and leaves me standing there with a now-impatient woman.

My Professional Mask was barely staying on my face when I came in; it's completely off now. I say a silent prayer, pleading for my shaking to stay in my bones and my Cloak of Invisibility to protect me from redirecting her Jody Attack to me.

She faces me and sighs deeply. "Okay. Let's see what you've got."

Still shell-shocked, I can't read her tone at all. I slam on my backup Professional Mask — the paper one that doesn't hold very well, and try to up where we left off, as if the past five minutes — that felt like fifty — never happened. "This is a first fitting. If anything needs to be altered, it's not a problem."

She takes the tail from me, shucks down to her skivvies, and slides it on, quite used to the fact that stage work forces her to undress and redress anywhere at any time, in front of anyone.

The tail zips up without a hitch, my added spandex panel making it fit just right.

With help from me and a crewman, she hops out of the dressing trailer and into her wheelchair, where we wheel her over to the soundstage for the director's inspection.

We're barely in the door when a stagehand approaches and explains that he's not going to be able to go on tour with them because his mother was just diagnosed with cancer and is going to have major surgery. He's extremely apologetic, knowing the show hits the road next week and all, and how that doesn't give them much time to replace him.

I wait for Jody to reappear, but instead, Bette hugs him. "Family comes first. You stay with your mom. And when the surgery is over, and everything is fine, you rejoin us wherever we are. Your job will be waiting for you."

Bette Midler is not *a diva* except by self-appointment. She is a queen — hardworking and devoted to her craft but just as much a human — a perfectionist human — but one able who distinguish between legitimate attempts toward perfection and thoughtlessness. I like her — she scares me, but I like her.

The man steps away, and instantly, the director focuses on Bette in the tail as if there was no interruption. "How does it feel?"

"It feels great." She spins her chair to the head costumer just joining the group. "I like it. Are we having her do anything else for us?"

"I was thinking of having her rework the background tails as well." — first I've heard of it, but okay.

"Can she get them done before we leave?"

He shrugs. "She can do them and ship them out to us."

"Great."

Before we wheel her back to her dressing room, he says he'll call me, and off I go with the blessing of the Diva.

He never calls me. He leaves town without collecting the baguette box or her original mermaid tail body — or paying me.

The problem with living behind Masks is making them work. I fake a lot of things, so I don't remember his first name, and never asked his last — something I clearly need to get better at doing — not that I know how to contact someone who's traveling (*before cell phones.*) I just did my first gratis job.

I don't blame Bette. After seeing how intolerant she is with unprofessional behavior, I think she'd rip him a new one if she knew what he's done.

FADE TO:

48. Squaw Valley, California — On a Hill

While I do genuinely love my job, my personal life still revolves around Daisy and a few close friends. Today is a perfect example. I'm a third wheel on Terri and Howard's road trip to see the five acres Howard inherited that lies just above the orange groves of Squaw Valley, California, in the foothills of the Sequoia National Forest.

The drive is okay. The conversation is good — but the view is tedious. Southern California is dried out in October. There's nothing to see save the stretch of white windmills standing like soldiers covering miles and miles of flat land. Still, it's nice to get out of the Valley.

I've spent so much time driving in traffic and cooped up in a shop full of clay, plaster, fiberglass, and ammonia that I've almost forgotten how nice space feels and how fresh air can be. As we hit the orange groves, I'm stunned. It doesn't smell like the Midwest — warm dirt and fresh-cut grass, charcoal grills, and juniper bushes. The day is young, moisture still hangs in the air holding the aroma of oranges, sweet and clear.

As we pass the last of the groves, the ground begins to rise. We wind and roll through the hills, the open road sweeping us left and right — a feeling I haven't felt in too long. The hills grow steeper, and the turns get tighter until Howard has to slow down to make the curves, and the land is no longer covered by orderly rows of trees but by fields broken by creeks with live oaks and boulders scattered across the countryside.

"It looks like some giants had a rock fight," I say. There's no rhyme or reason to where the rocks are. They seem to be just wherever they landed.

Visiting the property is short. We stay long enough to have a picnic and enjoy the open air, but no bathroom facilities on the hillside — or heavy bushes — we don't stay much longer.

The next summer, Terri and Howard invest in excavating a driveway and cutting a house pad for their second home, and I make most of the trips with them, falling more and more in love with the scent of hot wild sage and eucalyptus that carries so strong in the summer breeze.

Saying that living in the Los Angeles area is expensive is like saying walking on the sun will be a little warm. I've managed to buy a Honda Civic hatchback new off the showroom floor, and my apartment is gradually getting furnished with beautiful antiques. I go where I want when I want, buy any clothes I want, and I have a savings account with living expense money set aside to cover a full year of unemployment.

It's time to invest. Buying houses in L.A. is generally something for married couples, because it takes two incomes to afford one. Daisy isn't much of a financial partner. But I need to find something to do with my extra money.

As we stand on their hill, watching the tall, dry grass making golden waves across the valley floor below, I turn to them. "You're not going to sell this, are you?"

"No way." Howard gestures to the stand of live oak behind us. "This is the only thing I've ever had that was my own."

"Since no guy seems to want me, if I buy a piece of land up here too, then I'll at least have you two around until I'm old and crazy. But if I buy something, and then you sell, I'm out here in the middle of nowhere by myself."

"This land is ours, and it's staying ours."

By winter — if you can call cooler air *winter* — the work I do on the Aluminum Association commercial at Lazzarini's shop gives me enough for a nice down payment.

Three day-trips and one bizarre night in a spider-infested motel room with Terri and Howard while a couple screams at each other in the middle of the parking lot at midnight, and I become a land baroness. I own my very own piece of Heaven.

Our first trip in the spring brings us a new surprise.

The drive up is unrecognizable. The rolling hills scattered with giant boulders are now blanketed in lush green grass and wildflowers that smell like honey butter and spice. It's how I've always imagined Ireland to be.

I look across the way. My five acres sit on the neighboring hill from Terri and Howard's parcel. "We can send messages back and forth by raising flags on poles."

Terri laughs. "When we're old and gray, we can move up here and keep each other company."

I may not have a family of my own, but Terri assures me I'm never going to be alone. If I never marry, I'll turn it into a bed-and-breakfast for movie industry people who need a country escape. Always have a plan — subject to change due to life. I have to. It's another one of my Rules. Surprises cause chaos, and I don't do chaos.

I draw up plans for a house I want to build on it someday. I invest in the groundwork by taking on extra moonlighting jobs, initiating my pay-as-I-go plan. Residuals from the Aluminum Association commercial pay for the driveway and pad; and a few McDonald's commercials pay for electricity and a well so deep I thought we might hit magma before we hit water.

With Cleve Hall — still dressed in black, even in the hot sun — helping me anchor foundation pylons one weekend, and then Terri, Howard and Terri's dad, and his buddy, working with me the next weekend to build a four-by-eight shed complete with screened windows and furnished with a card table and four chairs, I now have the perfect place for Daisy and me to relax in the fresh air, and maybe — just maybe, I can ditch my obsession for perfection — even if only for a few hours.

FADE TO:

49. Van Nuys, California — Lazzarini's Shop

Striving for perfection isn't a bad thing — that's what I tell myself, but it doesn't stop me from crying myself to sleep at night.

It's not the drive that hurts; it's the hollowness eating away in my chest because I'm not perfect. I watch my friends succeed, and no matter what I do — or what I have accomplished — I'm still a step behind them. I'm certain I'm that second choice, the alternative hire, living off referrals that come when someone is too busy to take the job, so they refer me. I'm not good enough. I have to do better.

The person eating at me the most is Lisa. She's a better talker, so matter how many jobs she screws up, her facade is so solid that she's taking jobs I'm sure I can do better.

I have to adjust my top few Rules of my God-only-knows-how many Rules. Below, *I can never fail*; *I must keep my weirdness my secret*; *I must always consider everyone and everything's feelings*; and *I must check all closets and window locks before locking myself in*, above the basic Rules like *Don't breathe where somebody else has just exhaled*; *Always eat M&Ms in color-matched pairs*; and *Rotate your wardrobe to be fair to all your clothes*; and *never step on a doorway threshold*, My Rule: *I cannot sneak or lie* will officially allow the caveat: It will not be a lying to claim I can do something I've never done before if my Hyper-drive proves to me I'm capable because — unlike Lisa — the claim will ultimately be backed by my top Rules.

With this new justification — endorsed by Terri — I'm soon working so many simultaneous jobs that I'm sacrificing taking photos and even sleeping to keep up. I must shake my second-string status.

By the time Rick calls me to build a giant dog for something called *Sandlot*, I'm already a proficient foam fabricator, so I don't have to lie about that. The fashion design degree that taught me how to drape, pattern, and sew makes me faster than many others doing the same thing, and I've worked with fake fur enough to have a pretty good idea of how to make it pass for real.

What I don't have experience in is making two-man suits — which is what this giant dog will be. It's one thing to make a birthday party horse with two people inside, where looking silly is okay. It's another when it needs to look like it might actually be alive. Coming from a kid's imagination allows for some leeway, but I still have to make sure it's within the realm of believable in the mind of the storytelling kid in the movie.

I'm working with Cleve Hall on this one. Rick supplies us with a set of bars that stretches between two men, so the back man can lean on them while he's bent forward to help his balance, because he'll also be walking on stilts to accommodate the bend of the dog's hind legs. It's simply a matter of standing the two men in this barred-stilted contraption, tracing them onto the wall, and then projecting a St. Bernard on the wall big enough for them to fit in. From there, it's like building any other thing. Foam fabricate a dog, figure out the closures and attachments to get the men in and out of it, drape, sew, cover, figure finish, and send it over to the painter.

The other challenge is *fur transfer*. I have to do it on a set of paws that need to duplicate the real dog when it can't or won't do specific actions. With nothing in my brain's library of learned techniques to show me how to do fur transfer, I confess to Rick that I've never done it before, and instead of lambasting me, he offers to teach me.

Fur transfer, I learn, is when the backing on the fake fur is too stiff to follow the shapes, so you have to adhere the fiber to a finer cloth and then shave off its original backing. Since the paws are going to be used for tight shots, the off-the-shelf fur would turn Samson's feet into Teddy Bear feet that would jam the joints and kill the movement. Transferring the fur to cut-flat pantyhose gives Samson a set of very nice toes — and me a new skill for my ever-growing toolbox.

I have to get better, more efficient, smarter, faster, smoother. I need to become as close to perfect as I can. If I can become one of the best, maybe people won't forget me anymore. Maybe then they won't dread having to settle for me.

(TWO WEEKS LATER)

Everything for *Sandlot* is almost ready to go and I've not heard one word about either Clever or me going with it. Cleve just interviewed to build the giant creatures for *Ultraman* and he tells me I should go there too, so we can keep our little team together. I squeeze in an interview during our lunch hour with the shop head, Kevin Carlson, and lock in a twelve-week position as not only one of the builders, but also an on-set for maintenance and as a SAG (Screen Actors Guild) union puppeteer.

That shop is yet another temporary warehouse space in North Hollywood, but it's in the best location. Next door is Cinema Secrets. A few more doors down is Ted Rae's shop, and at the driveway entrance, across the way is Buechler's shop, MMI. *Ultraman* is going to feel like working on a monster-making campus.

A week before my position at Lazz's shop ends, Rick stops me while I'm sewing. "I'd like you to go to set with the dog. It'll be two weeks of SAG and maintaining the pieces."

My heart drops. "If you had only said something sooner. I have a three-month job lined up that starts the Monday after I finish here." Having jobs lined up back-to-back shop jobs is an art form that I've pretty-well perfected. This time, my efficiency is backfiring.

"Can you delay your start?"

I've heard of people doing this, but I can't. It's against my Rules. I committed to a start date. Changing it now makes me unreliable — a liar. I have to say, "Unfortunately I can't."

The next morning, Cleve is practically dancing in his shoes. "I'm going to set with the dog. I'll see you in two."

I'm blown away. *Ultraman* is several months of work, including six weeks of SAG. If I had said yes to Rick, I would've been able to have both and get SAG on two different film projects instead of just the one. "Rick offered the job to me, but I just couldn't bail on Kevin. I'm surprised you're going and losing two weeks building kaiju. This is your dream job."

"Yeah, I know. Big Godzilla monsters are my thing, but if I can get two weeks of SAG pay, I'm taking it."

"But you're not SAG."

"I know. I'm not going to join either." He shrugs. "I'll take the pay and then not join. It's not like the residuals are going to be enough to justify the initiation fee, but weekly rate is too good to pass up."

Sandlot has a green director, with no recognizable actors as far as we've been told. I'm not going stab Kevin over the difference between two weeks at my shop pay vs the SAG wages. In my head, I can so vividly see the pained look on Kevin's face when Cleve pulled the rug out from under him and left him to recalculate his schedule to compensate for one of his key builders disappearing. My Rules won't allow me to hurt someone like that, nor will they let me lie or change a deal after I've committed to it.

At any price, I cannot break the rules.

50. North Hollywood, California — The Kaiju Warehouse

"Well, Lynette, it looks like you're the lead fabricator alone." Kevin plops down a pile of monster design turnarounds, while a small group of guys stand around us. "I'll lead the crew sculpting of Ultraman himself and the creature heads and hands, and you'll be in charge of foam fabrication."

I look around. I'm the only female in the shop — no surprise there — but I'm in charge this time. Most of the guys have skills departments other than foam fabrication. They know how to wield a razor blade and use Barge, but I'll be doing all the engineering and patterning until Cleve gets here. The creatures are all kaiju of some sort. Several are similar to Godzilla, while others are extremely one-of-a-kind concepts, inspired by bugs, ocean creatures and dinosaurs. If I create Godzilla-shaped base form, the gang can work on the similarly shaped monsters, leaving me to direct my energy to the more elaborate suits.

After creating a body pod using walkaround suit techniques, with a zipper in the back, a basic tail shape, and fabric gusseted legs and arms patterns, I turn the guys loose in teams of two to build Red King, Mrs. Red King, Tendon, and the others, while I start on the winged dragon fly inspired creature called Dorako.

Cleve joins us as after I've finished Dorako and started on Kemular — a quadruped amphibian creature with a hard shell that needs to open like Delorean wing doors, exposing a fleshy area underneath. He only stays for a couple of weeks before Kevin fires him, after wandering in hours late or not showing up at all.

I bring in Terri to help, but she's only there for about a week before she is called to puppeteer on *The Flintstones* movie.

The fact is, I am going to stay the lone Key Foam Fabricator for the duration of this project — and I'm thrilled. The creatures are fun; they're mainly mattress foam, which is a very forgiving material to work with, and their skin is brushed latex, which is simply time with very little skill needed.

Sunday is normally our one day off, but I stop by to say hi to my new friend, a guy who's a Hasidic Jew and needs Saturday off instead of Sunday.

"Hey there!" Yus is already gone for the day, but another one of the guys bounces over, with a big smile on his face. "Check this out."

He proceeds to show me how he's using the pod piece I designed for the kaiju to make the walkaround suit he's building for a moonlighting job he managed to snag.

This guy is standing right in front of me, bragging to me about how he — with no foam skills beyond what I've showed him — has stolen a copy of my pattern from Kevin — from me — to use for his project, so he can cut me out and claim to be a foam sculptor …and turn a fat profit by not actually putting in one single hour of prototyping hours he's billing the client for.

If he thinks I'm flattered — I'm not. If he thinks I'm going to congratulate him on his ingenuity — I'm not. What I would like to do is rip his head off and shove it up the behind of his half-done pig suit.

"Don't tell Kevin. I know it's technically his pattern" — and mine but he seems to have forgotten that, even while he keeps calling it "your pattern" to my face.

I smile dumbly — stupidly — because he's so enthusiastic. Maybe he's just oblivious and excited about using the new skills I've taught him. Maybe he thinks I should be proud of him for being such a good student. I can't confront him. I might hurt his feelings.

"Do you have any suggestions for me?" He hands me the character artwork.

I can see this pod pattern is not the best place to start. The proportions are wrong. The subtle curves of the design are missing. While he's going to deliver a pig costume to his client, I don't see them calling him again. But I can't tell him that — that would be mean.

He asked for my thoughts, but I don't feel inclined to help him steal credit from me in the future. So, I keep my Nice Mask firmly nailed in place and give him a couple of benign tips to improve the shape enough that the client isn't royally screwed — it's not their fault they hired a con artist — and then I exit the shop as quickly as possible.

"See you tomorrow," he calls out to me.

"Yep. See you tomorrow."

I want to stomp my damn Nice Mask into the parking lot cement, but I can't. I'll need it to keep living by my damn Rules.

(WEEK FIVE)

Kevin hurries around the shop, telling us to tidy our work areas. This afternoon, the director and producing team from Japan will be coming by to check our progress.

I straighten up my area, but I leave my wall intact. Every day, I buy a banana from the food truck, and each time, I make sure to take the one with the label stuck to it. I've been sticking the labels on the wall next to my table the same way we did at the ice cream parlor my family owned during my teen years.

Among the stickers are little pieces of brown table paper with words and sayings on them. They are quotes from the dumbest girl I've ever had the agony of working with. She only lasted a couple of weeks. After everyone got so tired of her perpetual yammering that when she went to the bathroom, one of the guys tied a rope between the doorknob and the industrial sewing machine just so we could have a few minutes of peace and quiet, and Kevin let her go. I heard she went to work for Rick Lazzarini — for two whole days before he fired her, too.

"I mistook *sunny* for *bright*," he said.

That quote is the center post on my Wall of Idiocy. The girl had no idea what any of the wall meant. If she had, hurting her feelings would've killed me. But we're hot and dirty, and I hated her lack of professionalism, her lack of skills, lack of consideration, respect… This is not a playground, it's a job — one that I live for — and the only way I could keep from going all Jody on her was to find some humor in the bedlam she created.

The wall stays as-is. My banana sticker and quotes mingled among the kaiju designs, check lists, and construction notes still hang when the Japanese men in suits arrive.

While Kevin hosts the dog and pony show, I continue my work on Baltan.

Baltan is one of the *Ultraman* royalty among their kaiju villains, and his design is one of my favorites — followed closely by the robotic beetle-looking Zetton suit I've already completed. Knowing how popular Baltan is and the fact that Terri started him during the week she filled in before going to work on *The Flintstones*, I'm taking great pains to honor Baltan — and Terri — to the best of my abilities.

Prior attempts, in my opinion, haven't done many of the designs justice. Kevin and I have agreed that we want to stay as loyal to the original artwork as possible.

Kevin leads the men through the line of foam latex Ultraman suits, past the paint area, and around the shop, eventually stopping in front of my table. "This is Lynette. She's in charge of the creatures' foam fabrication."

The group barely looks at me before turning to the Baltan pieces laid out before them. One man turns to Kevin. "How will someone get into these pieces?"

Kevin defers to me.

"There will be hidden closures here," I point to the side seams, "and here." I point to the shoulders. Many of the pieces will be attached to a body stocking"

Without ever acknowledging I had spoken, another man turns to Kevin. "The claws? Will they be as big as in the drawing?"

Again, Kevin looks at me.

"Yes." I pick up one of the claw pieces and offer it to one the man. "The rest of the pieces are what I'm working on right now."

When the man doesn't take it, Kevin takes it and hands it to him. Now the man accepts it. "What is this material?"

"L200." No matter what I say or do, none of the men even look at me.

In Japan, I know building kaiju is a well-regarded profession, and a position held by men. I'm getting the distinct impression that it bothers them to have a female responsible for the construction of their kaiju.

Until the men leave, I submit to my role of second-class worker. Kevin tries to include me, but he can't change their minds, nor can I do anything in less than an hour to help. If I push, I'm only going to verify whatever ugly thoughts they have about an American woman being in their creature shop. If my work can't speak for me, I need to let it go.

Letting it go is what I have to do. I'm sure this won't be the last time I'm passed over, looked past, looked over, forgotten, or flat-out disregarded. I'm used to it. It's happened my whole life. My Cloak of Invisibility is strong.

If I speak up, I might hurt Kevin, and he tried so hard to get me some respect. Hurting his feelings is against the Rules. If I speak up to the pattern-thief, I might make him feel bad — and that too is against the Rules. If I speak up to the Japanese producers, I might offend them — breaking the Rules — and that will stop me from gaining work through any American-based companies they are involved with — breaking my #1 Rule.

As Steve Johnson says teasingly to his crew: "Suck it up, cupcake."

That's what I'm going to have to do, and it has to be the end of any feelings I have about it. I close the door on that Room in my head and walk away.

(But that wasn't the end of it.

After a short-lived theatrical release, Sandlot exploded in the video rental market, becoming one of the biggest sleepers of its time. Meanwhile, Ultraman pretty-well disappeared. When I finally saw a few episodes, I realized my name was left out of the credits. Hence, I wasn't receiving a dime in residuals from Ultraman, while the crew from Sandlot had been seeing a steady flow of some pretty fat checks.

By my Rules of not allowing me to ask Kevin for a delayed start, I missed out on literally thousands of dollars in residuals.

I called SAG to inquire about the lack of residuals from Ultraman, and the guy on the phone informed me that while there had been residuals distributed, since my name was not on the credits, I wasn't entitled to anything. I have my SAG contract, but apparently, SAG doesn't pursue negligence. He also told me that with the company being from Japan, the chance of them doing anything on my behalf was nil. He assured me he would add my name to the list, so any residuals run through SAG in the future would be divided with me included. While my fellow puppeteers on Ultraman have continued getting checks, I have yet to receive a single dime.

Invisible enough to my co-workers that they don't even consider the fact that they're stealing my work even while admitting it to my face, invisible to the men paying me to give them the monsters making their series continue, invisible to my own union.

To follow my dream, I'll suck it up, cupcake.

RETURN TO:

51. Van Nuys, California — Stan Winston Studio

It took me forever to get into this shop. I couldn't get an interview to sweep the floors.

The third time I sent over my resume Stan starting the dinosaur construction for *Jurassic Park*. I even followed up with a phone call. The receptionist verified they had received my resume and that it had been forwarded to the department head. She said it there were any openings; they'd be in touch. "Thanks for sending it over."

I waited — again — and nothing happened — again.

I knew several people working there. Was this another one of my invisible moments or was I being blackballed by someone I considered a friend?

More and more I was becoming an outsider.

When Kevin Peter Hall died, I didn't even go to his funeral because I didn't feel I'd be wanted there. I didn't work with him, but after meeting him on *Harry and the Hendersons*, I went with friends to Camilla's apartment to dye Easter eggs one evening, and Kevin was there. He was such a sweet person. He looked adorable batiking an egg as it nestled in his giant palm.

But I wasn't his friend. We only met through mutual friends. If I went, his real friends would've seen me as a fake — a liar — so while they all went to pay their final respects, I stayed home and cried alone.

Looking at my co-workers here at Stan's — the ones who like me and the ones who don't but pretend they do — I now know why I couldn't get in here before. The only reason I made it in when I did was by sheer luck. In this industry, sometimes timing is everything.

Sometimes, good timing is simply dumb luck; other times, it's figuring out just when to jump. And until that good timing happens, all anyone can do is push on.

CUT TO:

52. All Over the Place in Hollywood — Interviewing

I'm tired of hearing *Oh, I wish we'd thought to invite you. You would've loved it.* I hate wearing a Cloak of Invisibility, but it's just happened again — right here in Santa Monica, at a job interview. I show the guy my portfolio, and then he pulls out his — and shows me the same *D.C. Follies* puppets I just showed him I had built.

I freeze. What am I supposed to say? Calling him a thief will not get me the job.

"Um," he starts when he realizes I've quit flipping pages. "I puppeteered some of the puppets. I just use these pictures to show people what I can puppeteer."

If that was true, then he would've led with that. Since he didn't bother to say a thing until I forced him to explain, I know he lets most people assume he built my puppets. What else did he show me in this portfolio that isn't actually his to claim?

I smile. "Oh. I see." I should say more, but I'm speechless.

Suddenly, he looks at his watch. "I've gotta get going. I have a call with a client starting in ten minutes."

"Yeah, I'd better get going. Traffic is going to be rough heading back into the Valley." I close my portfolio.

Heading to my car, I know I've lost the job, and it's not even my fault.

I hate job interviews. I suck at them. Luckily, I don't interview much anymore. Most of my work comes from referrals or callbacks from shops I've worked in before. If I relied on job interviews to get jobs, I'd lose the job almost every time.

I can't brag myself up — it's embarrassing. If I claim I've done half of what I've actually done, it sounds like I'm lying. I haven't been working in the industry long enough to have accomplished as much as I have, in the eyes of most people.

So, I skim over my credits to keep from coming across like a braggart — and wind up seeming mediocre.

There's still nothing memorable about my looks either — I can't allow myself to do it. I don't wear makeup. I yank my hair back into a ponytail to keep it out of the glue. I wear whatever is clean that's comfortable and practical — usually baggy pants and cropped tees. I don't have an outgoing personality like Terri, give creative narratives, or have a cool accent. I'm only weird because I stay so ordinary to hide how weird I am because I can't possibly explain it to make it make sense to anyone.

So, I sit across, near, or beside someone — as I am again right now, on a sofa in front of a coffee table, with Darryl this time — while he looks through a portfolio of whatever photos I've been able to glean while on the job or given by the shop owner after the project is over, to see if he thinks I'm capable of making a dozen poseable vervet monkeys for a restaurant in South America.

"This all looks great."

This time, my portfolio does its job.

He hands me a brochure. "Here's what we do."

I open the brochure for his company and discover not one but two of my works in it. One photo is not just the same puppet; it's a copy of the exact same photo he just saw in my portfolio.

Before I shove this stupid brochure down his throat, I take a breath, smile, and point to the photo of Tiger, the giant cat from Universal Studio Tour's *The American Tale Theater* that I foam sculpted for Randy Simper. "This looks familiar."

While his justification is questionable, I'm able to keep my Mask from falling off well enough this time to save the job offer.

I don't know how many times I'm going to have to wear my newly added Oblivious Mask, but apparently, I'd better keep it well in hand.

FADE TO:

53. Sun Valley, California — XFX

When Bill calls me to work on a Duracell commercial with him at XFX, I jump at the chance. In Steve's shop, I don't have to be oblivious.

Getting any project done requires three things: time, money, and manpower. In the industry, we get to pick two — or one and you hope friends are willing to play with you. Commercials usually choose money and manpower. They carry tight schedules with long days in the shop and intense tempos on-set — but they pay well and generally come with small perks. When I won the Nintendo commercial contract, lunch on set came with on-site-made sorbet and a four-string quartet while we dined under umbrella-covered tables outdoors. And when I was on the Aluminum Association commercial for Rick Lazzarini, production flew us to New York and put us up in a hotel that was walking distance from Little Italy — and some of the best food in Manhattan.

This time, the advertising company for Duracell has put together a concept they hope will create an ongoing campaign, so they decide to treat the project more like a movie. They hire Barry Sonnefeld, the director of *The Addams Family* movie (and later, the *Men in Black* film series) and a major make-up effects artist — Steve Johnson's XFX — instead of contracting a freelancer like most commercials do. And they're giving it a more production time. This project will stay closer to normal ten-hour days in lieu of the big bucks and extravagance.

It's fine with me. I already have a side project at home. A job with major overtime would take the fun out of them both.

The stars of these commercials will be the Puttermans, a family of doll people who run on Duracell batteries. Working with Bill Bryan again is going to be fun. He's good company, fun conversation, and we've worked together enough to make a sturdy team.

Building the Puttermans is a job of precision. Every shirt, skirt, or pair of pants has to be perfectly designed to look like clothes even though we're making them out of L200, so every pleat, fold, and wrinkle is strategically placed and permanent

— and let's not forget the battery sockets we have to add to their backs to hold the giant batteries. Just in case the L200 doesn't dictate the shape enough, the fabricated clothing is coated in Urethane, so the actors can't move very far. One crease and the garment is ruined. Top that all off with swivel shoulder joints out of Styrene so their arms have to swivel in the armhole just like a Barbie doll shoulder joint does and we have very uncomfortable actors who look so much like live dolls they walk the edge of disturbing.

As for the hips, knees and elbow joints, the actors simply can't bend more than a couple of inches if they're wearing long pants or long sleeves — which makes it a real treat to get them in and out of the clothes.

During the first fitting, Steve asks, "Do you think we can make spandex move completely wrinkle-free? I don't want to make foam latex gloves and have female characters having pudgy fingers, but they can't have knuckle wrinkles."

Another new challenge. This project is full of them. Even better, the challenge is to achieve absolute visual perfection… I'm in Heaven — while I'm making outfits that imprison the actors in performer hell.

Perfect gloves, I believe I can do.

I make every female character multiple pairs of specifically fitted gloves that go all the way to their armpits and attach between their shoulder blades under their clothes. They're sewn and darted so precisely that no fold shows until their hand is so closed that the wrinkles are out of view. The spandex is so tight that off, the pieces look like they're made for children, but I can identify them simply by looking at the lifeline darts I've added to their palms.

Bill and I divide the wardrobe pieces, so we're both steadily turning out pieces of equal challenge, time consumption, and screen time. He works on Dad's outfit while I work on Mom's. He works on the son while I work on the daughter. He works on the aunt while I make the skin pieces. We cut and chat, glue and bounce ideas, lock folds and reminisce, build sockets, and ramble on.

Chattering along, we somehow get on the subject of pay, and I discover I'm doing the exact same job as Bill — but for thirty percent less per hour. Instantly, I want to slap him — but I don't. He's my friend and not the one who set my pay.

"I'm making a lot less than that," I say as casually as I can.

I tell him what I'm making, and with the broad smile that never seems to leave his face, he says, "I don't know why."

I don't either. It doesn't seem right. But then, I can see tons of reasons he's worth more than I am. He *is* Bill Bryan. He has more years in the industry than I have. He's more well-known than I am. He's one of my teachers. He's one of Steve's right-hand men. My head grows a list that goes on and on. He's simply more important than I am.

I'm…just me.

CUT TO:

54. North Hollywood, California — My Apartment

Terri shows up at my apartment to work on the suit refurbishment we need to complete for Mr. McGruff, the Crimestopper dog. Daisy greets her at the door before settling in between us on the living room floor.

While we stitch on the new paw covers, I tell her what I discovered at work.

"This industry will never pay us the same as the guys, but that's way too far off." Terri goes on to tell me what the average pay scale is for experienced foam sculptors and what I can expect as a female. "You have enough experience. You should raise your rate. You need to keep your rate in range with the rest of us, or you'll hurt yourself as well as the others."

I am one of *them*. The thought never occurred to me. I have confidence in my skills — even if, at the same time, I'm sure every client thinks I'm a screw-up. It never occurred to me that maybe Terri, Bill, and the others consider me a peer and not still a rookie. When that happened? How long have I been undercutting myself — and my peers?

Terri sticks McGruff's head on her own to reseat the helmet. "You should ask Steve for a raise."

"Really? Mid-project?"

"Yes. If you stay at your current rate, that's what he'll budget for you in the future. You're never going to be able to get what Bill gets paid — I can't either — but Steve has budgeted more than he's paying you."

"How can you stand it? You're as good as the guys are, but even you can't get the same pay?"

She stops working and sets the head down. "Let me ask you one thing. Are you happy?"

Now, I stop, too. I'm not sure how to answer that.

"I mean, do you like what you do?"

"I love it."

"Do you make enough money to buy what you need and have some extra for things you want? Everybody always wants to make more, but are you secure?"

I have a nice apartment and a brand-new car — for a steal because I forced a four-hour negotiation that ended in hard bargaining strictly to assure my dad would approve of my negotiating prowess. I own five acres in the county that now has a new well, a pad for a house, and electricity run to it — thanks to the Aluminum Association and the McDonald's Fry Guys and McNuggets commercials — and my savings account is still fat. "Yes."

"So? Are you happy?"

"Yeah. I'm happy."

"Then don't worry about what other people get paid. We can't help that. Look around. There are a lot of people making more money than us but who have less to show for it, and who make more money but hate their jobs. If you're happy and you're secure, then live your life and don't compare yourself to others."

I add another new Rule to my list: Never talk actual numbers with my co-workers again. Pay range — maybe. But locked salaries — never.

Still, I need to ask for a raise tomorrow — I tell Terri I will.

She'll ask how it went tomorrow evening when she returns, and I can't let her down.

CUT TO:

55. Sun Valley, California — Back to XFX

I've given myself every excuse in the world not to go to Steve's office to ask for that raise, even though he's been here for over an hour.

I still don't know how much to ask for. I'm hoping he'll make an offer. Left to me, I find it hard to believe anybody thinks I'm worth what they pay me already. I feel like I'm hired primarily because they're short-handed, not because they're dying to hire *me*.

By mid-afternoon, I run out of excuses.

The hours tick away. Two more hours and the day will be over. I can't go home and tell Terri I failed.

I cover my cup of glue and make my way past the sculptors working on the faces and male hands, down the stairs of the balcony to the ground floor — where it's much cooler than the corner Bill and I work in — through the tables of painters and mold-makers, to the reception area and Steve's office door.

His door — the door to my Fear Room — stands wide open.

He's leaned back on a sofa, taking a break with several of his anchor team members. "What's up?"

I certainly don't want an audience to see Steve laugh at me. "Never mind, I'll come back."

"No. Come on in. We're just talking." He situates himself on the edge of the sofa and waits.

He thinks I have a question about the project, but I can't think of one fast enough to fill that expectation. Besides, Terri will be asking, and I cannot fail her.

I scan the other faces in the room. Bill Corso, Lenny MacDonald, Norman Cabrera, Jim Eustermann, Tom Irvin — the gods of Steve's shop.

They all wait, looking at me with smiles on their faces. Probably remnants of whatever tale had been told before I interrupted, but now they seem ready for me to join them with another fun story.

"I've been talking with Bill, and I've learned that I'm being paid a lot less than him for the same job."

Steve laughs nervously as he looks from one of his comrades to another. "Hey, I just pay what people ask."

That is true. He's never once tried to talk me down in price.

"How much of a raise do you want?"

I can't ask for the full increase. I'll sound ridiculous if I do. He was supposed to make an offer.

The group waits for my answer. I have to make a decision fast, before my I-Am-Worthy Mask falls off.

"Three dollars an hour."

"Okay. You've got it."

Just like that.

Thanks to Bill, I see I can keep up with the pros in my field. Thanks to Steve, I realize it's my responsibility to decide my worth — not his. And thanks to Terri, I got my raise and learned that I need to reassess my pay from time to time or I'll get paid the same for the next one hundred years.

I was happy at the lower rate — but with $3 an hour more, I'm able to move across the hall in my apartment building, so I can have a shop and a real bedroom. That will definitely make me happier.

FADE TO:

56. Houston, Texas — Christmas with the Family

I don't get to visit my parents often because I work so much, but I try to make it back to Houston for Christmas every year. Working on *The Masters of the Universe Traveling Stage Show*, I missed one Christmas, and that left me feeling so guilty that I vowed never to let it happen again. While it's just a vow and not a Rule, so far, I've been able to keep that vow.

"Would you be willing to go to dinner at the house of one of my co-workers?" my dad asks before we even get from the airport back to the house.

He still works for the same company that coincidentally helped me with one of my first steps. But this time, instead of Dee Murr, it's another woman's attention I've gained, on with a son who's a big monster movie fan.

"He'd think it was a big deal if he could meet you and hear about your work."

I don't know what he thinks he'll hear from me, but…"I guess."

Two nights later, we go to dinner at Shirley's apartment, where I meet Chaney. To say Chaney is a fan is an understatement. My dad and I don't even make it to the living room before he breaks into a twenty-minute monologue about how much he loves watching effects films, how long he's been a fan, what kinds of movies he watches, how many times he's seen them, what magazines he reads to further his knowledge, and… Oh my goodness. He just doesn't stop.

Shirley detours the conversation by interrupting Chaney. "Your dad tells me you worked on Beetlejuice?"

Talking about myself is even more awkward than I imagined. Considering how big *Beetlejuice* is and how short my parts in the film are, it hardly feels worth mentioning. I give him an abbreviated story and barely finish before he starts right in where he left off, as if I hadn't said a thing.

After ten more minutes of his enthusiastic rattling, my ears are already tired. I excuse myself to the bathroom so I can wash up, relax the numb grin I've had plastered to my face for forty minutes now — and, more than anything, have a moment of silence. Surely, he's running out of steam and will calm down once we're at the table.

The lasagna's delicious aroma permeates the whole apartment. Sheila held the start of dinner an extra twenty minutes so Chaney could calm down — which doesn't seem to be happening — and frankly, I'm starving.

I'll do anything or listen to anything, if this kid will let me eat something before my hunger beats out my manners and I snap. Separated from my three-thousand calorie, roach-coach subsidized eating habit or the on-set perpetually available craft services table, I'm not doing well with this three-meal-a-day routine anyway. If this kid won't let me eat soon, I'm either going to rip off his lips and eat them to shut him up, or I'm going to get the shakes and burst into tears. Either way, it's not going to be pretty.

I dry my hands, use my shirt tail to open the door, and then flush the toilet with my foot before dashing out before the water stops swirling, while simultaneously bracing myself for another attack as I enter the dining room.

My absence has allowed them to migrate to the table. With Shirley across from my dad, that puts Chaney and me directly across from one another.

As my butt hits the chair, I hear, "You worked on *Ghoulies*, didn't you?"

"*Ghoulies II*, actually."

And you worked on some of the *Puppet Master* movies too, didn't you?"

Before I can ask how he knows all this, the answer comes.

"I freeze the videos when I see the crew credits, so I can find out who worked on what.

My name made the credits? I didn't know that. I haven't seen *Ghoulies II* or any of the *Puppet Master* movies.

"What was it like working on *Demonic Toys*?"

And we're off and running again as if I never left the room. The only difference this time is that now Chaney is asking questions, leaving me to do all the talking — and none of the eating.

I'm sorry I came.

FLASHBACK

57. Burbank, California — In a Dark Warehouse

"Oh good, you're here!"

I join Ken with John Buechler, Mike Deak, and a few others gathered in a circle, contemplating how the next scene for a movie called *Dangerous Toys* (before its release, it was renamed *Demonic Toys*.) I'd already made Baby Oopsie Daisy's blue nightgown and Jack Attack's collar, so the creepy puppets don't surprise me. But Ken calling at nine o'clock on a Saturday morning, saying they needed a puppeteer immediately; that surprised me.

They need a puppeteer able to reach the puppet into the scene while keeping their body out of frame. My skinny, long arm is much better suited for the job than any of the thick-armed men I see standing around. My dance training has given me the coordination, strength, and flexibility to be a decent puppeteer, even if I didn't grow up with a puppet on my hand.

I take another look around. I'm the only female in the building, meaning I must be perfect and never complain about anything. I have yet to get any grief for being "the girl" in this Peter Pan world. I need to be doubly sure I don't give them any reason to worry about having a girl in their clubhouse.

An hour later, we still haven't filmed a single shot. As I wander around, visiting with the other crew members, I catch Buechler, Ken, and two other men with their heads together, staring and me and whispering. I have no idea what they're talking about, but they can't possibly do anything to make me feel like more of an outsider than what they're doing right now.

After a few nods, a couple of smiles, and another nod, Ken leaves the group and joins me. "The actress we've been waiting for just called. She has the flu and can't make it. But from the back, you look a lot like her. We need you to double for her. Are you willing to do that?"

It wasn't what I was called in to do, but "Sure, I guess I could…" My voice faded off. They want me to act — in front of the camera. At least it will all be shot of the back of my head. I feel stupid pretending I'm somebody I'm not — especially since I already have to work so hard just to pretend to be *me*. But Ken trusts I can do it, and he brought me in. I can't let him down.

I'll be fine — that's what I just need to keep telling myself. *I'll be fine.*

Soon, I find myself in a flannel shirt and denim jacket, with my long hair teased into a tangled mess and no makeup other than dirt smudges, standing with my back to the camera, Baby Oopsie Daisy stabbing my eye out. This isn't so bad. I just have to jerk and pop like I'm taking a hit, in sync with the hand puppet's swinging arm. It's like dancing.

"Okay, now lay down. You're dead."

I lay on the floor. They lower the camera angle nearly level with my body.

"There's no way I'm going to be able to stay out of the shot," Deak says. "I can't get low enough — unless you can dig a hole in the floor."

Within minutes, I find myself on the floor, with Baby Oopsie Daisy on my own arm, as I puppeteer my killer walking away from my dead body. I'm the killer and the victim in the same shot.

"Perfect!" Buechler says. "Now, stay there while we move the camera."

They move the camera around and bring in the actor so he can discover the body, react, and continue to do whatever it is he's supposed to do. But as I watch the reset, I wonder, "From that angle, won't you see my face?"

"Yeah," Buechler says, "but you look so much like Ellen Dunning, it'll be fine."

It'll be fine. That's exactly what I've been telling myself all day, but now I'm beginning to wonder. Surely, I can't look *that* much like Ellen. But then, I'm just a generic brown-haired girl. Ordinary. I look like everybody.

It'll be fine.

DISSOLVE TO:

58. Houston, Texas — Back to the Eternal Dinner

"That was you?!" Chaney blurts between bites of cherry pie.

I didn't get to eat much of my lasagna or the salad because I was too busy answering questions and responding to interruptions and off-base theories about how the movie industry works. Now I understand what it must be like for real celebrities try to go out for dinner — to try to be normal for an evening — with the endless interruptions and people making mental notes on how you hold your fork, or like Chaney's mom, the servers stressing over whether you like their cooking because you haven't eaten much.

The difference between a celebrity in a restaurant and me at this dinner is that a celebrity can pay the bill and leave. I'm stuck until my dad figures out a way to get me out of here.

We adjourn to the living room, where I end up on the sofa, with Chaney parked right next to me, showing me crumbled drawings, pieces of masks he's made, and a heap of photos of things he's made or wants to make or wants me to tell him how it was made or wonders how he can make it or…oh, boy.

Shirley forces a laugh. "Give her a chance, Chaney. I'm sure she's getting tired of all the questions." The suggestion is more token than anything.

Chaney doesn't slow down.

She just chuckles and shakes her head and leans back to let him continue to eat me alive. For the fifth time, my dad tries to chime in, but Chaney is undeterred.

"Give me just a minute to go to the bathroom, and I'll be right back." I saunter into the bathroom again.

I'm dying of thirst. Sheila had already poured my water before I sat down, so I couldn't drink it. Using the sink as a sideways drinking fountain, I stick my lips under the faucet — being sure not to touch any part of it.

There's nothing else I need to do in this room, other than soak up its silence. I stand in front of the mirror. I'm tired, and it shows. My Pleasant Mask is falling apart. I don't know how much longer I can keep going, but surely the evening will be able to come to an end fairly soon. We've been here over two hours. It wouldn't be rude to leave now. I work on my expression in the mirror until I can play this bizarre celebrity roll a little while longer, take a deep breath, and dive back into the deep end of this too-hot pool.

"I have this magazine that has an article on *The Blob*. You worked on that, didn't you?"

My Mask must be slipping because my dad stands up.

"Well, Lynette, I think it's about time we get out of here." He says it like it's a joke, but I know he's saying what he knows I'm thinking. It's a talent of his. His big smile and honest face allow him to blatantly state the truth without people catching the offense. "Are you about ready? Because I am."

I pose with Chaney so his mom can snap a few pictures, and then we say a quick goodbye — or as quick as Chaney lets it be — before making a break for it.

As we slam the doors on the truck, I catch my dad looking at me. I don't know what my expression tells him this time, but he busts out laughing — wheezing, he's laughing so hard. "I'm sorry. I had no idea…"

"How could you? That was something." Now, I'm laughing too.

He throws the truck into drive, and we cruise through the quiet apartment complex and back onto the freeway toward home.

As I watch the taillights in front of us, broken by the streetlight glares running over the windshield, I can't help but replay the conversations of the evening, Chaney's questions, and my stories. I look for missed facts, things I shouldn't have said, ways I could've made him feel better about his efforts. Luckily, the words coming back to me are nice — which is good. If I'd crushed his enthusiasm in any way, it would haunt me the rest of my life. He was overwhelming, and annoying, and way too enthusiastic, but now that I can breathe again, I can see that he isn't a normal movie fan.

He didn't ask about the famous people I've met or dig for behind-the-scenes gossip, or even try to score the movies I worked on to find out which one was the biggest. He was more enthusiastic about my work on the low-budget stuff than most of the bigger titles. He asked questions about how things were built, how things were shot, and why things were done this way or that way.

I get it now.

Chaney isn't a movie fan; he's a movie-making enthusiast. He was absorbing education, not dirt. He can't see himself building creatures for *Beetlejuice* or anything else that's going to end up in a Hollywood movie any more than a little league baseball player can see himself pitching for the New York Yankees — he can dream it but he can't envision it in reality, but that little league player can see himself pitching in high school, and then college, and then making it to the big show, and Chaney can aspire to do low-budget movies from his bedroom or garage, his backyard, or a buddy's house that gains attention, so he can progress to Hollywood.

I don't have to be embarrassed by my work on the low-budget films. These are the movies that inspire the Chaney's of the world to dare to try, and I'm proud to be a part of that inspiration.

I am not invisible to him. I am humbled — I'm also still hungry. "Can we swing through a McDonald's drive-thru? I'm starving."

RETURN TO:

59. Van Nuys, California — Stan Winston Studio

I'm as content now as my head will ever let me be — not quite as invisible and, like a good cook, appreciated through my craft. Even after the Van Nuys Airport's attempted manslaughter of Alpha, we're back on schedule. It's a good thing, too. Terri and I have another side gig, making a prototype mascot suit for The Noodle Company that is about to kill us both.

It's just one foam and spandex spiral noodle costume. How hard can it be? The key word here is *spiral*. Humans aren't spiraled. We're having to hand-sew almost the entire cover over the foam form. It's killing my fingers — Terri's too.

What's worse, they requested — no — insisted the noodle be a tomato noodle. I tried everything to talk them out of it, but nope. The thing looks like a giant ketchup squirt. We're bruising our fingertips over a suit that they can't possibly want more of — and if they do, Terri and I have agreed to over-price it just to make the project go away. This is only the second time we've ever done this. The first time was…well…never mind. Let's just say I'm glad this suit is almost done and doubly glad I'm making necks for Raptor insert heads.

Making those is painless.

Shane saunters through the door behind me and stops at the end of my table. This time, he has a foam latex skin for a baby T-Rex. "We need a hand puppet of the baby. The mechanical one is too heavy for the actors to carry all the time."

Again, they're coming directly to me and not going through Kathy. But this time, it's worse. Baby T-Rex is her baby, the same way the Raptors are mine. If there was ever a chance of her liking me, this is the kiss of death. But Shane is above her. My Rules demand I only consider his needs. My feelings cannot become his problem.

We're pulling a shell now."

Instant Hyper-drive. I doubt there are many patterns for him because he's a one-of-a-kind — Like the Raptors, there's a fiberglass shell — If I cut and joint the shell... "How soon do they want it?"

"Two days. The painters will need it tomorrow afternoon."

Forget Hyper-drive, brain. There's no time to think.

By the time I've cleared my work surface of Raptor bits, Baby T-Rex's shells arrive. I scribble some lines on the pieces, and they disappear back out to the shop to be cut while I dig for foam scraps, spandex, elastic, and anything else I think I'll need to pull off this miracle.

When Baby comes back in pieces, I shut off my mind and start building. If I don't think and instead just do, I'll have this done without enough overtime to affect the noodle suit.

Afraid the head fabricator will see me building a Baby T-Rex without her, I let my mind drift. It starts looping a word the DJ said on the radio this morning. *Fascination...fascination...fascination...fascination...*

I've built enough shelled pieces and hand-puppets to know what the result needs to be from the get-go. It wasn't always like this, but I learn something new in every job I take and apply it — somehow — sometime in the future. ...*fascination...fascination...*

Suit or puppet — big or small — I will deliver this puppet to the painters tomorrow afternoon. No excuses. Excuses don't keep *The Chain* moving.

...fascination...fascination...fascination...

DISSOLVE TO:

60. Pacoima, California — My Workroom at a Sound Stage, Upstairs, at the End of the Hall

I expect anyone I hire to have the same work ethic as me. In other words, if they are going to be on my project, they had better respect the importance of *The Chain*.

Nancy is doing a great job hand-sewing for me, and it's working out well for us both. She's the receptionist for the sound stages, and her boss is allowing her to sew at her desk — as long as the stage takes precedence. Since I'm at Lazz's during the day on a Miller Lite Commercial and doing this project nights and weekends, tag-teaming the pieces keeps us from battling to get our hands on pieces simultaneously. It's perfect.

This is deadline weekend. I have to deliver the puppets to MCI's office first thing Monday morning. There's a lot of work left to do, but I've been religiously following the daily deadline schedule I create for any project I take on. So, I know to the hour what time I'll be done on Sunday night — nine o'clock.

Nancy works weekends at an exotic animal rescue, but I considered that when I created the schedule on day one. Friday afternoon, she'll take two puppets with her to finish sewing while I spend the weekend on the other two. She will drop them off Sunday evening by seven o'clock, giving me two hours to complete their figure-finishing before nine. I'm all set.

I order a pizza, settle in for a weekend of no movie-going or restaurants, and get to work.

Sunday night, Nancy returns with the puppets — completely untouched — and her right hand is wrapped in bandages. "A baby tiger bit my hand."

I don't care about her hand or the fact that her injury was caused by a baby tiger. She could've sewn with her other hand — maybe not as fast, but... I'm on a deadline. All I see is that I sacrificed my whole weekend to stay on schedule, and now I'm suddenly screwed.

As she elaborates and I listen to one of the most unique injuries I've ever heard. My head immediately pulls out its calendar to follow the line of events as she narrates. It's not like I'm looking for a trip in her story — after all, there are holes in her hand to corroborate her tale. There's simply no stopping my head. It's what happens every day with everybody, about everything. But in the process, I discover that the baby tiger didn't bite her hand until mid-afternoon today, meaning she easily had a full day and a half with two working hands to squeeze in the six hours or so of sewing she had with her — six hours that she committed to doing while watching TV Friday and Saturday evening.

What had she done Friday and Saturday evening? Frankly, I don't really care. She certainly wasn't sewing.

She didn't keep her commitment to me. She lied to me. And now, she thinks I'm so stupid that I can't do basic math, like I'll be so enamored by her baby tiger adventure that I'll forget she didn't keep her promise. She lied. That's all I care about.

Liars are failures.

I didn't lie — yet her lie will sink me tomorrow if I miss my deadline.

I practically have smoke rolling out of my ears.

She can tell I'm ready to rip that bandage off her hand and throttle her with it. "Can you call the client and ask them if it's okay to deliver everything on Tuesday? It's only one extra day."

My head flashes me images of Ken Forsse and the Space Challenger disaster.

This time, it's me that explodes.

"First of all, why should an amusement park in Asia, who hired a company as big as MCI who in turn sub-contracted the puppets to me, care that my part-time help — a person they've never met and will never meet — got her hand bit by a baby tiger on a Sunday afternoon?!"

"Second, how do you propose I do that at eight o'clock on a Sunday night? No one will be in the office to take the call, so my client won't even know I'm going to miss the deadline until I've already missed it."

She hasn't moved, except for her eyes — which are much bigger than they were when I started.

But I'm not done yet.

"And third," — the biggest reason of all — "missing a deadline — rescheduled or not — is the equivalent of professional suicide, because no client rehires anyone who misses a deadline." I point my finger at her. "*You* will *not* be the reason my reputation goes up in flames."

"I'd help if I could" are the only words she has to offer.

I can't think of any words more useless to me.

I finish my last two hours of work — alone — and then start on her job. I'm mad to no end, I'm tired, and now I'm imagining the *Jody Attack* waiting for me in the morning to top it off.

People trust me — rely on me. Ken showed me the importance of this. I will not miss this deadline.

I finish the last of the work, it's one hour until sunrise. If I go home, I'll be able to squeeze in in a nap and a shower before I deliver the puppets.

I've put off getting my Jody Attack for one more project.

FADE TO:

61. North Hollywood, California — My Apartment

While I'm still excited and scared of every project I take, I still have to say yes to every call I can.

When the phone rings this time, it's Steve calling me directly, instead of Bill calling me to help him at XFX. He wants me to make a padded suit for a Corin Nemec and, a bunch of corpses for a miniseries of Stephen King's novel, *The Stand*. After asking for a raise mid-project last time, I'm relieved Steve isn't holding that against me.

He asks what my rate is now.

I picture his office manager adding my name to the payroll without having to update any information. "Same as last time." If I don't say the actual number, maybe he won't remember the raise and regret calling me.

"Okay. See you tomorrow." No hesitation, no wincing, no snort of disapproval. Just *Okay. See you tomorrow.*

I get up early so I can watch the morning news and play with Daisy before heading to work. I collect my laundry, hang my towel properly, and make my bed in case I die while I'm out — I don't want them to think I'm a slob. Then I make Daisy's bed, fluffing her elephant Puffalump just so.

I still have an hour, so I get out the hula-hoop and hold it close to the floor so Daisy and I can play lion tamer and lion. She walks through the hoop. I raise it a little. She jumps through the hoop. I raise it higher. She jumps through the hoop.

Eventually, it's too high for her. I slide the footstool to the middle of the floor.

It doesn't take her long to figure out how to use the footstool as a vault, so she can jump higher and farther than her little beagle legs can go on their own.

"It's now eight-forty, and here's a look at our local weather," the newscaster says.

Eight-forty. I'm not dressed yet.

I hurry to the closet to grab something — anything — to wear when I catch a glimpse of a black-and-white flannel sleeve on the hanger against the wall. I still have a set of *Beetlejuice* shirts in the back of my closet. They're XLs, so I assume they're Alec's. Michael is much smaller.

Beetlejuice has become a huge success. Even so, if I wear it, nobody is going to know it's from the movie. Geena's dress would be recognizable. These are a basic red T-shirt and black-and-white flannel shirt set anyone could buy at Sears. If I said it was Alec's wardrobe, who'd believe me? I'm just me — the last-call invisible dork. My head reminds me of that fact every single day.

I put on the flannel shirt. It's soft and already nicely broken in. They'll both make really comfortable work shirts.

FADE TO:

62. INT. — Back to XFX

I walk through across the shop floor, and all the way up to my regular place on the balcony, and not one person recognizes Alec's shirt from *Beetlejuice*. I'll be able to kill guilt for having what I shouldn't without creating more guilt by throwing them away, by having them fake being normal — just like me.

After shunning the shirt for so long, I owe it a lot of happy adventures and start wearing it and its red T-shirt counterpart on a regular basis, just not together where we might draw attention while working on the pieces for *The Stand*.

The padded body suit for Corin is really easy. Just spandex and some subtle padding. Nothing to write home about. The corpses are another story — they're fun.

Steve has the mold department run five copies of five different bodies in polyfoam and pile them beside me on the ground floor. "I need you to carve these so they'll each look like a different body." He spreads out the first few. "They can be freshly dead or half-decayed and emaciated. Just be sure we have a good range."

I carve the first ten and call Steve over to check my range of dead people.

"Go further. You can change them into anything you want. But they'll be wearing clothes, so make sure to carve them enough that they'll look different once they're dressed."

Go further. I can do that.

I squeeze the trigger on the carving knife and dig into the gut of one of the bodies, scooping out its entire stomach. This one has been dead for a while. I carve away its arms and legs, turning it into a slightly fleshy skeleton.

The one beside it, I turn into a freshly dead athlete.

I carve and carve, all the while keeping a mental inventory of how many males I have vs how many females, their natural form, and how many are at what stage of dead and decayed, giving each body a different personality and its own story, until I have twenty-five dead people lying on the shop floor.

I intentionally mixed them up to look like they've randomly fallen in a crowd. Steve isn't requiring me to display them any particular way for his final inspection, but it makes them look better — and better is *my* requirement.

Steve weaves through the corpses, nodding at one and then another. "Hold on a second. Did you — " He stops, pointing to the late term pregnant belly I carved into one of the corpses.

"You said I should make all kinds of bodies. Surely somebody in town was pregnant when they died."

"That's too far." He's smiling but shaking his head at the same time. "We can't do that."

Hearing Steve's sputters, several other guys gather around my floor of corpses.

"It's too real. That's just wrong." He's still just short of laughing. Looking around the group, "What do you think? We can't. Can we?"

The rules he gave me were to make them all different and realistic. "It's a horror film, isn't it?" Seems logical to me.

"You're going to have to change that one. "That's too disturbing. We can't do that."

I changed the corpse, but I wasn't correcting a wrong. I had done the impossible. I had freaked out Steve Johnson, one of the kings of horror.

I touched perfection.

(*We won an Emmy for our work on The Stand. I wasn't one of the few who got to attend and receive a trophy, but those few represented a lot of us — and my corpses.*)

FADE TO:

63. North Hollywood, California — Close To Hell

Adrenaline slams my blood from my head to my toes. My eyes fly open, but I can't see anything.

Somebody is shaking my bed.

Please, God, not again.

The clock on the nightstand says four-thirty-one — the cops will want to know.

Daisy takes off, barking down the hall.

The shaking grows to crazy shifts and jumps. The room bangs and rumbles until my bed is in the middle of a thunderhead. It's an earthquake — a big one.

I dive for the doorway — standing or walking is impossible — and sit with my back against the frame. "Daisy!"

She keeps barking.

I don't know if she can hear me over the rumbling, crashing of dishes and falling furniture, but I keep calling, non-stop, hoping she comes to me before something falls on her. "Daisy! Daisy! Daisy!" As long as she keeps barking, I know she's okay.

With the floor still in the throes of the quake, at last, Daisy whips back down the hall and into my arms, and we ride the earth's tantrum together, the building swaying and creaking, the windows rattling so loudly I wait for them to shatter.

The building was built in the forties. This isn't its first earthquake. Surely, it can withstand one more.

The picture hanging in the hall flies off the wall. I can't see it, but I know from the smack-crash of it hitting the opposite wall and the glass shattering from its frame that's what it is.

A half minute that feels like a half-hour.

As the world slows from a rock to a wave and finally goes still, I stand and reach for the light switch. No more power. It's pitch black, and I know there's broken glass everywhere. Fumbling around, I find the flashlight I always keep by my bed — flashlights and water in California are as much a staple as the Thomas Guide — and my shoes. Carefully, I carry Daisy through the spears of broken glass, into the living room and adjoining dining room. My mannequin displaying my latest Halloween costume looks up at me from where she lay on the floor, stopping me from running into my antique armoire resting across the rocking chair, its door splintered, the mirror shattered.

This time I hear the rumble just before the world goes into another round of bucks and throws. I dive back to the hall door frame — making sure not to sit in the broken glass — and wait for this round to end.

I rode out a tornado at church camp and Hurricane Alicia in Houston; this is so much worse. No place is safe when the ground under your feet becomes a liar.

The quaking won't stop. I don't know how much more this building can take, but I know I need out of it — assuming it's still standing when this hell ends.

The world goes still again.

Still carrying Daisy, I make my way through the fallen furniture and destroyed dishes, to join the rest of the apartment residents in the courtyard, where we listen to the radio and wait for the sun to come up, so we can find out if we still have homes.

FADE TO:

64. Burbank, California — New Places

After the Northridge Quake, the aftershocks continue, but like in *Princess Bride* when Wesley hears the popping right before fire spurts out of the ground in the Fire Swamp, I hear a rumble or see the power lines ripple toward me as the quake travels underground, so an aftershock of much size isn't nearly so scary. And when the tremor ends, I'm pretty darn good at Guess-the-Magnitude — the newest game in the shops.

Taking inventory of my place, I find I lost about half of my Autumn Leaf dish collection as it flew across the room, chipping the opposite wall. My bedroom/shop floor is so deep with overturned boxes that the pile is level with the workbench; and my kitchen smelled like pumpkin pies for weeks, from my spice rack dumping into my gas stove burners. But the apartment building rode the wave no buckling or new cracks.

Nonetheless, soon there are so many people moving out of the Los Angeles area moving companies are dead-heading trucks back into the state to have enough trucks to move everyone out. The cost of homes drops in a way that probably won't happen again until the Big One hits, and the west side of the San Fernando Valley becomes beach front property.

It's a buyer's market. I have a steady job working for Tony Gardner at his shop, Alterian, building a silverback gorilla suit for a movie called *Katy*, so it's time to buy a house.

Terri buys a house in Burbank, and I find one just two blocks away.

It's a little two-bedroom bungalow on a half-lot with a detached one-and-a-half-car garage, and a little yard — and the earthquake didn't do one lick of damage to it. It's perfect for me and Daisy.

Juggling the loan process while sewing muscles for my silverback, my life settles into a new kind of chaos. It seems that in order for freelancers to get a home loan, we have to show three years of tax returns, the current year's pay stubs, and three years of canceled checks for every rent payment and utility bill — both front and back — to prove financial diligence.

As I explain this to Debra Galvez and TaMara Carlson (later Carlson-Woodard) — the two girls on the other side of my worktable, working on a different movie — *Tankgirl* — Tony Gardner asks for me to join them during their fittings.

Before we get in earshot, Tony explains, "We'll be running sixteen foam latex suits, total. One for each actor and stuntman. The budget only allows enough for us to sculpt one suit, but then production hired actors ranging from five-nine to six-two to wear them." After introducing us, he asks, "Can you see any way to alter this without ruining them."

Hyper-drive…with an audience waiting for my answer. The pressure is on.

One wrong cut and the suit will be trash — As it was, it already looks like trash — The torso is too short — I have to release the tension first — The sculpture has places to hide corrections — The first cut has to be…

I start cutting and safety pinning, and the time I finished, the suit fits perfectly and moves just as well.

For every performer who comes in for his fitting, I step away from my gorilla suit long enough to become the fitter. Then, I return to my gorilla while Debra and TaMara sew and glue the alterations.

My gorilla is going well, the Rippers are going well, and my three years of paperwork is at the bank. Everything is going smoothly.

"Lynette, can you come into my office for a minute?" Tony asks.

What have I screwed up? If he lets me go, I'll lose the house. I have to fix this.

In his office, he closes the door. "Would you be willing to go on location to Tucson, Arizona, to be in charge of the Ripper suits?"

I hadn't expected to go to set with the Rippers — it isn't my project. But we've known each other for years. When he explains that he needs someone strong enough to heft the suits onto a bunch of grown men night after night for seven weeks in Tucson's hundred-degree weather, of course, I have to say *yes*.

I come home and let Daisy out. And she finds two naked baby mourning doves in the grass in the courtyard.

Somehow, I find myself in my car, following TaMara — someone I barely know — across the desert, on our way to Tucson, Arizona. Just me, Daisy, two mourning doves, and three years of taxes — just in case — to live in a hotel for seven weeks and work nights in an abandoned copper mine.

I sure hope TaMara likes me.

RETURN TO:

65. Van Nuys, California — Stan Winston Studio

I know my mistake this morning the minute I pull to the curb in front of the shop and see the other side completely empty. It's street-sweeping day. I'm going to get a parking ticket, but I don't have a choice. There are so many people working at Stan's that there's not enough parking.

The elites have parking spaces in the lot — I'm not elite.

Thanks to Tina — Daisy's dog that I call my witness protection dog — I was late leaving the house. But since Tina is just learning English and still cowers if I even cough too abruptly, I'll pay the penalty with pleasure if it keeps me from having to push her into a panic by rushing her. Her feelings matter more than the fifty-dollar ticket. At least for now, I'll keep telling Daisy what to do and let our starved, petrified newcomer catch on by example. With Daisy being such a cheery little girl, it's working well so far.

Crossing the street, I see a Hummer H1 parked dead-center of the lot. Arnold Schwarzenegger is here again. I doubt he's here for any reason other than just to hang out with Stan. He's been here several times, but I've only seen him once when Stan took him through the shop sightseeing. Most of the time, he comes and goes unseen. So does Steven Spielberg, for that matter.

I guess even celebrities are entitled to drop by to visit their friends without everything having a professional purpose. It's no different than among us monster-makers, most of our best friends come from within our work circles.

FADE TO:

66. Tuscon, Arizona —
An Open Pit in the Desert

The set is cool, but that's the only thing that is. It's over a hundred degrees today, and the forecast for the next ten days promises to keep it that way. If TaMara and I don't get along, this shoot is going to be miserable. At least filming at night, we have the advantage of the desert temperatures dropping into the eighties — still not great for the guys wearing foam latex suits from head to toe, but better.

I know TaMara is strong and not afraid of hard work, and she thinks Daisy is adorable, so we're off to a good start. And production gives us two locals to help us. I certainly hope not all sixteen performers need to be dressed at once.

Within two days — nights, actually — I realize every actor needs things to endure the discomfort of these suits.

"We need to each take two actors and their stunt equivalents and be responsible for just them." I take eight pieces of paper and write the names of the actors on them. "Being in charge, I could just take the two I want, but to be fair, we'll all draw names. We each get who we get. Deal?'

Everybody agrees. So, we draw.

I hate that I don't have the nerve to simply take who I want and leave the three of them to draw from the rest, but my Rules require me to consider everybody's feelings, so I have to play fair. For the most part, any name is fine, except one. Jeff Kobar really isn't enjoying being wrapped in skin-tight foam latex with no way out until one of us pulls off his gloves and unzips him. The suits don't breathe — and Jeff hates it with a capital HATE. He's already given TaMara such grief that I took over once to shut him down.

"If you don't shut up, I'll make sure you are the last person taken out of your suit every …single …night." Probably not what I should've said to one of the stars of the show, but this is going to be a long shoot in uncomfortable conditions, and I have to choose between protecting my crew, or pleasing Jeff — I can't do both.

Tony is hundreds of miles away, expecting me to represent his shop and protect his suits — suits not normally expected to survive this kind of abuse for this long. Ultimately, I work for Tony.

Jeff is only one of sixteen we four are responsible for. He's going to have to get in line.

TaMara gets Scott and Jeff.

"Sorry, TaMara" — Scott is terrific, but Jeff is… well… Jeff.

I unfold my strips of paper. I get Ata — who's wonderfully polite and cooperative — and Ice T. Ice T has a great sense of humor. I tested it the first time we met.

He strutted in all cool rapper Ice T-like, and put on his Ripper suit, so I could alter it.

Curious to see if his posturing was real or an image, I raised my scissors and chopped the air — snick-snick. "Okay, spread 'em."

His eyes grew big. "You're kidding, right?"

"Actually, no." I couldn't keep a straight face.

Needless to say, he and all the guys held very still while I made those first few scissor cuts. By the time I finished altering his suit, he was very conversational. We bantered back and forth, him accusing me of being dangerous, and me keeping him laughing enough that he could let go of his nervousness — and his cool — and just be a person.

Now, getting to be his dresser for seven straight weeks, we're going to have a good time — or as good of a time as we can have in the middle of the night, in an abandoned copper mine.

The nights stay smooth with Ata and Ice T, and all of the other Rippers, too. We catch our stride and get the timing of the dressing down to an art. We know exactly how many minutes it takes to get them into their suits, and how to quickly get the sweat-saturated, skin-tight suits rolled down off of them at the end of the night.

Back in the abandoned office TaMara and I use for a drying room, I pick up one of the suits and give it a twist. The sweat runs out of it like a wet dishrag, leaving a puddle of water on the floor.

We hang them up, spray them with End Bac until their interiors are an utter cloud of germ-killing spray, turn on the four dehydrators, and leave to get back to the hotel before the morning sun gets too high in the sky, where we pull the drapes and grab a few hours of sleep.

Around ten in the morning, we awaken. Our call time isn't until six this evening, but we counted enough holes and tears, that I set TaMara and my call for two o'clock to be prepped by the official call, in case we're the first shot up.

We're never the first shot up. In fact, we almost never put any of the guys in suits until after our midnight lunch. But we must be perfect, so we must always be ready, with the suits dry, sewn, re-glued and repainted — just in case.

After spending three or four hours of the afternoon repairing these poor fatigued suits, TaMara and I — and Daisy — hang out in the back of TaMara's pickup truck, playing Yahtzee by flashlight. Always the first ready; always the last needed — that's us.

It's become a joke among the actors. They show up at six, knowing they're not going to have anything to do. They read, hang out in the makeup trailer, build model kits, and do everything but act, because Rachel — the director — can't stick to her own shooting schedule for love nor money.

Four weeks in, we're a good two weeks behind schedule, and tempers are hotter than the air. The comic book creator gave up and left. The producer, who was great friends with Rachel at the start is not even on speaking terms with her anymore. I don't know which came first, Rachel's attitude or the communication breakdown. It doesn't matter. Filming is turning into an A-number-one disaster.

I get a call from my realtor.

"I've arranged for your closing to happen on Sunday. We'll meet at the bank, sign the papers, and you'll officially have the keys to your new home. But the bank wants you to bring one more piece of paper with you."

I've had enough. I've faxed them tax returns, fronts and backs of every check they asked for, and the copies of every single pay stub with coinciding bank statement for last year and all of this year so far. I was pre-approved for almost twenty percent more than I'm trying to borrow. This is getting to the point of harassment.

"They want a letter explaining why you have a group of bills that were paid late."

"I already explained that was because when I moved across the hall to the larger apartment, and out of habit, the mailman kept putting my mail in my old box. I didn't have that key anymore and nobody rented the place for a while, so I couldn't get my mail."

"They want that in writing."

"So, they're meeting me at a bank — on a Sunday — to close my home loan. And they're saying they're not going to close if I don't bring this one stupid piece of paper?"

"Honestly, I don't think it's a big deal. They just have to have something for the file."

I've been baking my brains for weeks, paying for enough faxes from the hotel office to buy stock in the company. I'll be flying in and back on my only day off... They want their stupid letter; I'll give them a stupid letter.

Sunday morning, TaMara drives me to the airport.

I kiss Daisy on the nose, "I'll be back this evening. You be good for Auntie TaMara," and then I fly into Burbank airport.

My realtor picks me up and takes me straight to the bank.

"Did you bring a letter?"

"Yes, I did." I hand the loan officer a sheet of paper towel with my note written in Sharpie on it. "I was at work. I used what I had."

She holds it like it's a dirty tissue.

I'm wearing my I've-Had-Enough Mask. If she doesn't like it, I'll remove it and shatter her to bits.

"This will do just fine." She tucks it into my folder and puts the folder in a drawer. She closes the drawer — and the deal on my house.

(WEEK FIVE)

This is week is the worst set week on *Tankgirl* to date. We put guys in the suits, and we sit.

We sit for hours.

We take them out of the suits for the midnight lunch break, put them back in, and sit some more.

By Friday, Rachel has managed to get two days' worth of shots completed.

She's cutting shots left and right, trying to save the schedule, but so far, she's shot all the talking, but almost none of the fights or action. The stuntmen are bored out of their minds, and their suits still look almost new. At this rate, there's not going to be enough footage to put together a movie when leave here.

My only consolation is two more weeks and I'm out of here.

Saturday, we're up in the catwalks of one of the rock-sifting buildings, with all eight actors sitting on apple boxes, their suits peeled down to their waists, all of us out of sight but within earshot.

"Are you up there?" Rachel yells.

"Ready whenever you need us."

"I don't know what it is you even do." She starts so abruptly, I feel like I've missed something. "Frankly, I don't know why I keep you around. You never do anything." Her voice echoes through the abandoned building as she continues to berate me from two stories below. There's not a soul on the set who can't hear the tear-down. The entire cast and crew — most don't know me and have no interactions with me — now consider me worthless.

Never do anything? Of course, she doesn't see us do anything. We stay an hour after everybody else leaves, hanging up the suits and accessing the damage, and then come in four hours early, so the repairs never hold up the twelve-hour shoot day — if we stop on time.

The set is chaos, but I've never heard her outwardly chew out anyone else.

I want to cry — but that would break a Rule. I want to scream back at her — but that would break a Rule. I want to quit — but that would break a Rule. I want to die — but that would break a Rule.

So, here I stand, the obedient follower of my head — stifling everything that makes me human — taking it.

"What the hell is she talking about?" Ice T stands up.

Many of the rest of our little gang, still in the protection of the shadows peer over the edge, trying to see her below without being seen themselves.

She must catch sight of Ice-T, because she stops and takes a breath. "Just get Jeff and Scott down here," she snaps and turns away, disappearing under the floor below. "The rest of you can get out of your suits until after lunch. Maybe after lunch you'll be ready to actually work."

It's the Jody Attack I've been waiting for my whole career. Degrading, humiliating — depressing. All the work I've done for the past five weeks hasn't even been appreciated. I've endured this merciless heat wave and harassment from the teamsters. I've wallowed in other people's sweat — which is a huge challenge for me. I've lost sleep, learned to live with perpetually sore fingertips from sewing through the latex-impregnated spandex suits day after day. I've dined on Spaghetti-Os warmed in a coffee maker pot. I've made production wait on us. And I've even become the owner of a house I have yet to sit in. All this for this woman who is in the process of single-handedly screwing up so badly that when it's all said and done, there's going to be very little to show for all this torture. Yet, there's nothing I can say or do without breaking a Rule.

Two days later, I get a message from the front desk that Terri has called. Her dad is watching my apartment, taking in my mail, and relaying messages through Terri from my answering machine.

Since it's already morning, I call Terri right back.

"Steve Johnson called. You need to call him back as soon as possible."

I hang up and call Steve, who offers me a job working on the suits for a film called *Species*.

"I'm off this job in two weeks."

"Great. I'll see you the Monday after."

For two weeks, I work hard and lay low, praying Rachel doesn't target me again.

The final day of hell, when I stop in the office to pick up my previous week's paycheck, the coordinator hands me a new contract to sign. "They're extending the shoot two more weeks."

Not for me, they're not. "I have another job already lined up."

"You can't delay your start?"

My Rules say *no*. On *Ultraman*, I should've asked. I'm not staying in the hellhole this time, and I'm grateful to my Rule for saving me.

Rachel's attack verified everything my head ever told me about not being good enough to be wanted, and the threat of her telling the whole world this again has me quivering behind my Calm Mask every second I'm on set. "Maybe if you'd said something earlier, but this is too short notice. Sorry." — not really, but this poor coordinator isn't my enemy.

I'm not even sure Rachel is my enemy; she may be my reality check.

I return to my hotel room to pack my clothes, my papers, and my tools. Daisy and I are going home — to see our new home.

(I'm the one costume crew member who didn't get an invitation to the screening. Hated or forgotten. I'll never know. Though I am sorry I didn't get a chance to talk with the guys again, in my heart, I know our rapport was the best thing about that job. That, and meeting my dear friend — TaMara.)

FADE TO:

67. Sun Valley, California — XFX

The minute I walk through the door, the smell of Plastalina and concrete fills my sinuses. Even blindfolded, I'd know I'm at XFX, one of the shops I call home — and after the *Tankgirl* terror, home is what I need.

Steve seems to hire a lot of odd ducks. I call his shop *The Island of Misfit Toys*. I think that's why I love working for him. He's willing to adopt the weird ones and give us a home. But even at home, I wear my Mask of Confidence to pretend I'm not any weirder than the rest of his crew. So, I stay plain. I'm still just the brown-haired girl with a ponytail and glasses, in boring clothes that might as well have come from Goodwill — except I can't wear somebody else's clothes, no matter how many times they're laundered. It's another one of my *things* — *w*ith the exception of the shirts from *Beetlejuice*. They hung in my closet long enough to somehow become mine before I put them on.

I settle my Mask, unload my lefty scissors and tools onto my regular work counter, and wait while the crew brings up a body cast so I can get started.

(ONE WEEK LATER)

Dana Hee comes in for her first suit fitting. Dana is the stunt woman wearing the Sil suit, another foam latex suit, even more skin-tight and streamlined than the Ripper design. Standing side by side, Dana is only an inch taller than I am and roughly the same weight. I envy her the job of performing as Sil.

Usually, SAG suit performers fall under the definition of puppeteers, so many times, puppeteers and suit performers are whoever is in the shop who's the right size. This time, the creature is a female, and I'm the only female in the shop, but production insists Sil be worn by a SAG stuntwomen — which I am not.

After cramming and squeezing Dana into the suit, Steve points to the wrinkled stomach as Dana leans forward. "Can you do anything about that?"

Having just played this game with sixteen Ripper suits, I know exactly how to fix it, but I know it's nothing anybody else has done. "Do you trust me?"

Steve is always antsy, but this question makes him squirm more than usual. "Why? What are you going to do?"

With others standing around for the fitting watching him growing nervous, it's *The Stand* situation all over again. "Do you trust me?"

Steve takes his unlit cigarette from his lips, fiddling with it like it's a toothpick. "Sure, I trust you, but what are you going to do?"

Offer nothing more, I pick up my scissors and turn to Dana. "Lean forward again."

Steve can't sit still, sputtering half-words and unfinished thoughts as I make a gaping hole from hip bone to hip bone.

I grab some safety pins, change the fit along the gash, and step back while listening to Steve regain his voice. "Did you see what she just did? I…She…"

I step back.

Dana stands up and bends. The suit stays smooth.

"I can do that to all the buckles and fix the whole thing."

Others mess with Steve from time to time, and he heckles them back, but this is the first time I've ever dared to nail him — and it was fun.

Rachel can suck it up without me. I may still wear a Mask, but with these guys, I'm safe. I'm home.

(THREE WEEKS LATER)

When TaMara finishes *Tankgirl*'s extended shoot, which turned into even longer than the two-week extension, I pull her in to help with the Sil alterations. After what she endured for me, I owe her this. Besides, working with her under better conditions is nice.

I don't always go out for lunch. I prefer to save my splurging for Thursday night bowling with my effects buddies, or sushi dinners at Chiba's — my version of *Cheers* — where TaMara and I sit at the sushi bar, visiting with Shig, while continuing the Yahtzee playing we started while living in hell together. I pull out my sack lunch and prop my feet up on my workbench, so I can eat in the peace of an empty shop.

Just me and Sil alone.

Sil's design is truly unique — H. R. Geiger at his best. Half-human, half-techno anatomy. She's beautiful. I could play her. I know I'd fit the suit.

TaMara returns early. "Whatcha looking at?"

"I'd fit that suit."

"Have you tried it on?"

I can't do that.

She sees my hesitation. "There's nobody else here. Take it in the bathroom and try it on."

I take it in the bathroom, and with nobody looking but the titty calendar girl taped to the wall beside the toilet, I work my way into the suit.

TaMara is waiting for me when I emerge to wedge me in the rest of the way and zip up the back.

It fits like it was made for me.

My heart sinks. I'd almost hoped it wouldn't fit, so I wouldn't feel so bad about not getting to be Sil. With that hope dashed down, being overlooked hurts even more.

"If only you were a stunt woman."

"Yeah, but I'm not." I look at the clock. "You'd better unzip me, so I can get out of this thing before somebody catches me in it."

As fast as I can, I peel out of the suit, taking care not to tear the still-delicate unpainted suit, and take it back upstairs to our corner before anyone catches me.

TaMara and I get back to the alterations, and when the guys return, the day goes on with nothing different — except I'll forever be tortured by the fact that I *could've* played Sil.

During my afternoon break, before going back upstairs, I grab some water from the cooler and wander the shop, checking out others' progress on the project. While I'm talking to Lenny, Steve calls across the room, "Hey, Lynette, TaMara says you fit the Sil suit."

I have no idea why TaMara ratted me out, but Steve's going to fire me now.

"Is this true?"

I step closer — but not too close. "Yeah," I manage to eke out before I shrivel too far to say anything else.

"Put it on. I want to see."

I'm not sure what's happening, but I guess I'm getting in Dana's suit again.

I put it on, TaMara zips me up, and I come out to show Steve. Sil has sewn-on heel spikes that don't really hold weight, but with my ballet training, it's easy for me to stay on tiptoe, so the suit can look just like it does in the art.

After I turn, pose, bend, and twist, Steve says, "Humph. That's pretty cool."

Then I take it off, and that's the end. Still, somehow, I feel better knowing that at least Steve appreciated me in the suit — even for just those ten novelty minutes.

CUT TO:

68. Burbank, California — NBC

I may not get to play Sil, but I get a consolation prize when Ted Rae calls to ask if I want to make three demon suits for *Days of Our Lives* and also perform the lead demon. The demons only film one day, so Steve has no problem giving me that day off.

The design of the demons is simple. I'll be able to do them in the evenings after I get home from XFX, but with the tight schedule, I'll need help.

I call Terri to help me, but she's onset with *Indian in the Cupboard,* leaving me leaning on TaMara some more.

I feel terrible asking her. I don't have a personal life, but she has a boyfriend, and now I'm taking her evenings away from him. After being together day and night on *Tankgirl* and now day and night for *Species* and *Days of Our Lives*, she'll be so sick of me by the time we're done, she'll regret moving into the house across the parkway from mine. At least the late-night commute home will be just a quick walk across the grassy field.

It's a good thing she does live so close because we're falling asleep with our sewing needles in our hands by three a.m. deadline night.

While I keep an eye on her as she goes home, I'm stunned. She doesn't act like she hates me yet — though I'd lay a bet her boyfriend does now. Maybe she does, too, but she still has to put up with me a while longer at XFX.

I'm going to miss her.

Friday morning, hiding behind the Professional Mask I always wear tight for Ted and a burst of nerd adrenaline, I park in the NBC Studios lot that I haven't been to since my days on the *Thundercats Live Stage Show*. This time though, instead of being tucked away in a storage area, I'm on one of the soundstages, as an actress.

It's not my first suit performance. My first was wearing Terri's still suit from *Dune* that we redressed as a sea witch at a promotional event while Terri wore her mermaid tail. There were the transportation-themed children's videos called, *Hobart the Platypus in Cosmo and Hobart Presents,* that Terri and I built and performed the characters for where I played Hobart the Platypus. Being McGruff the Crimestopper Dog, Poofy the Samoyed, Vreidle the wolf scientist, and a few other gigs gave me more experience, but this will be my first performance see around the world.

I like suit performing. I've always felt I could perform at a pro level if I was given the chance. I have the strength. I have the endurance. I have the coordination. But I'm an average height and too average-looking for anyone to believe I have the guts or ability for it.

Ted is giving me another first chance, and I'll make the best of it. It may not be Sil, but it's a creature performance. I'll possess Deidre Hall's character of Marlena until my arms are too tired to reach for her anymore.

FADE TO:

69. Sun Valley, California — Back To XFX

Maybe taking a day off for a suit performing gig will let Steve recognize me as a suit performer. It's just not something I can work into a conversation without sounding desperate or vain — or high. But if he would just give me a Mask to hide behind, I could act like whoever he needs me to be. After all, I do it every day already, and I'm so good at it, nobody knows I'm doing it.

"Hey, Lynette, can you help Lenny with a film test next door?" Steve calls from the floor below.

I close my glue container and join the guys in the neighboring warehouse unit, where I find a plywood box with a giant plastic chrysalis in the corner Bill Bryan has been working on.

"This will be part of a train compartment." Bill leads me to the back side. "We need you to raise up through here" — he points to a hole in the plywood just behind the chrysalis — "and grab that bar, so we can pull you up out of frame. The camera is upside down, so it should look like you're falling out of the cocoon headfirst." He hands me a sleeveless beige leotard. "Natasha will be naked for the shot. Wear this so you don't have clothes catching."

As the guys yank me to the ceiling by the makeshift trapeze, my shoulder clips the edge of the wood. I adjust and go through again, and again. While we smooth out the motion, my body bumps and drags every time I go through. It hurts, but I won't — I can't — complain.

The crew looks up at me from below as I hang high above them. Nobody else in the shop can do this for them. I am important.

We finish the test, and I go back to work with the glory of knowing I contributed to designing a special effects stunt.

By the time I return from lunch, the bruises and abrasions are coming in bright all over my body.

Steve is in his office with a few of the guys, so I poke my head in.

"I can show you where you need to fix the rig." I turn, showing them the scrape on my shoulder and knee, the bruise under my ribs, and the huge raspberry on my hip.

"Jesus!" Steve looks horrified. "Guys, you can't do that to Natasha. They'll kill us."

No doubt about that. We have to test the rig some more.

I can tell from Steve's tone that he wouldn't blame me if I didn't want to go another round as he asks, "Are you willing?" but he needs me.

Bruises will heal.

I shrug and give him my canned answer. "Sure."

I'm taking the beating, so Natasha doesn't have to — but I'm still not a stunt woman. I can't be Sil.

CUT TO:

70. Hollywood, California — MGM Studios

The first day on set with Dana in the Sil suit, and my first day at MGM Studios. By this point, I've been on most of major studio lots, but this is different. This time, I'm here for longer than a few days. This MGM soundstage will be my home for a few weeks with Dana — who I don't fault for being Sil; she is a great person to work with.

I step out the side door of the box truck we're using for Dana's dressing room and my maintenance/storage area.

The day is the kind of day that shows exactly why Hollywood is perfect for filming. Sunny, but not too hot; and no clouds to ruin filming continuity. I'm almost sorry I'm going to have to miss it by spending all my daylight hours on a dark soundstage — almost. I never regret the opportunity to work on an actual soundstage or on an actual backlot, walking ground very few outsiders get to see — even on paid tours. It feels like success.

Across the way, Ben Kingsley steps out of his Star Waggon trailer.

"Good morning," I call over, just so he knows I see he's a person. "Beautiful day, isn't it?"

He pauses, obviously savoring a warm moment. "I'd rather be gardening,"

If anyone else had said that, it would've sounded a little like a complaint, but through his English accent, I catch a bit of humor in his tone.

We go inside the concrete box better known as a soundstage, me to my side of the set and him to his.

Waiting for the grips and gaffers to finish the lighting for the first shot, I have nobody to stand with or talk to. The rest of the XFX crew is working with makeup and special effects rigs. I'm the sole Sil suit crew, so I'm that new kid who doesn't know anybody, standing on the playground, hoping to see a friendly face — but the only face I recognize is Ben's.

I step over beside him. "You said you'd rather be gardening. What kind of gardening do you do?"

He starts right in, telling me about the four acres in England he bought that he's landscaping with roses and wisteria, paths, and a pond. He's very descriptive, and I can see its grandeur in my mind. "It used to be a broken-down parking lot."

"Wow. I just bought my first house, and I've been putting in a trellis and roses up the walkway, myself. Nothing like the scale of your garden, but..." my voice trails off. I can't possibly pretend my four rose bushes and one climber over a trellis compare to anything this Oscar-winning movie star might have.

If I keep talking, he's going to hate me for being a Hollywood phony who's just trying to saddle up to him. I see it all the time — people claiming they're friends with a movie star after a two-sentence conversation. Okay, I spoke to him initially just to be nice, but I like him. He's a real person — a co-worker — just like Ice T and the other actors I've worked with. Sets should be safe places for stars to walk. It's the one place outside their homes they shouldn't have to worry about feeling fan-stalked. I won't be the on-set auto-graph chaser.

Ben turns to me. "Everybody has to start somewhere."

"Okay people, we're ready," the Assistant Director calls.

And we're back to our spots, Ben on his side of the set and me, alone in the dark, on mine.

The next morning, driving through Hollywood, I see a little plant nursery. I have a few extra minutes, so I stop in and pick up a miniature rose bush and some small snips.

I place them on the top step of Ben's trailer with a note that reads, *I know it's not a garden, but maybe this will help you pretend you're gardening.*

Dana and I work the morning on-set with her as Sil, but after lunch, since she doesn't have to suit-up immediately, we stay in the trailer, her in a chair and me on the floor with the suit, checking it for small tears.

No holes. No nicks in the foam. The suit must stay perfect. If Steve comes down and finds it's not, he'll never trust me alone on-set again.

There's a knock on the door, and Ben pokes in his head. "Are you who left the rose bush on my doorstep this morning?"

"Yes. You said yesterday — " as if he doesn't know. Just shut up.

"That was lovely to find. Thank you so much. May I come in?"

"Sure."

The next morning, Dana and I arrive to find two dozen roses in our trailer, a dozen for her and a dozen for me. From that moment on, if Ben isn't on set and Dana and I are in the trailer, Ben is in the trailer with us, with his newspaper and cup of tea. He says there's nobody to talk to in his trailer and "it's boring."

I'm certain the real draw is Dana. She's a fellow actor — his peer. And she's pretty. I expect to take a backseat to her. Still, we have fun together, talking about everything from movies and our thoughts on other actors to our wants for our own careers to our families, pets, and hobbies. We talk day after day like real friends, and Ben makes me able to forget that he — Ben Kingsley — is a huge movie star, and I'm just me.

(WEEKS LATER)

Ben's last day on-set is well before Dana and I are wrapped. He comes to the trailer to say goodbye and tells us how much he enjoyed our company.

It feels presumptuous for me to assume he wants to stay in touch (email isn't a thing yet) so despite our great relationship, I lose my new friend.

Being on-set in this industry is like when I'd go to camp when I was a kid. New friends always swear they'll continue to write, but after the first letter, it stops, and life goes back to normal. As adults, we know better than to even make that promise. So, I'll keep working in Hollywood, and Ben will return to England.

He doesn't need me as his friend. I'm sure he has plenty.

I slide back under my Cloak of Invisibility, where nobody but Dana sees me — because she needs me — and I continue to do my best to be perfect for her …until she doesn't need me anymore either.

CUT TO:

71. Northridge, California — Back to Another Warehouse

Today on the *Species* shooting agenda, we're filming the underwater dream sequences. The water feels much warmer now than it did two days ago for rehearsal, when we showed up and the tank had just been refilled after springing a leak. Tuesday, the water was hose temperature.

Dana has gone on to shoot *Mortal Combat* and isn't available for the second unit filming. Overlooking me again, production has hired another stunt woman, Theresa, to step in. Mike Deak is wearing the male Sil that I altered and finished between shoot days. As far as I know, he's not a SAG stuntman and more than ever; I want to scream, "I'm right here, people! Let me double for Dana!" But I don't, because as much as I want to be Sil, Rules are Rules.

I'm underwater for the shot and underwater resetting the shot. The only time I can breathe is while I count down before we all go under for the next shot.

For hours, I hold my breath — easy enough. I hold my breath if someone coughs, sneezes, or even yawn anywhere near me anyway. I hold my breath in crowded corridors.

I've held my breath since I was ten years old. A woman pointed out that my mouth was open — because I can hardly breathe through my nose at all. Because of her, I hold my breath randomly throughout the day, just so I can look normal.

Holding my breath is normal, but doing it while working and calling the shots is exhausting — but I won't give up. Bill Bryan is standing by to tag off, but I was the one here for the rehearsals, so I need to be the one in the tank. It's me Deak and Theresa trusts, and I can't fail them.

"I need out of the suit, "Theresa announces. "I have to use the bathroom."

I told her not to keep drinking tea, but she has yet to care anything about what I have to say. To her, I'm an underling.

The A.D. turns to me. "How long will it take?"

The time it takes for me to unglue and peel her out of the suit and then get her back in… counting the glue work… "A good twenty minutes if we hurry."

She's out and back in thirty minutes later, after she drinks another cup of tea while I'm re-gluing the back closed. We take her out of the suit for lunch — and more tea.

Partway through the afternoon I cry uncle. Holding my breath and running around with this nut wears me down, and Bill has to replace me. I failed.

After an hour Theresa wants out for another pee break.

"That's okay. We got what we needed," the director says. "Go ahead and take her out."

Theresa and I go back to the room we're using as a dressing room — again — and I take her out of the suit for the last time. It's only as she starts to leave that Steve mutters, "Hold up," and I see Deak is still completely in his Sil suit — Bill hasn't been undressing him.

The A.D. calls over his shoulder from the exit door. "She just pulled away."

"Lynette, get in the suit."

I dress myself and Bill closes up the back, and I climb back into the water tank — not to tend to the actors, but as Sil. For at least a couple of hours, they see me — and I'm going to do my best to make sure I'm a worthy Sil performer, so I don't fade away again.

(Productions doesn't give me a screen credit as a suit performer for wearing Sil for part of the underwater shots, or for the childbirth and cave shots they use me for on another day — or even after I wore the Sil a third time for the photo shoot used for the movie posters, and video and DVD cases.

However, a year later, when Ben and Natasha are guests at Comic-Con, TaMara and I go just so I can say hi.

The second Ben spots me in the crowd, he stops signing autographs, comes around the end of the table, gives me a big hug, and asks me how I'm doing. Every head in the hall turns to watch me and Ben together.

Even with all the work I did on Species, the minute Ben steps away from me, I'm instantly absorbed by the ocean of bodies, ignored by everyone around me, and in minutes, I feel myself disappear to, once again, live beneath my Cloak of Invisibility.

But for that one moment, I am special because Ben shared his light with me.)

FADE TO:

72. Augora Hills, California — Animated FX

I'm so easily forgotten that I'm not sure how someone I've never met gets my phone number, but TaMara and I are going to be carpooling to Animated FX to work for Norman Tempia. His is a name I've only ever heard before — thanks to Terri. He's one of Henson's crew on Fraggle Rock — so building realistic chimp suits for the next couple of months for a movie called *Ed*, starring *Friends*' Matt LeBlanc, will be a privilege.

Outside of the rental gorilla suit Terri and I made for Michael Burnett and the silverback for *Katy*, I haven't delved into the ape suit world. Camilla Henneman is still Rick Baker's suit queen, and Rick does most of the films that need ape suits, so this is an opportunity to advance my muscle suit skills to her level.

Norman sets TaMara and me up in what would otherwise be a front office. This means everybody comes and goes through our workspace, but being off the main work floor also means we can keep our work cleaner.

Cleanliness is key with these suits. While chimps are dark-skinned and dark-haired, this chimp will be wearing a white baseball uniform, so Norman wants the muscles and all the coverings to be white.

It doesn't take long for me to see that Norman has his way of doing most things. He insists that all the muscles be sanded into shape.

After working on *D.C. Follies,* I thought I knew how to sand foam better than most, but Norman doesn't sand foam with a Dremel or even a pneumatic sander as Randy taught me to do. Norman wants us to use a sanding wheel — specifically, a twelve-inch floor-model disc sander. And every muscle must have edges that feather to the point that no edges are visible anywhere on the suit.

This takes quite a bit of doing — and blood. After bloodying our knuckles, shredding innumerable muscles, chipping fingernails to the fingertip, and scuffing cuts into our fingers, I get the hang of it.

By the second week, I can make edges so whisper-thin that my fingerprints have been sanded off through the foam.

Norman is just as particular about how we sew the covers on the muscles and the muscles onto the suit. If we don't secure our stitches often enough, we tear them out and sew them again. If the cover is too tight, we sew it again. If our stitches get too wide, we sew it again. And if he can feel a muscle edge after the muscle is sewn on, we take off the whole thing and start from scratch.

It's the *Karate Kid* repetitive stroke training all over again. By the time the suits for Ed are ready to go to set, my obsession for perfection has met its match. Norman is proud of our chimpanzee suits — and I'm proud of how well I've learned to make muscle suits. Though, if I had one wish, the costume department would let me make Ed's baseball uniforms. The one they made for him is so skin-tight that they don't help hide the human proportions we worked so hard to camouflage. Personally, I think that if a chimp joined a baseball team, his suit wouldn't fit like it was made for him; it would be an altered human's uniform on a chimp. But then, that's just my opinion.

FADE TO:

73. Burbank, California — My House

Finish one job and get another. That's my life. I'm obsessed with my career, constantly juggling three simultaneous jobs because I can't say no. Someone calls asking if I can do something, my head instantly runs its Hyper-drive program and shows me how to build it, and I say *yes*. I fight so desperately not to be invisible that as long as I leave myself seven hours a night for sleep, I work seven days a week.

At one point, I found myself going into Sequoya Creative at seven-thirty in the morning to start a crew working on full-size whales for a touring museum display, before arriving my day job at nine to build Tiger for Universal Studios' *American Tale Theater*. When the day's work was done, I went home to build Myrtle, a hand puppet for Lois Young, and two buffalo heads for Buffalo Bill's Casino on the California-Nevada border.

With my house payment doubling what my rent was, I'm even more obsessed with assuring I'm never unemployed — even though I've only been unemployed for six weeks since I moved to Hollywood over a decade ago.

I get another call.

"Are you available?"

I'm up to my eyeballs in work, but instead of saying *no*, I find myself asking, "Why? What do you need?"

So, I'm back at Lazzarini's, building King Kongs for casinos in Atlanta and Chicago, while in the evenings and weekends, Terri and I make a cow, a horse, and a pig for a children's video called *Farm Pals* on the heels of making Bimbo Bear pieces for the second time — first for the Chiodo Brothers, and this time for Screaming Mad George.

With the luxury of my new, much larger home-based garage shop, at least there's plenty of space for the three chubby body pods and bulbous heads without sacrificing my living room.

As I drape the pig head while Terri works on the horse, she says. "I know a guy you should meet."

"Oh yeah?"

"He works down at the float. We need to go down there when we take a break so you can talk to them about the dragon's neck."

Terri's high school sweetheart and she reunited after her divorce. While she and I bought houses near each other after the Northridge quake, her sweetheart purchased a house as well — one that just happened to be next door to a woman very active with Burbank's Rose Parade float committee. This woman talked Terri into submitting a design for this year's float, and it won, so Terri has been frequenting the float construction site for months.

During our lunch break, sweaty and marred with glue and markers, we swing by the Burbank water treatment plant, where the volunteers build Burbank's float. Terri walks me over to a man standing near a welded neck frame big enough for a person to crawl through. "This is John. He's helping with the neck."

My heart deflates. John is nice, but he's not my type.

There is a guy there who interests me, but I doubt he paid much attention to me. We only talked for a few minutes — and only about that neck.

"So, what do you think of Jim?"

Jim. She means the Mac truck of a guy with a goatee and pleasant voice who first caught my eye.

The premiere of *Species* is coming up. With Terri already hinting to me that he's interested in me, too, I call and invite him to join TaMara, Scott, and me at the screening.

That night, Jim meets me at Lazz's shop, where I change clothes in the bathroom before Jim drives us into Hollywood for the movie.

It doesn't matter that I try my best to look good and be conversational. It doesn't matter that afterward when we all go to Big Boys to get desserts and to discuss the movie, I know this first date will be our last. I didn't get to read *Species*' script. I had no idea *Species* has a naked chick going around killing men in it.

Saturday, while Terri and I alter the butt of the cow, I tell her about my horribly awkward date. "Definitely not first-date material."

Two days later, I get a message on my answering machine from Jim. He wants to dare a second date with me. I don't know what he means by *puppeteering a baby dragon with me in a parade,* but it can't be worse than him wondering if watching *Species* is any indication of what dating me will be like.

FADE TO:

74. Burbank, California — Yet Another Warehouse

Jim is willing to endure my crazy lifestyle, so we start dating — much of which is working on the float for the City of Burbank. It's the only way we can date and get the float built, with my work schedule.

It's tough having a job that requires me to make a cool design look bad, but Ken Hall needs me to do just that.

Kamen Rider's Hydrasect already exists, so I can't match the beautiful concept art the way I was allowed to do when I rebuilt the *Ultraman* creatures. This time, I have to match the ugly interpretation built before so they can match footage, with all its wrinkles, buckles, and slop. To be perfect this time, I have to match sloppy work to the best of my abilities.

"Lynette, call on line one," comes over the shop's speaker.

I find the nearest wall phone and connect the call. "Hello?"

"This is John Rosengrant at Stan Winston Studio. Would you be available to come in for a two-week job?"

I may die right here, right now. For years, I haven't been able to even get an interview at Stan's. Now, they're inviting me in, but — "Oh, no. I have one week left here. I can't leave before the work is done." I hope he hears the regret in my voice. "I've been dying to show you my portfolio. I'll meet you at Denny's for lunch or anything to show it to you."

"No. Thanks. That's okay."

Yep, I'm going to die.

"I've asked three different people in the shop to recommend somebody for this job, and they all said you. We'll wait for you."

We finish the call with *we'll wait for you* echoing over and over in my head — not *nobody wants you*, or *you're screwing up* — the common earwigs I'm stuck hearing — but *we'll wait for you*.

I can't wait to tell Jim.

I return to my work and give Ken the best tacky Hydrasect he could ever want because I'm going to be working at Stan Winston Studio without even showing them my portfolio.

They're waiting for me.

FADE TO:

75. Van Nuys, California — Stan Winston Studio

As John takes me from one room to another, I'm walking into Heaven — with TaMara there to greet me. She's been working for Stan for a few weeks now and is one of the three who recommended me. Too bad we won't be working together — or even in the same room. She's on a different film.

I haven't been in a shop big enough to have different rooms for each department since Alchemy II. A few shops have a clean room and a dirty room, but this is so much more. There's a full conference and display room, a fabrication room, mold-making room, a room for the mechanics and another for the electronics, and an open floor area for building large things, each area carries the smell of the work done in that room. There are multiple sets of bathrooms, and offices for the human resource department and designers, and more rooms I can't even see.

Every room is filled with hustling people. I recognize a few faces, and we wave hellos to one another, but John doesn't slow down. He keeps flying low more than walking, and I stay on his heels, speed-touring the areas on our way through what — I think — is supposed to be my orientation tour.

With my head whipping left to right as we breeze through, John introduces me to Chris, who's heading the construction of a creature called Kathoga, for a movie called *The Relic* — the project I'm here for.

Chris leads me upstairs, where TaMara and the team she's with are making lion parts for *The Ghost in the Darkness*. We join the other two builders for the Kathoga team — Dave Monzingo and Dave Grasso — around a rigid carbon fiber shell of Kathoga, with a torso about half the size of a Volkswagen. To tail tip, add another five feet. "This needs to be a suit in the next two weeks."

They didn't just wait a little bit; they completely waited for me.

"Okay, where would you like me to start?"

"I was hoping you could tell us."

The water just got very — very — deep.

I turn lose my Hyper-drive, ask for a Sharpie, and start marking places to begin cutting this thing into pieces. Like a butcher breaking down a carcass, I can already see where the body should be jointed, how to control the shin movement, how to keep the skin from catching in the shell joints, and where to put the closures.

From that table to the main floor where we set up Kathoga's work area, even while Chris and the two Daves follow my lead on two full suits and several insert pieces, I live in my Rejection Room. I may have finally made it within the Stan Winston walls, but my head reminds me all day, every day, that I'm not one of them.

A week and a half into the project, Chris says Stan wants to make me part of his permanent staff.

Stan hasn't said anything to me. I haven't been called to the office to complete more paperwork. For that matter, I haven't even met the head of the fabrication department because she's been ill since before I started.

I can't handle being the butt of a joke, so I mark where I need rivet holes to join the legs and start cutting strips of elastic, and pretend Chris didn't say anything.

Stan stops by to check our progress, and I narrate my plans for the rest of the suit. He stands with his hands hooked in his front pockets, listening calmly. When I finish, he nods and walks on to see how the mechanics are progressing. He didn't act impressed or disappointed.

A while later, he passes back by. "Did Chris tell you?"

I assume he's referring to the offer of a permanent position. "Yes."

"Are we good?"

"Sure."

"Good." He strolls on, leaving as casually as he appears.

Chris smiles. "Told you, Netty. You're a lifer now."

But the voice in my head whispers, "You'll never be one of them."

(THREE WEEKS LATER)

The only thing better than being trusted by Chris and the two Daves is the glory I feel from seeing all the new construction theories I'm using on Kathoga succeeding.

My obsession with perfection has turned my head into a trouble-shooting calculator. Every piece I build, my Huper-drive runs through every what-if scenario it can imagine. That still leaves me perpetually worrying that I haven't thought of everything and I'll be doomed tomorrow, but at least for the day I'm living, I'm moving forward and happy in the moment.

That is, until I hear the head of the fabrication department has returned and has just thrown a fit because I was hired without her approval.

"Kathy just went to Stan and tried to get you un-hired," Chris laughs.

He may think it's funny, but what I hear is: *You're working under someone who hates you before she's even met you.*

There's no way to fix this. I can be nice. I can avoid her while I'm working on *The Relic* since she's on a different project, but this won't last forever. Eventually, I will have to work in the same room with someone I know doesn't want me here — someone hoping every single day that I fail.

The obsessed voice in my head is right; I'm not going to be able to stay one of them. And it's going to feel the need to remind me of this every minute of every single day.

FADE TO:

76. Burbank, California — Home to Hollywood and Back Again

I can't give up my side projects. If Stan decides he doesn't want me after all, or the department head can convince him he doesn't need me, I have to have my doors open. So, while I'm in a shop with TaMara during the day, I keep moonlighting with Terri.

This time, I'm handed twelve three-feet-tall skeletons to dress in shreds designed however I like. The only rules are: No two can look alike; focus on textures; and they must all be wearing white with dark gray and black distressing.

With no art whatsoever nor a script, I fish for hints for styling, use, preference, and mood through our conversations with the producers handling the project.

Free reign is one of the scariest things a client can do to me.

This project reminds me of my days on *PanGalactic Pizza Parlor*. Instead of a park in Japan, the park is in Korea, but it's still a mass of puppets with little reference and even less oversight, that Terri and I will create and puppeteer for prerecorded footage. Also like the Disney Project, we'll probably never see the end result, or get any feedback to know if they like or hate our work.

What should be a simple little project full of creative freedom, instantly becomes a high-pressure job. I've spent so much time giving everyone else what they want that I don't know how to create things from my own imagination anymore.

More than I realized when I took this job, I need this job because I'm getting stuck behind my Masks. I need to allow myself time to be freely creative — but pleasing others has become such an obligation that I don't know how anymore.

Saturday, I head over the Hollywood Hills to explore the fabric stores for inspiration. As I sit at a stoplight, imagining all the things I can do to these skeletons, a public transportation bus passes through the intersection, wrapped in an advertisement for *Species*.

It's me! The photo taken of me as Sil during the photo shoot, curled in fetal position, covers the side of the bus.

No one can see it's me — I'm hidden inside the suit — and I don't have a camera with me. Like so many things I do, the only proof there will ever be is my memory.

The voice in my head tells me that with no evidence or validation from someone else, nothing I do matters. Alone, I'm not enough.

After shopping for fabric, I return home and back to my version of normal life.

Terri and I finish the skeleton project — and never see the results. Thousands of people see the bus — and never see me. But I know what I saw, and that image will forever hang in my Good-Memory Room for me alone to enjoy.

(MONTHS LATER)

I'm not nearly as alone these days. Compared to most of my friends in relationships or marriages, Jim and I haven't been dating very long, but I've already told my parents if he doesn't propose to me by Christmas, I'm proposing to him.

This evening, we went for a nice dinner at Damon's Steakhouse and a walk on Brand Avenue. Most of our dates have been to the water treatment plant to work on Burbank's Rose Parade float, eating sushi at Chiba, and going to movies. And even though he has a seven-to-four, five-days-a-week job, he supports the wacky hours my career — no — my work obsession demands.

He's the first person I've dated who doesn't make me feel afraid to be me — minus my secret Rules, which he can't know about — nobody can. I can be silly, or target-focused on my work, sweaty and dirty or dressed up and girly. He accepts it all. Most of all, for reasons I can't explain even to myself, I trust him enough to eat food he brings me, even if he doesn't eat the same thing — and not because I'm willing to die to please him. Without knowing he's doing it, Jim gives me permission to stay away from my Fear Room door for a little while.

Daisy likes him too — although after she escaped for the umpteenth time to go mooch cheese toast from the bus boys at Sizzler, I'm not too sure how Jim feels about her.

We've been sitting in my living room, talking about one thing and then another long enough that Daisy is pacing between the bedroom and the living room. It's past her bedtime, and she wants to be sure she's making it very clear to us.

He's going to have to leave soon. After a couple of half-attempts to wrap up the evening, he drops to one knee in front of me. "I know we haven't been together very long …and if it's too soon, say so …but …will you marry me?"

I find myself staring at the little dark blue palm trees on his light blue shirt, half-stunned. Someone actually wants me for forever.

I already know what my answer is — and I'm so happy I don't have to ask him. The threat of rejection might've been too much for me to dare to pop the question.

"Yes. Yes, I will marry you." Saying it like that sounds so formal, but his proposal was formal and clear. I owe him a kind of response in return, so there's no doubt that I'm saying *yes* to the proposal and not to the too-fast part.

As traditional romance goes, he stays the respectable gentleman, saying goodnight at the door and going home, leaving me and Daisy officially engaged to a man and a cat named Plywood.

(THE NEXT MORNING)

Before Jim left, he told me to call him in the morning. I think he wanted to let me have time to reconsider — which I have no intention of doing. Still, I take a couple of hours in the morning to Hyper-drive the idea the same way I do everything else.

Which house we should live in? — Are our lives truly are compatible? — How long I'll need to make my wedding dress before we can get married? Because I'm absolutely going to make my wedding dress. — Should call him first or my parents? — I'll call him first. — It makes sense to make plans to go tell his parent's house today to tell them, so I'll know how much time I have to call my parents and get ready — What about a budget for the wedding — I'm allergic to cats…

My brain never stops. I can't stop it.

I dial his number.

The call connects. "I'm sorry, but this number is no longer in service," the recording recites, completely unaware that it's ripping out my heart. "Please hang up and try again, or call the operator for assistance."

He's disconnected his phone. Of course, he doesn't want to marry me. I'm too weird. And now he's hiding. Do I go to his house? No. I can't let him reject me twice.

I slam the door on the Fear Room in my head and open the door to the Logic Room. Dial the number again.

I do, and the line connects again.

"Hello?" It's Jim, oblivious to the trauma I caused myself by calling the wrong number — and I won't tell him about what just happened until I can tell it as just a silly incident that we can laugh about.

"Hi," I say cheerfully, turning the key in the lock on Fear's door. I won't go in that room today. Today, I'm going to allow myself to be happy.

(MONTHS LATER)

My wedding dress must be perfect. Each pearl individually tied on Italian rayon lace; boning worked into the torso, so the fit is perfectly smooth; swags of pearls draping across an open hole in the back. The dress is almost complete. Five of the eight panels, I beaded on the set of *The Relic*, with the lace barely poking out from a garbage bag and a flashlight tucked in my armpit — part of the time on-set, I was even covered in dried blisters from losing a battle with a patch of poison oak on my property — poison oak I was told was dormant.

It wasn't.

I won't let Jim see the dress before I walk down the aisle. In return, he won't let me see his plans for our honeymoon until we're on it.

Being in the dark is uncomfortable. I can't plan. I can't trouble shoot. I don't even know what to pack. I'm trying really hard to relax and enjoy the surprise he's building. He has no idea just how hard I'm trying because I've got my Fun Mask bolted on hard.

As we near the big day, I hustle even faster, making sure the Raptors at Stan's are perfect as well as the wedding plans, but I feel like a shaken can of soda. I don't know how much more I can take — or what will happen when I fail. I've invited several people from Stan's to the wedding — including Kathy — but not wanting to hurt anybody's feelings, I didn't ask Terri to invited them to my bridal shower. There isn't room in the Tea House for them all.

The day before the shower, I start to wash my hands and realize my engagement ring is missing. It was on my hand yesterday when I showed it to my mom after picking her up from the airport.

"I lost it. I lost my ring." Saying it aloud makes it real.

Frantically, I push everything around on the kitchen counter. I stick my hand in the garbage disposal. I sweep the floor. My mom checks the bathroom. We both check the bedroom, the bed, the pillowcases.

I call Jim. The minute he answers, I say, "I've lost my ring. We've looked everywhere, but…" I can't finish. I'm crying too hard. He'll hate me. "I'm sorry. I can't find it."

"I'll be right there."

Of course he'll be right there. He paid two-hundred dollars more than he'd budgeted for, so he could get the biggest diamond that would fit the antique setting we both fell in love with.

He must've flown from his house to mine, because there aren't enough green lights to get Jim to my door as fast as he gets there.

I melt into his arms. "I'm so sorry. We've looked everywhere." I don't want to let go of him. This might be the last time he'll ever hold me.

He pulls back — I want to die.

He doesn't look around the kitchen or bathroom long before he marches into my bedroom, with me trailing behind.

I start to explain where we've already looked, but he's already throwing back the comforter and sheets, shaking the pillows before dropping them on the floor, and swiping his hand along the edge of the mattress. Without slowing down, he hefts the mattress up on its edge.

There, on the bed platform is Jim's diamond ring. He'll be able to get his money back.

He picks up the ring, leads me around the bed, and slips the ring back on my finger, just as he did the first time. "You're worth more than a ring to me."

FADE TO:

77. Burbank, California — Wedding Day

I drop the black trash bag on the ground next to one of the brick pillars outside the church. My trash bag stresses everyone out. *You need to hang that dress up,* they say. *Will you at least let me iron it for you before the wedding?* They ask. The dress doesn't need ironed. With the weight of the Italian lace and pearls, being on a hanger would ruin it. Perfection means using different Rules.

Terri and I got here first, but we have plenty of time. So, I sit in the shade, against the wall, to wait.

Michael, my hairdresser, arrives minutes later. "What are you doing out here?"

"We're locked out of the church," I say it jokingly, but it's the truth.

"Is someone coming to let us in?"

"I certainly hope so." I've already recalculated our time. We're still within a safe range. No worries yet.

Michael rolls his eyes the way only he can do and leans against the other pillar to wait.

We wait. For twenty more minutes, we wait.

Recalculating again, we're still good but we're closing in on *not-so-good*.

"Can we call someone?"

"Not on me. Who would've thought the church would forget to unlock the doors when there's a wedding?". This is not going perfectly.

"Well," Michael scans the building until he finds a covered outlet. "we'd better get started on your hair, or we're not going to make it." He plugs in his curling iron and props a mirror against the wall.

"I'm going to call Jim and tell him not to come yet." With her hair still in rollers, Terri grabs her flip phone and punches in his number.

We're double dutying now, Michael styling my hair, while I'm doing my makeup. This should buy us enough time to avoid going into panic-mode a while longer.

Michael finishes my and Terri's hair — and styles his own as well. We're passing through *not-so-good* fast and well on our way to *disaster*.

A car pulls in. We're saved — nope.

It's the first of the guests arriving. "What are you doing out here? Where's Jim?"

My insides are running up and down the hall, looking for any place to hide to keep from getting sucked into the Panic Room, while outside I straighten my Casual Mask and say lightly, "We're still locked out of the church."

More cars pull in, and more nicely dressed guests emerge for me to greet in my sloppy pants and Oxford shirt.

"Where's your dress?"

I point to the trash bag against the pillar, where it's been for almost an hour and a half.

This is not going perfectly, and there's nothing I can do about it. I've always heard that something going wrong on your wedding day blesses a marriage with good luck. If that's the case, Jim and I will be extremely happy together — provided we ever get into the church.

FADE TO:

78. Valencia, California — A Few Weeks Later

Jim did a wonderful job planning our honeymoon without me. We went to Victoria, Canada — a far cry from where I am right now.

The Raptors were supposed to shoot in Kauai. Instead, the Monday I start back to work after our honeymoon, I'm in Valencia, freezing my butt off in a damp wheat field in the middle of the night.

Hefting a tail over my shoulder, I follow the thin path of stomped-down wheat to the clearing where we've already placed Alpha. While the shortest distance to any point may be a straight line — and convenient for making umpteen trips with hydraulic Raptors and bulky puppet parts — we don't get that luxury. The field must stay pristine from the camera angle for the shot. No shortcuts.

We prep our spot with our Raptor parts and hot chocolate, and we wait.

We rehearse some more. And we wait some more.

Filming *Jurassic Park: The Lost World* is going to give Jim a hard introduction to what will be like being married to me. In the morning, I'll get home just in time to say hi as I climb in bed, while he's getting out to get ready for work. And every week will be different until I'm back in the shop full-time. He'll either accept this life or ask for an annulment soon.

Jim says he understands, but I don't believe that's possible.

He thinks he married someone who's weird because she's a monster-maker. He's also aware of my obsessions toward perfectionism and organization — I can't hide those — but like everybody else, they think I'm a perfectionist because I'm picky, and I have to let them believe that.

Over the lone assigned walkie-talkie Chris carries, through the static, we hear Steven Spielberg has arrived.

Keeping our ears turned toward the walkie-talkie, we listen closer. Steven has his gear and is heading toward the camera crane.

The crew discusses the set-up and first shot, but only partially over the walkie, so more and more we don't know what's going on.

The walkie goes silent as Steven rides the crane up to check the shot. Up goes the crane.

I've kept most of my issues hidden for thirty years behind Masks and performances. I'm pretty skilled at it now. So, I won't have to make Jim deal with the parts he can't help — my constant feeling of being unwanted; my aversion to second-hand clothes, touching other people's socks and sharing towels; my hand-washing; my sensitivity to the direction every arm or eyebrow hair, eyelash and facial peach fuzz lays — mine or anybody else's.

Down goes the crane.

More silence. More waiting.

I won't tell him about my tailing invisible string threatening to tangle if I can't break it; my fear of failure, of flying.

The next thing we should hear is that the cameraman is in position, Spielberg is at the monitor, and we're ready for the one rehearsal for camera we do before we roll, but we hear nothing.

My hot chocolate is cold — I'm cold. We haven't moved in over half an hour, and the dampness has wicked through the shins of my jeans. This is going to be a long night. Still, a part of me is glad we didn't go to Kauai — the part that hates to fly.

Every flight, I'm already dead from the moment the airplane's wheels leave the ground until we are close enough to touch down that I'm reasonably confident I wouldn't die if we crashed. Flying more frequently doesn't worsen the fear, but it doesn't get better either. I get myself on planes the same way I'm able to eat food I fear is poisoned. I've forced myself to do things I thought would kill me so often that I simply accept my fate. I do life-threatening things, survive them, and enjoy realizing I'm wrong again …and again …and again.

The walkie explodes with voices cutting in and out, talking almost nonstop. Through the back-and-forth broken chatter, I hear, "Where'd … go?"

More chatter — more chaos. "Does anybody…eyes on…"

Silence. Static. "He's … … car …"

Chris grabs the walkie and heads out of the clearing. "I'm going to go find out what's going on."

I don't have to tell Jim my concerns about hurting inanimate objects' feelings, of doorknob germs, of flushing toilets, of breathing recently exhaled air, of defying my Rules, and so many other particular things that I don't realize I'm over-analyzing until I'm over-analyzing them — and probably many more concerns I'm not even aware I have.

Twenty minutes later, Chris returns. "Okay guys, that's a wrap for tonight. Let's get everything out of here. We're coming back tomorrow night. Same call time."

What the…?!

Apparently, when the grips set up the lighting, they came in using the shortest distance theory. When Steven went up in the crane and saw the trampled paths in every direction in what's supposed to be virgin field, he came down from the crane, walked to his car, and left. No yelling. No tantrum. He just left.

He doesn't like making his film crews work overtime, and there's no way to move the entire camera camp and Raptor setup to a completely new location in the field and still get it shot tonight.

Well, I guess it'll be one more day before I can go with my new husband for that sushi dinner at Chiba.

Jim is aware that I'm somehow weird, and he's okay being my anchor while I bounce in the waves. That counts for something.

I trust him so much that I'm not afraid to eat anything he gives me. I haven't felt this safe in a long time. So, I'll add whatever Rules I have to, to keep up with my career while double-timing it to be Jim's perfect — though secretly weird — wife too.

FADE TO:

79. Hollywood, California — Universal Studios

We've been filming for a few weeks now, and Steven seems to be happy with our new interpretations of his beloved Raptors. I know because our shots aren't getting changed.

In general, Steven has a three-take allowance. Either you get the shot within three takes — or so close that he can see we'll get it on the next one — or he's moving in and will "fix it in post." *Fixing it* can be anything from CGI to rewriting the script to dodge the scene entirely. Yet, he works with such assuredness and professionalism that he's never threatening. He simply thinks fast and needs the film schedule to keep up with his vision.

I can relate to that, and I'm enjoying the fact that we've been able to deliver for him so far.

Right now, he's on the soundstage next door, shooting a different scene while we rig the Raptor for its death scene. We've already shot it getting kicked out the vent of the kiln house by Vanessa Chester. All we have to do is lay the Raptor down and dress the bamboo spike through its side.

It takes five of us to get the Raptor onto its side, because she probably weighs as much as a real Raptor — if Raptors had ever gotten this big. Once down, we rehearse her movements to give Steven his shot in one take.

"What's that?" Chris asks.

Our Raptor has sprung a hydraulic line, and the fluid is dissolving the foam, turning it to goo.

He cuts open the skin so the mechanics can clamp off the hose and repair the break, before he dashes over to the other soundstage to see how much time we have before Steven comes over expecting to shoot. We don't want another drive-away moment — especially not one that's our fault.

The mechanics put the Raptor through its movements.

It's running safely.

David replaces the lung bladder, and then I realign the joint pieces. We re-rivet the joint elastic before I sew the skin closed.

By the time Chris returns, our Raptor is moving, but looks like hell. We can't glue the skin shut because the foam is too gooey, and we can't repaint it for the same reason.

Chris grabs his trusty makeup kit, pulls out some good old grease paint, and stipples a paint job that's a pretty good match to the airbrush pattern — if nobody looks too closely.

Steven and the camera crew show up twenty minutes later.

This time, it's not just me wearing a Cool Mask; it's the whole lot of us — but I have more training than the others, so I'm probably the only one not growing an ulcer at the moment.

The whole time Steven keeps asking us to raise the head just a little further, while I — all of us — pray we can lift it far enough to satisfy him without ever showing him the sequel movie we're prepared to shoot. *The Incredible Melting Raptor.* Somehow, thankfully, the shot goes off without a hitch — and without working overtime.

FADE TO:

80. Van Nuys, California — Stan Winston Studio

Stan doesn't like overtime any more than Steven does. Sure, overtime costs him money, but he also says that artists will burn out if they don't have time off — which is true. He goes home on time and, unless there's a tight deadline, he expects us to do the same. If it weren't for the two projects I have at home, I'd have my evenings and weekends mostly free.

With my additional new Rule, I do make sure to take most Sundays off for Jim's sake.

It's nearing the holiday season, we've completed work on ...*Lost World* and the Stan Winston Studio is in a bit of a lull, yet I'm completely happy for the first time in a long time that I can remember.

I have a husband who still wants to keep me and who I undoubtedly trust — though I don't know why. I have a side job in my shop with Terri, making a *D.C. Follies* style puppet and a marionette head of Jamie Foxx; and I have Stan Winston for a boss, who I also believe actually wants to keep me because he didn't lay me off with the free-lancers.

Meanwhile, Stan is keeping us busy making wooden boxes padded with velvet for Christmas gifts for Steven Spielberg, Arnold Schwarzenegger, and a couple of other of his closest friends.

I have to admit, I'm a bit jealous of Kathy. She's covering a chair that'll be used in a music video for Michael Jackson. The rest of us don't know anything about the video. Covering a chair for a video isn't all that exciting for a monster-maker, but at least she's touching a Michael Jackson video, which is more bragging rights than the rest of us will have. She's the department head, though. I can't blame her for keeping it for herself.

We've been warned to keep our work areas clean today because a guest will be getting a tour. This can mean anything from a future client or simply a friend wanting a sneak peek at something in the shop. One day, Arnold Schwarzenegger came through with Stan just to see what we were working on. The shop isn't open season for tours under non-disclosure agreements, but since Arnold is in and out of the shop for lunch and film projects, he can split that friendship/professional hair every time.

Shortly after ten in the morning, the door behind my chair opens, and I hear Stan's energetic voice chattering with his guest as they enter. I glance up from my velvet box to see Michael Jackson pause at the end of my table while he waits for the rest of his entourage to gather.

He wears the black face mask he's famous for wearing in public. If only I could wear an actual mask like he does… I'd love to be able to hide like that. Despite his mask, his eyes are undeniable and can't be ignored. They're big and clear and surprisingly inviting — which I can only imagine is difficult for him, since he has to live such a guarded life.

It wasn't that many months ago that the gossip rags and then the actual press condemned him for inappropriate behavior with a young boy, yet here he is with his makeup artist, costume designer, and many others on his staff — and several of their children. Apparently, when he's touring, many of the families tour together. It's not hard to see that Michael loves his crew; they are his family. It's also not hard to see that the moms don't seem to be the least bit concerned about their kids being around Michael.

Stan introduces each of us to Michael as they pass through, and he greets every one of us, keeping it brief, with his soft, quiet voice that's as inviting as his eyes.

The following week, the mold department wheels in two fiberglass body forms of Michael.

I'll be working on body-altering suits for him. One is a fat suit that I'll be teaming up with one other fabricator to make, turning Michael into a fat, middle-aged white man. The second suit I'm solely responsible for will turn him into a ghoul. Both suits need to be as light-weight and simple as possible, because Michael will be doing his famous dance moves from beneath the build-up. I'm back to my first-suit theories, with Alena doing acrobatics under padding.

I've built enough muscle suits, that especially since *Ed*, building muscle suits comes easy. Looking at the human frame as a skeleton, breaking down the movement needs so my designs aren't just bulk lumps making the silhouette of the creature or character, but instead have overlapping muscles mimicking the shape and movement of actual anatomy, I've done it so many times that it's second nature.

Michael is so slender, he's a perfect skeleton. Turning his shape into any other human form is going to be a cake walk. The only challenge is keeping it simple, because this means compromising my design anatomically, and I don't like making compromised designs. Compromised designs force me not to give perfection, and if Stan doesn't take that into consideration, it'll reflect badly on me. With this being my first muscle suit for Stan, the idea of him thinking I can do no better… I start sweating on the inside.

FADE TO:

81. Van Nuys, California — Back to the Warehouses

My fitting with Michael is today.

Luckily, the mold shop had a giant sander similar to the one I used on Ed, so I was able to crank out matching biceps in minutes. Even with the short deadline, I had time incorporate some muscles movement from the joints. Suits with muscles playing bumper cars drive me nuts, and I won't do it — even on simple suit like this one.

At a nondescript building not far from Stan's shop, I find myself in a mansion ballroom with Michael and his full dance team rehearsing part of their routine. I have no idea how long this has been in the works, but clearly the brevity of the deadline for my part hasn't pertained to the rest of the production.

Before I arrived, I was warned that the production team isn't allowing any dilly-dally on-set, and they aren't kidding. I'm immediately whisked away from the set and into Michael's dressing room as quickly as possible.

Five minutes later, Michael joins me. This time, he's alone and I can feel how much more relaxed he is without a crowd watching his every move — and he smells amazing. Light and slightly clove scented. I don't know what cologne he's wearing, but even after dancing all morning, he smells like he was ready to go out.

There's no hint of an ego and, instantly, I'm not invisible. I almost feel too big, and I try to think of something — anything — to say to soften any tension I'm causing. But everyone in the shop has been told — and retold — to be brief and not engage any more than our job requires. Now that I'm in a one-on-one with him, I wonder how much of that rule is Michael's and how much is his team's, but with no way for me to know, I can't break that rule.

I force my Polite Professional Mask into position and get to work.

Michael is full of kind smiles and *thank yous* — never *thanks*, always *thank you* — and he's willing to do whatever or stand however I need him to, to finish the fitting. Even in his underwear while he switches from one suit to the next, he stays cooperative and fairly quiet, always professional and friendly — and always listening.

Having several friends who have worked with him prior, I know he can get chatty, but with another costumer in the room, I'm so afraid of getting ratted out for breaking the keep-it-brief and don't-engage rule that I don't try.

The longer I'm there, the more I get the impression that he isn't the one making the demands, but his legal team trying to protect him. I think that protection — proven necessary by the recent public condemnation coming mostly from gossip rags — is keeping him fearful.

Maybe if I told him we had many mutual friends, he'd feel safer. Tim worked with him not only on *Thriller* but again on *Captain Eo*. After Tim and Michael spent time cutting up on the set of *Thriller*, Tim told me he was surprised that on the first day of shooting on *Captain Eo*, Michael waved and called out a greeting to him by name from across the parking lot, even though they hadn't seen each other for a few years. And when Terri was on *Captain Eo* with him, they had a long conversation about what he would do if a genie gave him three wishes. This isn't the behavior of someone who doesn't want to make friends with his co-workers.

I look up at Michael from the pectoral muscle that needs to get shaved down a little on the top.

Michael's big brown eyes meet mine and he smiles — but I can feel the eyes of my co-worker behind me.

"Well, it looks like we're close. Just a few little tweaks and you'll be good to go." I let their orders push me back under my Cloak of Invisibility.

Without making any particular connection, Stan keeps me in the shop to start work on *Instinct*, and my co-worker gets to go to set to maintain the suits as Michael's dresser. Knowing I build one-and-a-half of the two suits, that hurts, but Stan is my boss, and I follow the rules — even when it means not being able to make friends.

82. Van Nuys, California — Stan Winston Studio

Making friends with co-workers isn't something I do well. If they don't like me right off, nothing I do ever changes their notion of me.

Kathy and I work in the same room and converse cordially, but it's professionalism not friendship that keeps the room smooth.

We four fabricators have our own gorilla suits to make for *Instinct*, but Stan insists we confer as a group, to assure all the suits will be made using the same techniques. He doesn't want us creating a gorilla fashion show.

Both of my gorillas are young males. While I've only made a couple of gorillas prior, this time I get to make the ultimate gorilla suit — meaning, there's the time, the money, the mechanical movement, and the materials to make these suits look as realistic as possible, without having any asterisks footnoting the reasons they aren't perfect.

This challenge will be glorious.

Instead of picking up the scissor to trim-carve my foam pieces, I head back to the sanding wheel.

The speed the wheel eats away the foam is fast. Sure, I wind up with a bloody knuckle or two from time to time, or a fingernail ground to the quick before I can get my hand back when the whirling disc grabs the foam and crams the entire piece between the wheel and the metal guard, but that doesn't happen often anymore.

The rest of the fabrication room has decided they aren't fans of the threat of lost skin, so they're sticking to the traditional method of scissor-trimming the foam into shapes. For me, the benefit of the speed is gold when it comes to keeping up with my vision of what the final piece should be.

It's all good. Ultimately, our suits will all look the same under the fur.

I leave the fabrication room with my bicep chunks, sand them into shape, and return ten minutes later. I check their shape against the photos of the real gorilla

Stan supplied, mark the places I want to finesse, go sand the tweaks, and they're done and ready for spandex covers in just a few more minutes.

Watching the shape of my first gorilla come together so quickly is a blast. I can see the whole form in my head already. Even the sanding speed is frustrating, but I'm ahead of schedule, so the only person frustrated with me is me — and I'm used to that.

"You need to slow down."

I stop and turn to see all three other fabricators looking at me. "You're making us look bad."

They have to be kidding — their expressions say they're not. "I'm not hurrying." If I was, they wouldn't just look bad; they would look dead. "I'm just working at the rate of what I can see." Before they have time to counter, I duck out of the room with the triceps I need to sand.

In my head, I hear the echoing *Slow down. You're making us look bad.* My whole life, I've worried that people don't want me around. This time, I know for sure it's not just the voice in my head — It's the literal voices of everyone in the room.

I work hard; I don't fight with my co-workers; I try to be nice; I mind my own business and don't offer uninvited comments on their work. Now, none of them want me around. It's no longer just Kathy who has a problem with me. They all do, and there's nothing I can do about it.

I work for Stan — not them. The person I must strive to be perfect for is Stan. I can't be their compromised version of me. That goes against the Rules. I've worked my butt off so that even if people never remember me, they'll remember my work. Like so many other things I've grown accustomed to about myself, I'm used to not being liked.

Jim likes me, though. People come and go. People are nice to me, and then they're not. But I'll always have Jim. He thinks I'm okay, and Stan thinks I'm okay. That has to be enough.

Not many days go by before Shane struts in from behind my chair. People all come with signature walks. Shane's is a strut. He saddles up to my table. "I'm working on a mouse, and I need a mouse that can go from stretched out to balled up in the same body."

I suddenly find myself the lone fabricator on an entirely different team, making a hand-sized mouse for *Mouse Hunt*. At the same time, I'm making my *Instinct* gorilla suits, and like a man-eating Blob, the resentment I feel grows.

(A COUPLE OF MONTHS GO BY)

I'm comfortably settled with married life, working my two side-jobs by night and finishing my gorillas by day, and Jim giving me strength and security I haven't felt in way too long. Going back and forth between my gorillas and the mouse for *Mouse Hunt* has given the rest of the fabrication department time to catch up, so while the tension isn't gone, it's shrunk back into the shadows, with only glimmers from Kathy.

Joey, the Silverback sculptor, and Stan stare at Kathy's suit-in-progress. There's a lot of talking and pointing going on, and Kathy is looking at Joey the same way she looks at me.

"Lynette, can you come over here a minute?" Stan continues staring at the suit. "The proportions are off. What do you see that can be done to fix it?"

They ask me right in front of her — and I'm supposed to answer …right in front of her. While I respect them not doing it behind her back, she hates me enough without this. I didn't do anything to cause this.

But Stan's my boss — not her. I must march straight into my Fear Room, with my head up and take my punches.

The back is too short and it's throwing the shoulders and upper back out of proportion. "It feels like the bones need to shift." I'm being as tactful as I can because her feelings *do* matter.

"What parts can stay?"

Oh, boy. Hyper-drive time — not only for the fix but to find enough tact for the answer. "The arms are good" — but the shoulders have to be remade. "New bones to extend the torso… Just reposition the thighs and the legs are good." Changing those two things will make — "The back muscles would have to be remade, though, to accommodate the new torso." Trying to save Kathy, I add, "At this point, it would be a lot of work. I don't know if you'd even want to — "

"Okay, fix it." Stan's last words, and he leaves the room before any of us can say anything more.

He asked for my perspective, not for me to meddle. She and Joey have been butting heads, but I've never seen teams juggle mid-project. I didn't think he would... Oh geez.

Kathy returns to her worktable to focus on the baby gorilla and doesn't say a word.

I remove most of the muscles and build new bones, which ultimately affects the shape of the back, butt, thighs, shoulders and neck. Her arms, part of the legs, and the chest will stay. Then I step back, and Kathy makes the belly, and does the fur and skin work on it.

I'm proud of the way the Silverback turns out. I think Kathy is, too. We both made valid contributions. Are we a team? I don't think she sees it that way. And there's nothing I can do to console her — again.

FADE TO:

83. Hollywood, California — Raleigh Studios

Even though Lindsay MacGowen and I developed entirely new material usages and construction methods for *Mouse Hunt*'s mouse — and then the cat, too — to meet the movement demands of the bodies, they still came together faster than the whole tribe of gorillas for *Instinct*. And since the mouse barely fits my hand, I soon find myself bouncing from set to puppeteer the mouse, then back to my gorilla suits and back to the set again. This is the most fun I've had working since... maybe ever.

I don't know if Jim is having quite as much fun, but I share my enthusiasm with him, and he knows it's only for a few weeks, so he's enduring the chaos well.

Gore Verbinski, *Mouse Hunt*'s director, loves the mouse and loves to play with the mouse's scenes, challenging us to give him more and more; and he's so nocturnal that, unlike Stan and Spielberg, he's not against burning the midnight oil to play with his toy mouse a while longer.

I start each Monday with a call time of eight in the morning, and by Friday, I'm going in at five in the evening and coming home at ten o'clock Saturday morning — but the crew is a blast, and the challenges are glorious.

As I sit onset, waiting for the cameras to get set for the next scene, Shane calls from behind me. "Lynette, come over here a minute."

The guys huddle close, creating a secret conference circle in the dark.

"We want to talk to Stan about putting you in charge of the fabrication department, but we wanted to hear your thoughts first."

They're offering me my dream job — Kathy's job. For years I've had people asking me when I would open my own shop, but I never wanted to deal with the pressure, the constant overhead, the liabilities. All I want is to be the right hand the owner can't do without — a department head. Many shops consistently call me, but they never want to keep me. To them, I'm disposable. According to these guys, I'm indispensable to them — to Stan.

But more opinions matter than just these few.

As if they're reading my mind, they assure me they have discussed this with Stan's other key designers, and they have the support to make this happen.

I want to say *yes* more than anything — almost anything. "I can't do it, guys."

They all pull their heads back like I just burped in their faces.

"I've wanted that job for years, and I'm so flattered that you want to help me get it, but you can't do it. Jim and I have been talking, and I'll be leaving soon to start a family. I can't have you sabotaging the department by giving me the position when I'm getting ready to quit."

"Think about it," They push. "Just think about it."

I am thinking about it. (I still think about it — and I will until I'm in my grave.) The what-ifs are torture.

But life marches on. Jim and I didn't marry until I was thirty years old. We agree that we want kids. If I don't want to be so old that I can't keep up, I can't wait much longer to start.

I told Jim he can have as many kids as he wants, but I'm only pregnant twice. So, that's my Rule. "You can hope for twins or pick them up at the baby store. I don't care. But I'm only pregnant twice."

Dragging down my work momentum with pregnancy, I figure my career can survive doing that twice — maximum. Anything more, I'll be completely forgotten, and my career will be unrecoverable.

I've been offered the job of my dreams. I've made it to the top of the mountain. But I can't stay there. It's time to climb another one. But I can't let go of my love and obsession with my work.

I can't quit my career entirely, or I'm a failure, and now that I've found a man who I believe will always have faith in me, I can't fail him either — as the professional he knows or the wife he deserves. I don't know how I'm supposed to do this, but somehow, I have to figure out how to do it all. But it won't be able to include my dream job in my career plans — and it hurts.

FADE TO:

84. Van Nuys, California — Stan Winston Studio

Maybe Kathy would feel less threatened if she knew that I never tried to steal her job but that I didn't steal it even when offered it. Unfortunately, the only way to let her know would be to throw quite a few people under the bus, and I promised them I wouldn't do that — so I won't.

Until I leave, I'll keep my mouth shut and let her resent me for whatever it is she already resents me for.

The pain of leaving is easier to take, knowing I *could've* had my dream job, but my goals are always moving. Hit one dream and take on a new one. I've always had a plan — subject to change due to life. I didn't start out to be a monster-maker. I started out wanting to work for the movies. Life's opportunities lead me to this monster world, and while I'll be leaving Stan's soon, I love my career and don't want to leave it.

A few weeks later, I enter Stan's office.

I've never been in his office — I never had a reason to. It's not like I hold rank in the shop. I'm not a department head — though I could have, I'm not. And I'm not one of his key designers or project coordinators. I'm just me. In Stan's eyes, I'm just another fabricator.

He offers me a seat, but I'm afraid to sit down. I'm dirty and covered in fur bristle. Still, at his insistence, I take a seat.

After some small talk, I take a breath and throw myself off the cliff. "I need to give you my two weeks' notice."

I think he thought I was going to ask for a raise.

"Jim and I want to start a family, so I need to step away from the glue toxins for a while. It kills me to say this. Working for you has been — " I can't finish. The tears hit me, and my voice disappears. "I love working here."

He offers for me to stay on even after I'm pregnant until I near my due date, but to be the most responsible mother, I need to get away from the fumes before that.

He offers for me to stay until I get pregnant, but I already told Jim I was quitting.

Every offer he makes tears more of my guts out more than the offer before it. He's trying hard to be kind to me. He doesn't realize that the more generous he is, the more he's tempting me, and the harder it is to say goodbye. Building creatures here, always facing new challenges, always growing, always looking for that better technique; it's becoming more than an obsession. It's becoming an addiction.

I want to say yes to him. I want to stay. It would be so easy to keep saying yes to one more project and then one more. But to be perfect, I will have to be perfect for my family, too. If I don't learn to say no, my addiction will leave Jim and me eternally childless. I'm going to have to learn to fight my obsessions — and it hurts so very, very badly.

CUT TO:

85. Glendale, California — Backyard Shop

I haven't been gone from Stan's all that long when I get a call. "Are you able to go to Africa with *Instinct*?"

Just shoot me now.

Leaving Stan's was tough enough. Now, I have to say no to a paid trip to Africa.

"I'm already pregnant." I don't regret that part, but it doesn't make turning down work any easier — so I don't turn down any job I don't have to.

Steve calls. "If you can't work in the shop, can you come in long enough to do the fittings and mark the changes on the Sil suits for Species II. TaMara can do the hands-on part."

Lindsay, from Stan's shop, calls again later, asking if I can make the necks for the parrots he's making for a movie called Paulie. "You can just pick up the pieces you need for reference and bring it back when you're done."

Jim knew from the get-go that I couldn't give up my work, so he turned the guest house out back into a shop for me shortly after we married, so I had a place for my moonlighting. The bedroom is the foam sanding dirty room, and the living area is my sewing room. Being pregnant, the space has gone from my part-time shop to a full-time one.

I take on both jobs, making sure to say, "Keep me in mind. I won't be pregnant forever" — although some days it feels like I will be.

My big contribution to the household budget is the four-year contract, working under an NDA (Non-Disclosure Agreement) I started while I was still at Stans. For full disclosure with him, he knew about it, but nobody else did. I still have three years left on the contract.

Working under an NDA leaves it sounding like I'm not working much, but it's a good job. It's keeping my skills honed and pushing me to develop new techniques, so my obsession stays fed while keeping me working in a non-toxic environment from home.

Watching *Bewitched* when I was growing up showed me how to be the perfect expectant mother. Samantha was never overweight, lazy, or sloppy. She never had morning sickness or got emotional. I know sitcoms aren't real, but the dye is cast. I have to be a perfect pregnant lady.

I buy, borrow, and make maternity clothes. My favorite is a pair of overalls. They look cute with T-shirts and don't have a waistband.

Giving up my small waist is sad but obviously necessary. My waist was the only thing giving me a figure. Since I moved to Hollywood, I've gained fifteen pounds, but I still wear the same size clothes I did before. Throwing around giant suits and shaking grown men down into skin-tight foam latex has given me some serious strength in my skinny body. That's something I won't allow pregnancy to steal from me because I'm going to need it again.

I don't get fat — I can't.

The doctor put me on a diabetic diet as a precaution because big babies run in my family, and apparently, gestational diabetes causes big babies. "You need to gain more weight," she then tells me at the seven-month mark. "You've only gained fourteen pounds. It's not even safe for you to give birth until you've gained at least eighteen."

I'm dying to eat more chocolate, but her threat of diabetes is enough to reactivate my fear of sugar enough that I can't bend the low-sugar Rule. But if the doctor says I need to gain four more pounds, I'll gain four more pounds.

Ironically, I'm patterning a maternity belly when the phone rings.

It's Michael Burnett. I haven't worked for him for a while, but I've hired him for some mold-making recently, which probably floated my name higher on his list of contacts. "I have four months to make a full set of promotional suits for *Small Soldiers*, and I need your help. When are you due?"

"We're good. I have exactly four months. I can't work in your shop, though. Can I work at home?"

Two week later, I have a four-person crew working in the backyard with me. All the gluing is set up on the patio, with folding tables and brown paper covering the patio table and concrete under the arbor. I'm running a shop ...without a shop.

(THREE MONTHS GO BY)

It's five-thirty. The crew has gone home, and Terri and Jim insist I go for my evening walk, even though I don't feel like it. The doctor says walking is good for me, but this evening, I think an evening off sounds better.

"You can't give up already. You still have a month to go."

"Fine." I go as far as the corner. "Now, I'm going back to the house." Yes. I'm failing this evening's walk, and I don't care.

Three o'clock in the morning, I'm in labor. By evening, I'm holding Bryce — our son. This little man is my reward for starting motherhood right. He's my baby. He's here because Jim and I brought him into this world. We owe him the best life we can give him. This isn't a Rule — it's my Law.

He's a full month early — I didn't do that part exactly right — but that part works out well, too. Terri was my labor partner. A month from now, she'll be in Vegas doing a show. This fits my schedule better.

Two days later, we're home from the hospital.

When Bryce sleeps, I work. When Bryce is awake, he's in my arms, under the patio table umbrella, where I can oversee my crew still working toward our deadline.

I love my new baby boy, and I love my husband, and while caring for Bryce is my new Law, I can't — no matter what — allow myself to break all my other Rules. I simply can't. I know how weird it would sound to people, so I still keep it to myself.

I don't need to hear flippant comments like *You're too much of a perfectionist* — as if I enjoy living in the constant haunting fear of failure and rejection — or *Don't be so competitive* — if I am competitive. I don't care if I lose at Monopoly. It's more important to be a good sport than a winner, so I can be perfectly fine losing — as long as the winner isn't an ass about it.

People saying *There's no reason for me to feel so insecure* don't understand that every time I open my mouth, my gut tells me people are rolling their eyes behind me or seeing failures in me. And teasing me about it or saying *You're just being paranoid* is such a brush-off that it only proves the voice constantly telling me *Nobody wants to be inconvenienced by your feelings* is right.

I look at Bryce, nestled in the crook of my arm, sound asleep.

And I certainly don't need people telling me to relax. I have too much responsibility to relax. I don't relax by resting. Frankly, sleeping annoys me. It wastes time that I could use to help me not to fail. I have to be the perfect worker, the perfect wife, and the perfect mother, because *I cannot fail* is still Rule #1, and it doesn't include exceptions.

I take Bryce back to the house and gently lay him into his crib while I renegotiate with myself to organize my additional Rules.

FADE TO:

86. Glendale, California — Home, One Year Later

Everyone asks Jim and me if we planned to have our kids so close together in age.

"Of course, we did," I say, holding my rather tall one-year-old to the back of my hip, so my round belly doesn't cause him to slide off. Both times, I got pregnant the exact month I scheduled it to happen.

"Boy or girl?"

"We'll find out when it's born."

Their face turns to something between horror and confusion.

"Never open your Christmas present before Christmas morning. It takes the fun out of it. And what bigger present will we ever get than this."

For the people who think I'm a perfectionist, if I were truly a perfectionist, I'd demand to know my babies' genders beforehand so I could decorate the room according. But I'm not a perfectionist. I'm a Rule-follower, and the Rule is: *Never peek at your presents before you open them.*

We didn't know Bryce was a boy until he was born. We just painted the room mint green and I made a mobile to hang over the crib by stringing Bette Midler sequins-donned Beanie Babies to a couple of spiral-striped sticks. (Somebody told me the one Beanie Baby was worth five-hundred dollars *after* I'd hot glued a red metallic trimmed collar to it. After that, I didn't try to find out what the others would've been worth if I hadn't devalued them.)

As with my first pregnancy, I keep working. Last time, it was for *Small Soldiers* — one of the soldier suits even ended up in the movie — along with the NDA contract. This time, it's still the NDA and painting figurines for Terri. Terri has been commissioned by Disney to create a line of limited-edition sculptures of the six main rides in Disneyland's Fantasyland, called the *Jewels of the Park*. It's the perfect project for me.

I sit with my feet propped up on my workbench, overseeing my one helper helping me with the NDA contract; Bryce stretched out on my legs with his little legs splayed around his sibling in my belly; and my belly making a perfect prop to steady my hands while I paint tiny faces on Dumbos and Carousel Horses, and pinstripes on Mr. Toad cars. I've perfected recognizing the stir that comes before the kick from inside my belly so the bumps wouldn't smear my paint job.

TaMara calls. She's working at Stan's again. "I'm refurbing the Raptors for *JP3*. Can you come in and look them over with us?"

I return to Stan's long enough to talk with TaMara, and to loan her my personal notes from my initial designing. While there, I'm pulled into the sculpting room so they can ask me for any ideas for making the Pteranodon.

Over the course of a few weeks, I make regular visits to Stan's to consult and brainstorm. It hurts a little, watching others do what I want so badly to do myself, but I'm surprised it doesn't hurt more. This shop has called me four times since I've been away. They even made sure I got an invitation to the screening of *Instinct*. They haven't forgotten me, and Stan's not angry with me for leaving.

Maybe — just maybe — I'll be able to come back someday.

My labor pains start shortly after my shop help, and I have quit for the day. By the time Jim gets home from work, I'm sitting on the front porch, already packed and looking over the contract for the sale of my house in Burbank. We've been renting it out for the past couple of years, but with the kids, it's becoming too much work. The Realtor is supposed pick up the papers tomorrow. Jim changes clothes, while I make sure I have all the papers, and we're off to the hospital.

Like Bryce, our second baby is a month early, too, so he and Bryce are only fourteen months apart instead of fifteen, as I planned — to match the age difference between me and each of my siblings. Unlike Bryce, our second son's lungs are about one week underdeveloped, so he can't come home with me.

"We've given him the surfactant. Soon, his lungs will start developing it themselves, and he'll be good to go," the doctor says. "Don't worry. This won't cause any lingering effects on him or his life. He's just a bit too early. That's all." Shifting gears, he perks up. "So, what have you named him?"

"We haven't gotten a chance to meet him well enough to name him yet."

I learned with Bryce not to settle on a name before meeting our babies. I was sure Bryce was going to be Grayson — son of the gray-haired man — because Jim, at thirty years old is already nearly fifty percent gray. But when I held him for the first time, after one look, I told Jim, "This isn't Grayson. I don't know what his name is, but it's not Grayson."

We went back through our narrowed-down list of ten boy names and realized our firstborn's name was supposed to be Bryce.

I won't make that same mistake again. Once I say it out loud, it's supposed to be permanent. Change is too hard.

The realtor drops by the hospital with a bouquet of flowers, to pick up the papers I finished signing after delivery, ice cream, and a few hours of sleep. "What's his name?"

"We still haven't figured that out."

It takes three days before we've held him enough to feel certain of what his name is.

It's Conner. We've decided. We've said it. It's done.

I've been pregnant twice. We have our two kids. This part of my perfect plan is now complete.

(THE NEXT SPRING)

Bryce is in the highchair, and Conner is coasting in the wind-up swing, while Jim clears the dinner dishes and I talk to my parents on the phone. My mom just told me my uncle is getting ready to sell one of the houses he bought to restore but has since decided not to keep it after all.

"Ask him how much," Jim says from the sink.

It really doesn't matter. We saw the place when we visited right after we were married. It sits on thirty-five acres that are about a third farmland. The rest is woods with creeks running through it. The land is gorgeous, but the barns are falling down, and the two-story Victorian house sits empty with no furnace, no bathroom, part of the windows missing, the weather-worn clapboard coming loose, and raccoon footprints on the walls where they've been passing from room to room through the missing transoms above the doors. I can see its potential, and if it was in California, I'd be talking Jim into buying it in a heartbeat — but it's not. It's in Indiana.

Still, to show Jim just how different home costs are in California from the rest of the country, I ask how much.

A week later, my mom relays to me that he's selling the entire farm for about half of what our current little two-bedroom house is worth.

Soon after, Jim comes home from work. As usual, I'm on the front porch with the two boys and Daisy and Tina, my hours in my shop done and my help gone for the day. He leans against the porch rail.

I can't tell if he's looking at the ground or the boys playing on the area rug covering the cement, but he's clearly got something on his mind.

"I don't see us living here forever."

"You mean this house, or in L.A.?"

This house belonged to his grandmother. His mom grew up here, and we're buying it from the estate. Leaving it never seemed like an option.

"I mean California."

He's never lived further than four miles from his parents. When I married him, I knew I was committing to living in the San Fernando Valley for the rest of my life. I never said this to him, but then, I don't say a lot of things.

"I hate my job."

Over the past few months, his job has gone from Monday through Friday to five days plus random hours on Saturdays and Sundays, where he goes in just long enough to program the machines for their next steps to keep them running through the weekends. We can't even take the kids to the park without watching the clock.

"I don't see us raising our kids in the city. And if we can't be by my family, then we need to be by yours. And most of your family is in Indiana."

That's a lot of *and*'s to take in.

"I don't mean we need to move right now, but someday, before the kids get too old to adjust, we should consider moving."

Bryce is barely two, and Conner isn't even one yet. I'm burning out trying to keep up with everything, but I know that will change once the kids are in school, when I don't have to double-duty every waking hour.

"Well," I start slow, my head rushing through the various options like it's flipping through a deck of cards. "We have time. We can't really go anywhere until I'm fully vested in SAG retirement, and I still have two years to go for that. But we could buy that farm and hold onto it until we're ready to move. It's cheap enough, if that's what you're thinking."

I've never considered living anywhere but California — not before I'm old enough to retire. The only plan I ever made was moving to my five acres and turning it into a bed-and-breakfast so my movie friends would have a place to escape to, and I wouldn't wind up alone. But after Terri and Howard divorced, and then I got married and had kids… I hadn't stopped to imagine what might be next.

Jim is right, though. The city is changing. Watching Bryce peddling his Big Wheel in a circle around a patio table and knowing that if we stay here, our boys will never be able to run free and explore the world on their own… This isn't the life we want for them.

Our job is to give our children the best life possible — and that's not here. It's time for me to look hard at what it means to be perfect because I've hit a wall. I can't be the person I'm trying to be without failing another part of me.

FADE TO:
(THREE MONTHS LATER)

We are officially the proud owners of a house so uninhabitable that we can't get insurance. So, technically, we are the proud owners of thirty-five acres …and some broken-down buildings that may be able to be fixed up — provided we save them before they fall over.

The plan is to move in ten years so the boys can settle before junior high.

Then, the plan changes to a six-year plan so the boys can make friends before they get too embedded here.

Then, we decide on four years so Bryce can start kindergarten there and never feel the change.

Then, it changes to two years, which is how long I needed to become fully vested toward retirement.

Jim comes home even more depressed and frustrated.

"I'm going to have to quit my job. I'll sweep floors or pump gas or do whatever it takes to keep a paycheck coming in, but I can't keep working there."

Not only is he never able to have weekends off, his parents just offered to take us on an all-expense paid Hawaiian cruise, but his boss won't allow him to take his vacation time and go.

I hand him an envelope that just came in the mail. "It's from SAG. I've been counting wrong. I'm fully vested as of now."

The newspaper has also reported that Disney just purchased the entire campus of buildings near our house and is planning a vast expansion and remodel that will take eight years.

"If you're going to pump gas, we could afford to live better in Indiana than here. And if we don't move soon, we're going to be living the next eight years by a wrecking ball and jackhammers, and we're not going to be able to give this place away with a free dinner."

It doesn't take us long to see that life is moving us into the next phase of our life with a giant boot-swing to our butts. Ready or not, we don't have a choice. With our money tied up in the farm in Indiana, we can't buy a better place here. We're going to move to Indiana even sooner than we planned.

How soon is contingent on our realtor, Alina, when we list the house. "I'll only show your house if I think the client is a legitimate match."

I like the sound of that. "What about an open house? I know those are common."

She flicks up a hand. "I don't do those. They're time-consuming and generally only draw gawkers, not buyers." She's so confident, we believe her. "I'll put you on the Caravan listing so other realtors can tour it, but I won't be here that day. Just let them in when they come."

After the Caravan, a couple of other realtors show the house, but nothing comes of those showing, and Alina goes completely silent.

Knowing Jim only has to endure a while longer, he keeps his job and starts working harder and faster, trying to ensure we'll have as much money saved up as possible. I still have that NDA contract, and I'm painting another set of collectibles for Terri. This time, it's the organist at the organ, the gargoyle on the queue line rope posts, the gravedigger with his dog from *Haunted Mansion*, the skeleton in bed in the treasure room, and the three prisoners bribing the dog from *Pirates of the Caribbean*.

Paul, the Chiodo Brother's office manager calls to see if I'm available to help them with five giant heads they need to make of N-Sync for the *American Music Awards*. Michael Burnett calls to have me make two costumes of the Coffee Alien from *Men and Black*. And a producer asks me to figure finish a wolf head starting at ten at night for him to use the next morning.

I say *yes* to it all. Every job feels like the last. Once we move, I'll fade away the rest of the way and soon be completely invisible — forgotten.

Jim tries everything to keep me from feeling like I'm selling my soul. "You can fly back for work a few times a year and stay with my parents."

There's a sculptor I know who does that, but he's a fantastic talent. I'm just a fabricator. I doubt anyone will need to fly me in like they do him.

An entire month goes by before Alina shows any sign of life.

When she shows the house, we sit with the kids in the car, just around the corner where we can see them come and go from the house. It takes us longer to load the kids in the car and leave than the time it takes her to show the place — and I'm irked.

"That was nothing but her pretending to have a prospective buyer, so we can't claim she abandoned us."

The next week, Alina comes by with an offer. "They want a thirty-day escrow."

Thirty days? We're supposed to have a few months of showings, offers, negotiating, and then escrow. She only showed the house once. No open house; no parade of viewings forcing me to run around shoving quickly rinsed-off dishes in the cupboards; no baking those four cookies to make the house smell homey or stowing the toys under the beds. Now, she's telling us we have thirty days to pack up and get out.

"Thirty days is common right now."

We didn't know that.

"They have to be out of their house in thirty, so they need you to be out in thirty as well. And they need us to agree this week."

From a ten-year plan to a ten-week plan, life is throwing us out of the state — and there's nothing I can do about it.

(TWO WEEKS LATER)

My heart bounces so hard it makes my chest hurt. I have to say yes — I always say *yes*. Still holding the phone, I look around at the stacks of boxes that have been growing steadily for the past two weeks.

Cecil and Tracy watch me, their heads sticking out of an open box in the corner. Two of my oldest friends. Cecil's left eye is still misshapen from the chrome of that rear car window where I first found him; and I never have found Tracy any arms or legs. Their weirdities are more obvious than mine, but they get me. They've been on this wild ride with me all these years and will carry on with me as long as their bodies hold out.

Change still terrifies me, but I remind myself again that change means growth. That's not much consolation at the moment. I've spent my whole life chasing this Hollywood dream of mine, and now that I've caught it, I'm changing everything up.

With the phone still in my hand, I watch Bryce and Conner playing with their oversized Legos. We have to go. But Paul just told me he wants me to bid two complete costume sets for Bibleman, Cypher, and Biblegirl, as well as the two main villains and several henchmen for the Chiodos.

Altogether, he wants me to bid thirteen outfits. The Chiodos don't have the contract yet, so they'll be able to plug in my numbers into their bid, to assure there'll be enough money in the budget to cover me and my materials.

The job doesn't require anything I haven't done a hundred times before, and it's a big enough project to make me a decent amount of money — which is just what we need, considering our hundred-and-twenty-year-old farmhouse needs a roof that doesn't leak and an indoor bathroom. And a furnace. And, for that matter, glass in the windows. Who am I kidding? It needs everything.

I remind myself one more time: change means growth. Still, I can't stop myself from asking, "How long before you'd start, if you win the contract?"

"It's not a rush. We should know something in four to six weeks. Then, we'll have three months to complete the job."

Six weeks is bad. Add three more months, and the job was impossible. I have to remind him. "You do remember I'm moving away, right?"

"Yes." His Cape Brit accent makes everything about him sound so matter-of-fact. "So, be sure you include three plane tickets in your bid. One to take measurements, one for a fitting midway, and one for the final delivery and fitting."

I can't believe he's serious, but he sure sounds that way.

He tells me we won't hear if they get the contract until I'm already in Indiana. If the job doesn't come through, I still have two more years on the NDA contract, so I'll be able to continue contributing to the family financially, but silent work doesn't hold the same thrill as creating creatures for movies.

There's something special about going to the theater and seeing my work on the big screen while I sit with my cheap-and-sleazy nachos with extra cheese and a pile of jalapeños. I always have my drink in the cup holder on my right, and the Milk Duds in the cup holder to my left.

When the movie ends and the audience applauds, there's a special pride in knowing I was a part of that. And when the credits roll, and I hear applause from a few random people as they clap for the names of their friends — or for their own — and then my name appears among my co-workers, it's my turn to clap for myself, and for so many other I love working with and respect. Hearing others clapping together, knowing they aren't clapping for the show as a whole, but specifically for you and your work is a thrill that can't be matched.

Each movie I work on makes me just a little more seen, a little more remembered, immortal. I don't want to give that up — no — I can't give that up. It's too much of a part of me.

I wonder if the people in Indiana applaud at the movies. Even if they do, it won't matter to me anymore.

I've always believed if you're not dreaming, you're dying.

I don't want to die.

FADE TO:

87. Farm Country, Indiana

I sit on the back stoop, picking spatters of dried dusty lavender living room paint off my forearm, while I watch the contractor build my shop in the backyard — the one *Bibleman* is paying for — while the boys play in their new massive, unfenced world. Bryce is running laps around Conner, as Conner debates whether to crawl through the sweet-smelling grass or eat it. I don't think Bryce yet realizes he can run a straight line now.

Boys need to be able to run. They need to be here — I probably do too.

Living in Indiana is the only way I'm going to be able to control my work obsession. For years, my life was like I was an alcoholic living above their favorite bar. With the bar further away, maybe I'll be able to learn how to balance life and work. How I'm supposed to do this is beyond me. I've tried before, but my Rules always suck me right back down the rabbit hole.

For the first time in my life, I no longer have a clear plan.

We've been living in Indiana almost a month, and I'm not hearing much from California. Already, I'm being replaced. Forgotten. When I finish the *Bibleman* contract, the Chiodo Brothers won't need me either. Late next year, the NDA contract will be finished. Then what?

A year from now, word will have spread that I've moved, and everything I've done to try to be remembered will be old news. I'll be that person people ask, "What have you done lately?" and I'll have nothing to say. Without my career, my Cloak of Invisibility will swallow me up completely.

Jim and my boys are the only people who will want me — at least, I hope they will.

I check my watch. Jim should be back soon with the blasting caps — a full month, and we still don't have running water.

Right before we moved, Paul told me it would be six to eight weeks before they'd need me to start. "Are you going to be settled by then?"

"Sure," I heard myself say before I had a chance to consider the big picture.

We're hauling fifty-gallon barrels of water over from my uncle's well, because the pump in our well was seized up. The new one is too big to fit down the pile without the pipe getting cleaned first, and the well companies keep standing us up. Not a perfect start to living here — at least the outhouse now has all four sides on it.

We're using part of our house restoration money to build a six-hundred-square-foot shop for me in the backyard. I think four hundred square feet is plenty big enough, but Jim says I'll need the space.

He believes in me. He lets me dare to try, so I will keep trying. I can't disappoint him.

I can't imagine how I'm supposed to bring in enough work to justify the space he's having built for me, but I won't give up. I am still not allowed to fail.

FADE TO:
NOT THE END

After *Bibleman* covered the cost of building the shop, things were slow for the first year, and I quickly began to question our move and my turning down Stan's invitation to go to set on *JP3*. But more than anything, I questioned whether I was worth anything or whether I was forgotten the minute I left the state. I've always felt invisible. In my mind, moving away made it true.

After talking to Jim, we decided we needed one more child, so while the back of the house was torn away to build a kitchen, we had Trent.

A few months after Trent was born, the calls started coming. My shop gained projects — from Indianapolis, Las Vegas, and out of Hollywood, building characters for concept TV shows and web series, reenactment shows, commercials, and private commissions. Terri started using me as her painter on her limited-edition collectibles and a commission piece for Guillermo Del Toro. Randy Simper called me to build props for Terry Fater. I started flying back west a few times a year for work, and we introduced our family to the locals by opening a corn maze that we haunted every fall for the next fourteen years.

Meanwhile, I had dreams that someday Stan would call and ask me to fly back for another project, but before that happened, in the summer of 2008, he passed away. Stan Winston was the one person I believed could revive my career. When he died, so did a big part of my dream.

With little faith in myself, I pushed on, but every time the phone went silent, my heartbeat grew quieter while the voice in my head grew louder. *I'm not needed. I'm not wanted. I was letting down Jim and my boys.*

I needed a new dream, so I started writing. I wrote a novel that got representation from a big-name New York literary agent, but when the book didn't sell, the rejection broke what little confidence having an agent had built, and part of me died again.

Then, I wrote another novel and started on another. The writing wasn't paying me, but it gave me new hope — in case Hollywood never wanted me again.

Then, the movie project calls started accelerating — and so did my writing.

Soon, I was back on the fast track, working in my shop, flying west, and writing while pushing my boys to dare to follow their dreams — whatever those may be.

Now, I'm helping develop web series, flying west to work on everything from the movie *Dust Bunny* and Disney's new series *Skeleton Crew* to commercials for Legacy Effects — founded by the anchor team of Stan's shop. I've been a producer on a couple of films, written a couple of screenplays, created a published children's book series, written more novels, and started making appearances at fan conventions.

While my life is ever-changing, one thing never did change — my secret OC thoughts. Not until I started writing this memoir did I ever confess the darker parts of my OC, even to my husband. The parts that go beyond the specific placement of the sofa pillows, the spazz-outs if someone touches my face, the utter horror I feel if anyone uses my towel, stressing about how things will look if I suddenly die or get dementia — dementia is my most recent addition — and the innumerable other quirks on my list of physical obsessions have become simply daily encounters that we've come to accept as *another one of my things.*

It's the head games that are tougher to explain.

Every day, I still argue with my thoughts, never feeling worthy, always sure everyone is barely tolerating me, certain I'm an imposition even to my closest friends, and concede that my children consider phone calls from me an inconvenience.

I am not just fighting imperfection. I'm fighting to keep from falling into that black void. That fight keeps my head in a perpetual paradoxical debate. My strive for perfection, I'm sure, makes me still come across as overly picky and pushy, yet the idea that someone may consider me pushy or picky is crushing to me. Then, I push harder to be more perfect. There is no logic behind it — other than the logic I create that helps me justify my shortcomings to myself.

My saving grace is my Rules. I don't make my Rules because I have to win. I make my Rules because I care — maybe too much — but that's who I am. I can review my Rules, re-prioritize my Rules, add new Rules whenever I gain a new piece of information to obsess over, and I can even sideline a Rule if I can get my logic to create a valid compromise.

I still use my Masks because I still can't express my feelings well. Not because I don't feel — I feel very deeply and empathize even more — but my heart lives in a Room of its own. I can't be in two places at once. I can't spend time in my Heart Room, Pain Room, or Sadness Room while I'm in my Fear Room, Anger Room, Loyalty Room, Social Room, Responsibility Room, or any other of my rooms. For me, the sensation I get from emotions is quick before it becomes just another memory — information — to be used, referenced, and recalled at-will, rather than something I relive.

That fact remains, I am weird. I will always be weird, but I'm used to it now.

Weird is not a label; it's a descriptor. There should be no labels; there should only be descriptors. Labels categorize and divide. Descriptors acknowledge differences. And differences draw wonder — that's a good thing.

I will always be a brown-haired, blue-eyed, very ordinary looking female, with a vivid imagination, good math skills and a dry sense of humor, who loves flowers, food, monsters, baseball and elephants, who needs to always feel she is a part of a bigger Chain, and who has a hearty collection of obsessive compulsions that I still keep hidden relatively well.

I can't expect everybody to understand me, and I try with all my might not to feel rejected when people don't get me. They don't understand me any better than people from two different countries speaking two different languages can communicate without working at it.

Sure, my OC comes with challenges, but it's also become my gift. My OC helped me follow my dream — and succeed. I still need it, because I'm not done chasing dreams yet. Besides, it's a big part of what makes me ...*me*.

FADE OUT.

Dear Fellow Weirdkins,

If you think you have OCD or know someone with OCD, you don't have to live your life as I did, trying to figure out what it is and how to live with it, alone. There is a much better understanding of OCD now. There is nothing "wrong" with you. You don't need "fixed". But you are different. Find out what makes you different and use it. Gain power over your OCD, and become OCD.

Always with my love,

Lynette